THE SPIRIT OF ENTERPRISE

THE SPIRIT OF ENTERPRISE

The History of Pacific Enterprises from 1886 to 1989

Douglas R. Littlefield and Tanis C. Thorne

Pacific Enterprises, P.O. Box 60043, Los Angeles, California 90060-0043.

DESIGN: JOSH FREEMAN/ASSOCIATES

Table of Contents

Acknowledgments

RESEARCHING AND WRITING THE HISTORY of Pacific Enterprises would have been extremely difficult without the assistance of many individuals. Foremost among these are the officers and staff of Pacific Enterprises and its three major subsidiaries: Southern California Gas Company, Thrifty Corporation, and Pacific Enterprises Oil Company. Several people deserve special mention, particularly J. Foster Hames, the secretary of Pacific Enterprises, and Bruce B. Harris, a retired executive assistant at the company. Hames and Harris were indispensable in guiding us through the maze of corporate sources, directing us to appropriate people for special assistance, facilitating communication, and helping in other ways that are too numerous to mention. Without their generous assistance, this book would not have been possible. In addition, many employees — both currently working and retired — helped by submitting to interviews, assisting in locating documents, providing insights into particular events, proofreading drafts, and securing illustrations. Still others within Pacific Enterprises and its subsidiaries also gave generously of their time, making research and writing easier and more pleasant than it might have been otherwise. One department in particular deserves extra recognition. The staff of the Southern California Gas Company Research and Information Center provided us with work space, allowed us to use their telephones and copy machines, directed us to countless historical files, and in general tolerated months of disruption caused by our research and writing. A special thanks also goes to Cathy Sheppa, Foster Hames's secretary, who cheerfully took on a multitude of chores beyond her official duties to speed the project to conclusion.

Aside from the valuable assistance we received at Pacific Enterprises and its subsidiaries, many people and organizations outside the firm helped in the creation of this book. Professor Edwin J. Perkins of the University of Southern California played a major role in shaping the project and in editing multiple drafts of the manuscript. Joseph G. Dobbins, a UCLA history graduate, was an invaluable research assistant. Among his many duties, he kept over six hundred photos and other illustrations organized and in manageable order. Josh Freeman, Vickie Karten, and David Fikse at Josh Freeman / Associates also deserve our thanks for designing the book from cover to cover and for putting up with countless requests to redesign various pages as revisions were made.

We are also indebted to the following individuals and institutions for providing access to historical documents and photographs: the American Gas Association; Peter R. Antheil; the Bancroft Library at the University of California, Berkeley; the California Historical Society; the California State Library; Citrine Resources; El Paso Natural Gas Company; *Forbes* magazine; the

Los Angeles City Archives; the Los Angeles Department of Water and Power; the Los Angeles Public Library; the *Los Angeles Times;* Maguire Thomas Partners; the National Archives; the Natural History Museum of Los Angeles County; the Northwest Alaskan Pipeline Company; the Pacific Coast Gas Association; the Pacific Gas Transmission Company; the Pasadena Historical Society; the *Saturday Evening Post;* the Siemens Corporation; Special Collections at the University of California, Los Angeles; the Urban Archives Center at California State University, Northridge; the U.S. Patent and Trademark Office; the Utility Workers' Union of America, AFL-CIO, Region V; and the Wells Fargo history museums in San Francisco and Los Angeles.

Needless to say, in a project of this magnitude it is impossible to mention by name all who deserve recognition for the assistance they provided. To everyone who helped with this history project, your contributions are sincerely appreciated, while responsibility for any errors or omissions is clearly our own.

Douglas R. Littlefield
Tanis C. Thorne
December 11, 1989

Introduction

PACIFIC ENTERPRISES IS A SOUTHERN CALIFORNIA holding company
with a long and illustrious history. Founded in San Francisco as
Pacific Lighting Company in 1886 by C.O.G. Miller and Walter B.
Cline, a century later the firm ranks among the leading diversified
companies. Pacific Enterprises has earned this status because of
conservative business practices, the flexibility to adapt to changing
circumstances, an astuteness in recognizing sound investment
opportunities, and a boldness in expanding its economic base
when conditions warranted.

Much of the credit for developing Pacific Enterprises' guiding strategies belongs to C.O.G. Miller (president of the company
from 1898 until 1940 and chairman of the board from 1940 until his
death in 1952); to his son, Robert W. Miller (president from 1940
until 1956 and chairman from 1956 until 1967); and to his grandson,
Paul A. Miller (president from 1968 to 1972 and chairman from 1972
until 1989). The Millers' successful management of the firm's affairs
for over a century is a testimonial to their business acumen, and
their achievement of corporate growth and accomplishment is all
the more remarkable because it occurred under the leadership of
three members of a single family — a distinction of familial continuity rare among large corporations in the late twentieth century.

During C.O.G. Miller's tenure as head of Pacific Lighting,
the company found the southern California gas distribution business

to be fertile ground for its endeavors and took advantage of opportunities to increase the number of its utility holdings in the region. Overcoming strong competition, Pacific Lighting gradually consolidated these firms. By the late 1930s the company had grown from a handful of employees to over five thousand workers providing gas utility services to scores of southern California communities under the joint direction of two principal subsidiaries, Southern California Gas Company and Southern Counties Gas Company of California.

After Robert Miller succeeded his father as president in 1940, Pacific Lighting faced new challenges linked to World War II and the postwar period. Under the younger Miller's direction, the company expanded its ability to serve southern California in the early 1940s by initiating the use of underground storage facilities. At the same time, the firm's employees united their efforts to promote wartime defense measures, to encourage gas conservation practices, and to operate a manufacturing plant to produce butadiene — an integral component of synthetic rubber. In the years following World War II, Pacific Lighting piped in major gas supplies from outside the state and faced the need to justify higher gas rates to government regulators. In the early to mid-1960s, the company also defended itself against threats to its status as the dominant southern California natural gas supplier.

Shortly before Paul Miller became president in 1968, Pacific Lighting moved its headquarters from San Francisco to Los Angeles, and in this new location the firm continued to change and adapt. With over ten thousand employees by the 1970s, Pacific Lighting confronted the oil and gas crises of that decade by striving to find alternative gas supplies and urging energy conservation. At the same time, Pacific Lighting also faced the reality that southern California's population growth had slowed, thus limiting future expansion in the gas utility field. To deal with this development, the firm embarked on a diversification campaign to broaden its holdings. At first, new subsidiaries were gas-related, but Pacific Lighting soon moved into real estate and agriculture. Subsequent additions included alternative energy projects as well as oil and gas exploration and development. Pacific Lighting also became involved in the retail sector of the economy in the mid-1980s by acquiring Thrifty Corporation. In the following years, Pacific Lighting added other firms as subsidiaries, and eventually the diversification program brought the experience and resources of more than forty thousand employees into Pacific Lighting and its affiliates.

While some of the new acquisitions were subsequently sold or dissolved when conditions warranted, the diversification program was well established by the end of the 1980s. With nearly half the firm's assets in non-utility operations by that time, it was obvious that the company's name no longer accurately reflected its business interests, and in 1988 "Pacific Enterprises" was selected to describe the firm's diversified nature more accurately.

A few years before the name change, top executives had concluded that the drive to broaden the company's business activities would require the infusion of new management personnel. With retirement scheduled by the end of the 1980s for Paul Miller and Pacific Lighting President Joseph R. Rensch, these two officials undertook an intensive internal and external search for executive talent. As a result, in 1984 the company brought in as executive vice-president and general counsel James R. Ukropina — an attorney who had an extensive background in mergers and acquisitions. Ukropina was named president in 1986 when Rensch moved to vice-chairman and subsequently retired, and upon Miller's retirement in 1989, Pacific Enterprises' board of directors elected Ukropina chairman and chief executive officer. Filling the vacancy in the presidency, the board simultaneously named to that post Willis B. Wood, Jr. — an engineer and executive with nearly thirty years' experience at the company, primarily in utility-related functions.

Paul Miller's retirement as the head of Pacific Enterprises brought to a close 103 years of family leadership shortly after the company entered its second century of operations. This book documents not only the firm's first century, but it also suggests reasons why Pacific Enterprises prospered. The Millers' business skills were certainly central to the company's prosperity, but over the last century, the talents of many other employees were also at the heart of the firm's success. Pacific Enterprises and its subsidiaries have always benefited from the skills of people with diverse strengths in engineering, finance, human resources, law, marketing, and other fields. Such employees have made impressive contributions in serving customers and operating the Pacific Enterprises businesses efficiently.

The flexibility provided by employees with many different talents has allowed Pacific Enterprises and its subsidiaries to prosper, and it demonstrates that adaptability has always been a hallmark of Pacific Enterprises' evolution. The ability to adjust to changing times, however, has been tempered by an adherence to conservative business strategies. This fact is readily apparent in Pacific Enterprises' diversification program, which combines a continued commitment to the gas utility as the firm's principal subsidiary with the strength of well-established companies in retailing and oil and gas exploration and development. Such prudent business policies have complemented the skills and talents of Pacific Enterprises' many employees and will carry the company into its second century of operation.

Pioneers of the Gas Industry

Forebears of Pacific Lighting in Southern California.

IN 1936 CHRISTIAN OTTO GERBERDING MILLER, better known as C.O.G. Miller, reflected on the history of Pacific Lighting Corporation's business policies on the occasion of the firm's fiftieth anniversary. Miller, who was president and one of the founders of the firm, recalled that over the years, Pacific Lighting — a holding company with a large economic stake in southern California — had added cautiously to its investments in different firms when such expansion seemed prudent and practical. With this approach to business, Miller observed, Pacific Lighting had become in effect one large integrated company made up of smaller components, all coordinated for the most efficient and successful operation. Miller noted, however, that he could not say when or how the policy had developed; "it was a more or less natural evolution," he believed.[1]

The evolution that Miller humbly dismissed as a natural process was in reality more the ability of Pacific Lighting to take advantage of opportunities and create strategies for success. Founded by Miller, a native San Franciscan, and Walter B. Cline, originally from Stockton, California, Pacific Lighting arose out of technological advances in the nineteenth-century gas industry, which had provided a multitude of business opportunites for entrepreneurs.[2]

Birdseye view of San Francisco, 1878 — then the financial capital of the West Coast — where Pacific Lighting originated.

1867 | 1889

BETWEEN 1867 AND 1889, THE FOREBEARS OF PACIFIC LIGHTING LAID THE GROUNDWORK FOR THE SOUTHERN CALIFORNIA GAS DISTRIBUTION SYSTEM.

1849 | California gold rush.

1860 | Los Angeles's population is 4,378 and San Francisco's is 56,802.

8

Engraving of Albert Miller, father of C.O.G. Miller, 1870s.

San Francisco gas street lighting, around 1900. The city's streets remained lit by gas until the 1930s.

Shortly before Pacific Lighting's organization, Miller and Cline — then both young men — had been employed by Pacific Gas Improvement Company, a San Francisco utility firm created in 1884 by Miller's father, Albert Miller. C.O.G. Miller had joined Pacific Gas Improvement as a cashier, and Walter Cline was an accountant.[3] The younger Miller and Cline soon became close friends, and this bond enabled them to seize an opportunity to start their own business venture. During the 1880s, the introduction of electric lighting and advances in gas technology had stimulated the gas industry in the United States to improve its lamps and service to remain competitive. Thus, in 1886 when Albert Miller's Pacific Gas Improvement Company elected not to promote the newly invented "Siemens" gas lamp — which provided a brighter and more efficient flame — C.O.G. Miller and Walter Cline formed Pacific Lighting Company and bought a small supply of the lamps at sixty dollars each. They rented their lamps out, primarily to restaurants and saloons at two dollars per week, and within a short period of time, the two entrepreneurs had about one hundred lights installed.[4]

Miller and Cline's initial venture into the gas business was limited to renting lamps in San Francisco, but they soon took advantage of another opportunity — one that brought the company into the southern California utility business. At the time, southern California was not as well-established as the San Francisco Bay area. Southern California's population was a mere fraction of the northern region, which dominated the state's financial, political, and cultural institutions. Nonetheless, in the 1880s southern California began to experience a period of rapid expansion brought on by a variety of factors,

1861 | American Civil War, 1861-1865.

Montgomery Street in San Francisco, late nineteenth century.

most notably a railroad rate war. With this growth came many business opportunities, and one of the most promising appeared to be in the utility industry, providing service to the thousands of new settlers.

The chance for Miller and Cline to become involved in southern California utilities came through Albert Miller's firm, which held a half interest in a gas manufacturing plant at San Bernardino. Seeking to dispose of its property in that location, the senior Miller's company sold out to C.O.G. Miller and Cline, who then parlayed the San Bernardino gas works and other investments in gas companies in Colton, Eureka, Riverside, Santa Barbara, Santa Rosa, and Ventura into a sizable investment.

1866 | Los Angeles Gas Company franchise, 1866-1886.

1867 | Los Angeles Gas Company incorporated.

C.O.G. Miller

Cofounder of Pacific Lighting.

Christian Otto Gerberding Miller, known to his friends as "C.O.G.," was born in San Francisco on October 1, 1865. His father, Albert Miller, had arrived in that city in 1851 and had become one of its earliest utility and banking leaders. After attending schools in San Francisco, Oakland, and Berkeley, C.O.G. Miller formed Pacific Lighting Company in 1886 with Walter B. Cline. Miller served as treasurer of the new firm until 1898, when he was elected president. In 1940 Miller became chairman of the board, a position he held until his death in 1952. Under his able direction, Pacific Lighting became one of the major utility holding companies in the United States by acquiring many small firms — primarily in southern California — and interconnecting their networks for smooth and efficient operation.

Miller's business activities were not limited to just Pacific Lighting. In addition to his duties with that firm, he was

active in the San Francisco utility industry, first as treasurer of Albert Miller's Pacific Gas Improvement Company and later as president upon his father's death in 1900. C.O.G. Miller also became a director of northern California's Pacific Gas and Electric Company when it absorbed Pacific Gas Improvement during the San Francisco rate wars in the early years of the twentieth century.

Miller's other business directorships included Firemen's Fund Insurance Company, American Trust Company, and the Kennedy Mining and Milling Company. In addition, he was a charter member of the Pacific Coast Gas Association (and its president in 1908), and he held memberships in the American Gas Association and the American Gas Institute.

Aside from his business interests, Miller was a civic, cultural, and community leader. He was a trustee of Stanford University, a director of the San Francisco Opera Association, a director of the

San Francisco office of the War Trade Board during World War I, a founding member of the San Francisco Community Chest, and a strong supporter of the California Historical Society.

Miller was married to Einnim Havemeyer Tucker in 1889, and this union produced two children, Marian and Leslie. Einnim died in 1896, and Miller was remarried two years later to Janet McAlpine Watt. This second marriage resulted in two more children, Robert W. (who, like his father, eventually headed Pacific Lighting) and Albert.

After a long and productive life, Miller died on April 23, 1952, at the age of eighty-six. By the time of his death,

San Francisco street scene at the turn of the century.

Pacific Lighting — which Miller and Cline had formed with an initial investment of only a few hundred dollars in rental gas lamps in San Francisco — owned the largest distribution system of natural gas in the country, having assets valued at more than $415 million and serving almost two million customers. "No man's reputation for conservative progress and sound finance stands higher," observed one of Miller's peers.[5]

With business flourishing, in 1889 Pacific Lighting bought the Los Angeles Gas Company and two firms owned by gas entrepreneur Thaddeus S.C. Lowe — Consumers' Gas, Light, Heat and Power Company and Lowe Gas and Electric Company.[6]

The acquisition of these three Los Angeles-area gas and electric firms, whose combined assets totaled over $1 million, committed Miller and Cline to a long involvement in southern California utilities. Because of this responsibility, Cline gave up his position as secretary, general manager, and member of the board of directors of Pacific Lighting and moved to Los Angeles to assume the presidency and management of a new subsidiary created to take over the southern California properties, the Los Angeles Lighting Company. Cline consolidated the gas and electric facilities under his control and became the director of Los Angeles operations. Miller stayed in San Francisco to oversee the parent holding company, and his duties were largely in the realm of corporate finance, acquisitions, and broad policy decisions. By mutual agreement, Cline was given wide latitude in operating the Los Angeles Lighting Company, but Pacific Lighting was frequently involved with financial and other important matters.[7]

Walter B. Cline, cofounder of Pacific Lighting.

Los Angeles, early 1850s.

The pueblo of Los Angeles, late 1850s. On the left is North Main Street and the Plaza Church.

Gas for lighting and heating was originally manufactured from coal. This woman, advertising the product of Santa Barbara Gas Company — later acquired by Pacific Lighting — has a coal bucket on her head and a necklace of coal around her neck.

Los Angeles Lighting Company was the product of over two decades of development in southern California's gas and electric business. Before Pacific Lighting had become involved in southern California, the utility business had seen vigorous competition among rival companies, rate wars, struggles with local governments over street lighting contracts and gas prices, and increasing difficulties in meeting the energy demands imposed by the area's burgeoning economic growth. These factors were not lost on Miller and Cline, who closely observed the Los Angeles utility businesses. The story of Pacific Lighting properly begins with the history of these companies.

The utility industry in southern California had its beginnings in the 1860s when outraged residents of the pueblo of Los Angeles demanded that the town install gas street lamps to combat crime. At the time, the town had little claim to notoriety except for its street villainy. Fewer than fifty thousand people lived in all of southern California, and Los Angeles itself had one tenth of that number. The town had no organized police or fire departments, no banks, and no public transportation. The streets were unpaved and unlighted. Local reformers claimed that the installation of street lighting would do much to counteract the town's reputation of lawlessness — one that was well deserved. Crime was rampant after dark, particularly around the Los Angeles Plaza and on nearby streets, where citizens were frequently robbed and beaten if they ventured out after sunset. Critics argued that street lighting was desperately needed.[8]

Not only did Los Angeles need street lamps to help combat its after-dark crime, but existing

1873 | Thaddeus Lowe's improvements in "manufactured gas" patented, 1873-1875.

interior lighting also cried out for improvement. In the mid-1860s, the kerosene lamp was widely used indoors for illumination. Although it was a significant improvement over the camphene lamp, which burned a combination of turpentine and alcohol, the kerosene lamp had important drawbacks, particularly in southern California. Since early attempts to refine kerosene from California crude oil had failed, supplies had to be brought in from the East Coast, which kept prices high. In addition, kerosene did not burn cleanly nor did it provide a very luminous flame. The combined demand for improved interior and exterior lighting caused a public clamor for the construction of a gas plant to serve Los Angeles.[9]

To meet this demand, the Los Angeles Gas Company, the first firm to provide gas service in southern California, was organized on June 28, 1867, and capitalized at thirty-six thousand dollars. The company planned to build a gas manufacturing plant on two lots adjoining the church on the Plaza. The firm's processing method was unique. Since the use of underground natural gas had not yet been pioneered, gas manufacturing plants in eastern cities relied on processing coal or coke to create gas. This technique was also used in northern California cities such as San Francisco, but unlike eastern urban areas that were near coal mining centers, the West had no known deposits. Coal had to be imported by ship from Australia at great expense. Consequently, the organizers of the Los Angeles Gas Company proposed to make gas from a local product more readily at hand, asphalt (or "brea"), which could be found in large quantities in the area.[10]

Within a few months of incorporation, the firm had laid pipes along a considerable portion of

Kerosene lamps were used prior to gas lamps for interior lighting.

Los Angeles Gas Company bill to the city for one month's street lighting, 1868.

1875 | Sale of Los Angeles Gas Company to Charles Simpkins.

1876 | Southern Pacific Railroad completed to Los Angeles.

An early photograph of the Los Angeles Plaza taken shortly after the first gas lights were installed in the late 1860s. Note gas lamp on the corner.

Stagecoach stop near the Plaza, early 1870s.

Main Street, and laborers were completing the gas works. Finally, after much anticipation, on the evening of November 30, 1867, a handful of buildings were lit with gas lamps, although no street lights were yet included.[11] The *Los Angeles Semi-Weekly News* hailed the beginning of gas service as a step toward urban maturity:

> Los Angeles donned at least one of the habiliments of a city. On Saturday evening last the principal hotels and mercantile houses were lighted with gas. Great credit is due Mr. [James] Hagan, the superintendent of the company, for his energy in pushing forward the work to a speedy conclusion. Our citizens, who have enjoyed the reputation of having a large stock of native and uninflammable gas on hand, can now boast of the genuine manufactured article that burns beautifully and gives a clear bright light.[12]

In the same year, the town's first ice depot was founded, and an enthusiastic newspaper editor effused that another step forward had been taken in making Los Angeles a great city: "We have Water and Gas, and now we are to have the additional luxury of Ice."[13]

With the Los Angeles Gas Company's works successfully producing gas, citizens called for the city to sign a contract with the firm to provide gas lighting on the streets. After considerable negotiation, an accord was reached in December 1867.

1879 | Edison patents incandescent electric light.

The agreement provided that Los Angeles Gas would install twenty-five gas street lamps at a cost of thirty dollars each. The firm agreed to sell gas at a rate of $11.00 per lamp per month (soon lowered to $7.50), and additional gas would serve interior lamps at city hall.[14]

Many residents applauded the city for bringing lights to the streets, yet not everyone was satisfied. Those living in unlighted areas continued to complain and were impatient with the Los Angeles Gas Company's glacially slow pace of laying extensions, not fully appreciating the difficulty of importing cast-iron pipes from the East Coast. Residents insisted on more lights for upper Main, First, Second, Arcadia, Fort, Sanchez, and Spring streets. Within its budget, the city approved some of the additional lights, but as Los Angeles grew, requests for street lamps proliferated. Unfortunately, neither the city's finances nor the company's system could keep pace with the demand.[15]

The insufficient number of street lamps was one problem Los Angeles faced in relation to the gas utility, but another was the quality of manufactured gas. Within months of the initiation of service, company directors found that asphalt was not as satisfactory for gas manufacturing as they had hoped. Unlike gas made from coal, asphalt-based gas produced tarry by-products that contaminated equipment and clogged pipes. Moreover, asphalt-based gas did not burn brightly; it was smoky and had an unpleasant odor. These drawbacks prompted considerable unhappiness with the Los Angeles Gas Company's commodity, and after many complaints, the organization was forced to shift to gas manufacturing using expensive Australian coal.[16]

St. Charles Hotel on Main Street in the 1870s. On the right side of the photo is a sign banning weapons from the Plaza.

Horse-drawn streetcar lines were among Los Angeles's civic improvements in the 1870s.

1879 | First gas stoves introduced on Pacific Coast.

1882 | Era of electric lighting begins in Los Angeles.

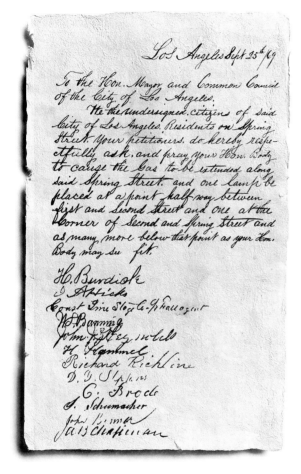

Petition by Los Angeles citizens for an extension of street lighting, 1869.

In addition to dissatisfaction with the quality of gas, other problems plagued the company. Foremost was the question of gas prices. Shortly after the first street lamps were lit, Los Angeles city officials objected to the rates the firm charged for service. The pricing issue first arose in December 1870, when the renewal of the street lighting contract came up for discussion before the city council. With sixty street lights in use at $7.50 per lamp per month, the city faced a hefty annual bill of over $5,000 for gas supplies. City officials demanded a reduction in rates, but the company refused. The company argued that the integration of Australian coal into its gas-making process to improve quality had increased production costs, and therefore a price cut was impossible. With the company declining to lower its rates, the city decided not to renew the street lighting agreement and to put the contract out to bid.[17]

By early 1871, several individuals had made proposals to undercut the Los Angeles Gas Company's prices and to provide street lighting for as low as five dollars per lamp per month. While city leaders and residents were inclined to accept one of these cheaper bids, a problem arose when the city attorney pointed out that the existing company held an inviolate franchise giving it the exclusive right to provide Los Angeles with gas until 1886. The attorney concluded that the city legally could not do business with anyone other than the Los Angeles Gas Company for the next fifteen years. Because the city's hands were tied and because the firm steadfastly refused to lower its gas rates, the city allowed its lighting contract to expire, plunging Los Angeles's streets into darkness for four years from 1872 until 1876.[18]

Pico House

Pio Pico and the Gas Works.

Pico House and the gas works in 1875.

The Los Angeles Gas Company faced many significant challenges in its early years. One problem was the need to overcome a smoky and poor quality product caused by the use of local asphalt in the manufacturing process rather than higher priced imported coal. There was also widespread dissatisfaction with service and monthly rates. These problems strained the firm's relations with the town's residents, but a more embarrassing problem confronted the company in 1869, when Pio Pico, a former governor of California and prominent southern Californian, constructed a three-story hotel on the Plaza directly across from the gas manufacturing plant. Named the Pico House, the hotel had all the modern conveniences of the day, including bathing facilities on each floor and gas lights in every room. Unfortunately for Pico and his guests, the prevailing westerly winds blew the smell of gas-making into the open doors and windows of the Pico House almost daily.

Pico lived with the stench for about two years, but finally in November 1871, he sued for damages claiming that the gas works had harmed the prestige of his hotel.

The gas firm argued that despite the problems caused by its gas works, the service it provided to the community outweighed any inconvenience to Pico and his hotel. When both the local court and the court of appeal accepted the company's argument, Pico used his influence with the city council to try to pressure the firm into moving its gas works

elsewhere. The city obligingly discussed the problem with company officials, but the firm refused to move its manufacturing works unless the city would pay all costs of constructing a new plant and tearing down the old. The city was unable to afford the estimated twenty-five thousand dollar expense for the move, and the gas plant remained where it was, much to Pico's dismay, until 1875 when the gas company voluntarily moved its plant to Aliso Street.[19]

Think of the Revolution

Utilizing Ordinary Garbage.

Although the Los Angeles Gas Company held an exclusive franchise to produce and distribute gas in Los Angeles until 1886, because of the high price and relatively poor quality product, the firm did not lack potential competition from entrepreneurs espousing various schemes — some more fanciful than others — to undercut the company's prices. One gas manufacturing plan utilizing ordinary garbage "of all kinds that is generally regarded as a great and unwholesome nuisance in a city" was proposed in October 1876. "It is really astonishing how so little quantity of worthless material can be utilized into a valuable commodity by so simple a process," an observer enthused. Estimates of the cost of making a thousand cubic

feet of this gas were as low as twenty-five cents. "Just think of the revolution this may be destined to make in the economy of our households," the observer exclaimed. "The gas man will look in upon us and beg permission, as a great favor, to be permitted to remove the noxious material!" When manufactured on a large scale, the garbage-gas process promised to produce ammonia and coal tar, which could be sold separately. Supporters projected that because of these by-products, the gas itself could be provided to consumers for free.[20]

A woodcut of an early experimental gas plant.

Although the city sporadically held further negotiations with the company over the next few years, nothing ever came of the talks, and the firm's finances suffered accordingly. The loss of the street lamp contract was unfortunate, but other problems proved equally irksome. With the streets still dark at night, the Los Angeles City Council repeatedly heard proposals from other entrepreneurs to build gas plants to supply both street lamps and residences. The exclusive franchise kept any of these propositions from becoming a reality, but the continuing threat to the gas company's monopoly rights was undoubtedly unsettling to the firm's executives.[21]

Aside from the lack of the street lighting business and the risk posed by potential competitors, in a larger sense the Los Angeles Gas Company faced an even more serious problem because of its failure to keep pace with Los Angeles's growth during the 1860s and 1870s. The city's population had risen to thirty thousand by the mid-1870s, a water company had installed a distribution system, two banks had been created, three daily newspapers were in print, Pio Pico had built his Pico House hotel, and a horsecar system served the downtown area. Yet regardless of the growth, the gas company found it difficult to attract new customers, essentially because prices were so high and because its lines did not extend to newly settled parts of the town. By 1875 it became clear to the firm's leaders that gas rates needed to be cut; the stagnating system required expansion; and the city's street-lighting needs had to be accommodated. Overwhelmed by these seemingly insurmountable difficulties, the company's directors sold a majority interest to Charles H. Simpkins, a San Franciscan who had substantial

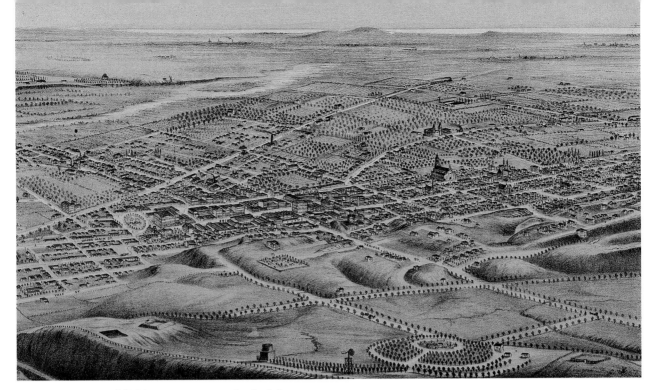

experience in establishing gas companies in Marysville, California, and Virginia City, Nevada, as well
as elsewhere.[22]

After Simpkins took control of Los Angeles
Gas, he improved the firm's relationship with both
the city and its citizens. One of his first actions was
to better the quality of gas by substituting a superior
grade of coal. This effort resulted in a brighter light,
but the bad odor remained a problem. Simpkins
also tried to solve another matter irritating local citizens: the location of the gas plant and the odor it
caused around the Los Angeles Plaza. In October
1875 he persuaded the company's board of directors
to approve the purchase of five lots on Aliso Street
for a new gas works, thus improving public relations
and simultaneously preparing for increased consumer demand for gas service. Simpkins also sent a
former Marysville colleague, Adoniram Pierce, to
Philadelphia to purchase equipment for the plant.
Pierce, who supervised the construction, estimated
that the new facility would produce 100,000 cubic
feet of gas per day.[23]

Despite Simpkins's efforts to upgrade the
quality of gas and to move the offensive manufacturing plant away from the Plaza, his honeymoon
with the city was short-lived because of continuing
battles over rates. Although Simpkins brought prices

Birdseye view of Los Angeles, 1877. Los Angeles, with its citrus groves, contrasted sharply with San Francisco's urban development in the 1870s.

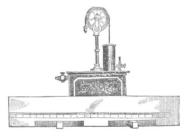

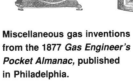

Miscellaneous gas inventions from the 1877 *Gas Engineer's Pocket Almanac,* published in Philadelphia.

1885 | Santa Fe Railroad
completed to
Los Angeles.

1885 | Southern California
real estate boom,
1885-1888.

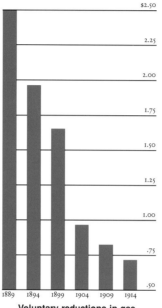

Voluntary reductions in gas prices, 1889-1914. The trend toward rate reduction began in 1875 when the Los Angeles Gas Company cut prices.

down in 1875 from $7.50 to $7.00 per thousand cubic feet, downtown merchants called for a gas boycott until the company reduced its rates even further. Fueling the merchants' grievances, the Los Angeles *Evening Express* charged that the city's gas prices were among the highest in the state; the paper's editors found no excuse for rates at seven dollars per thousand cubic feet when in San Francisco prices were only four dollars. Simpkins responded that rates in Nevada City, Grass Valley, and Marysville were all higher than in Los Angeles, but the protesters remained hostile. Within days, their ranks swelled to over sixty of the city's most prominent business leaders, all willing to forego gas in favor of oil lamps if rates were not cut. With such formidable opposition, Simpkins had no choice but to drop prices, and his company notified consumers that the new rate would be six dollars per thousand cubic feet.[24]

Whereas the threatened gas boycott had forced the company to lower its rates to consumers, the city's receptiveness to proposals from other gas companies for cheaper street lighting compelled the Los Angeles Gas Company to resume negotiations over street lighting. The result was that by December 1876, street lamps once again burned brightly under a new contract. The new agreement provided for one hundred street lamps to be lit in the central business district for nineteen cents per lamp per night. At the end of an initial two-year term, the city could extend the contract for three more years at its option. Rates were scheduled to drop to eighteen cents per lamp per night beginning with the third year if the contract was extended. The Los Angeles Gas Company was to provide service for twenty-five nights per month, with moonlight providing illumination on the remaining nights.[25]

In substance it's true. I was paying a sheriff $5 a day to postpone a judgment on my small factory. Then came the gas man and he cut off my gas. That made me so mad that [I] read up on gas Technique & Economics and decided I would try [to see] if electricity couldn't be made to replace gas and give them a run for their money and I stuck to it for 4 years but I was so poor an economist that I didn't hurt them at all except lately — 40 years —

EDISON

Thomas A. Edison claimed that his disgust with high gas lighting costs provoked him to invent the incandescent electric light in 1879.

This photograph of the Los Angeles Gas Company's Aliso Street plant was taken at the turn of the century.

While Charles Simpkins continued to struggle with Los Angeles residents and the city council over rates and service, another more ominous development was on the horizon. Thomas A. Edison's invention of the incandescent electric light in 1879 sent shock waves through the gas lighting industry, and gas stocks fell precipitously. That same year, the California Electric Light Company was founded in San Francisco to introduce the newly patented Brush electric light system to that city. The company completed a small plant to supply arc lamps in September 1879, and about a year later, the firm proposed the introduction of electricity to Los Angeles. The electric company touted its lamps as both brighter and cheaper than gas lamps, and by 1882 the Los Angeles promotion efforts had paid off with contracts to provide electric lighting to the Cosmopolitan Hotel, the Pico House, and the United States Hotel.[26]

This development was a major setback to the Los Angeles Gas Company, but the final blow came in mid-September 1882, when the city council voted to replace gas street lamps with electric lights. The electric firm, which had organized its Los Angeles system under the corporate banner of the Los Angeles Electric Company, then submitted a proposal to place seven tall masts around the town. Each mast would tower 150 feet above the streets and carry a three-thousand-candlepower arc lamp.[27] With gas rates still too high for city officials' liking, they eagerly accepted the Los Angeles Electric Company's plan. The new lighting proposition was even more attractive because it involved electricity and not gas and therefore did not run afoul of the twenty-year franchise held by the Los Angeles Gas Company.

By the end of December 1882, the electric street light system was in place, and the *Evening Express* described the momentous occasion when the lamps were first lit:

> Saturday evening [December 31, 1882] shortly after eight o'clock the electric light was turned on by ex-mayor [J.R.] Toberman. Only two masts were lighted, the one on Main Street, near Commercial, and the one on First Street hill. The Main Street light burned steadily and beautifully, and it cast a light similar to that of the full moon on snow. The First Street hill light was very unsteady, glowing at times with brilliancy, and again almost fading from sight. Three squares away coarse print could be read by the light from the Main Street mast. Last night newspaper print was read at the same distance from the same light. The distance was fully 500 yards. . . . The shadows of the telegraph wires were thrown so black on boarded street crossings that several times persons were observed to stop to pick them up for strings. . . . The only complaint so far is from young couples who find no shady spots on the way home from church or theatre.[28]

Regardless of the newspaper's enthusiasm for the new street lighting, not everyone was convinced that it was a good idea. Opponents argued that electric light:

> soiled ladies' complexions; that it produced color blindness, and besides had a bad effect on the eyes; that it magnified objects and caused optical illusions; that it was costly; that gas was good enough; that it kept chickens awake all night; that it was a new thing, and, therefore, an experiment and dangerous; that the wires attracted lightning; that the lights attracted bugs; and finally, that it was a speculation, and, therefore, a swindle.[29]

Nonetheless, such skepticism was rapidly overcome, and by mid-January 1883, the Los Angeles Electric Company had made arrangements to install about

Gas Appliance Promotion

Offsetting Diminished Lighting Revenues.

With the advent of electric lights, gas companies everywhere turned to promoting gas appliances to offset declining lighting revenues. The Los Angeles Gas Company was no exception, and on January 2, 1883, the firm inserted this advertisement in the *Evening Express* along with an illustration of one of its stoves:

The Los Angeles Gas Company have now on hand and for sale the Economy and Gas Cooking Stoves, the Eclipse Parlor Stove and Boiler for saloon use, which for neatness, dispatch and economy is hard to beat, consuming only 30 per cent of gas and 70 per cent of atmospheric air, making them the most economical stoves in use, requiring less fuel than any other stove for the same amount of work. Reasons why they should be in every household:

1st — They are perfectly harmless; no danger of exploding.

2nd — They are always ready; no trouble making fires, no ashes, no cinders, no smoke, no soot, no smell.

3rd — It is more easily worked than any coal or wood stove, and the oven will bake for twenty minutes after gas is turned off.

4th — They are portable, easily adjusted, and easily moved.

5th — They are the most perfect broiler, griller, toaster, roaster and baker in use.

6th — You can use any compartment independent of the others.

7th — Ornamental as well as in kitchen, there being no dust or smoke arising from same.[30]

I'VE GOT A GAS RANGE NOW

forty electric lamps in stores, saloons, and private residences in addition to providing street lights powered by a generating plant at Banning and Alameda streets. Electric lighting quickly became so popular that the firm could not keep up with demand and developed a waiting list for customers.[31]

Even though electric lights met the approval of most city residents, the Los Angeles Gas Company still valiantly submitted bids for gas street lighting to the city council. In late 1884, for example, the gas company proposed to light two hundred gas lamps for about fourteen cents per lamp per night. Assuming that the company only lit the lamps for twenty-five nights per month as had been its previous practice, the cost to the city would have been nearly nine thousand dollars each year. By comparison, the Los Angeles Electric Company offered to continue lighting the streets with electricity for one thousand dollars per mast. With fifteen masts in place, this reflected an annual expense of fifteen thousand dollars. Despite the gas company's substantially lower bid, the city council voted to give the lighting contract to the electric company, partly because of electric lighting's superior illumination and partly because the lights were a good promotion for the city.[32]

The Los Angeles Gas Company, like other gas firms throughout the United States, tried to offset this devastating inroad on the lighting market by aggressively promoting stoves and heaters, some of which were sold at cost or even given away for free. Gas stoves were introduced in Los Angeles and San Francisco in 1879, but the public was slow to accept them. Moreover, insurance companies strenuously objected to the appliances being used in homes, as

With the expiration of the Los Angeles Gas Company's franchise and the attacks by other gas and electric firms, Simpkins had had enough. Thus, when San Francisco's Pacific Lighting Company offered on November 20, 1889, to buy him out, he readily agreed. Lowe's firms likewise had suffered from the rivalry, and recognizing the futility of further competition, both also sold to Pacific Lighting.[38] It now remained for Pacific Lighting and its owners, C.O.G. Miller and Walter Cline, to consolidate the competing systems and bring economies of large-scale operations into play.

The first major California oil strike was in Pico Canyon near Newhall in the 1870s. Shown in this 1930 photograph are the ruins of one of the state's earliest refineries.

Southern Pacific roundhouse. Transcontinental railroad rate wars caused a population boom in Los Angeles in the 1880s.

Competition, Experimentation, and Consolidation

Pacific Lighting and the Early Southern California Utility Industry.

AFTER PACIFIC LIGHTING COMPANY formed Los Angeles Lighting in 1889 to take over the Los Angeles Gas Company and two of its rival firms, Walter Cline — general manager of the new organization — began to make improvements to the gas system. Using a fund of $100,000 that Pacific Lighting had set aside for this purpose, he reinforced existing gas mains and extended service across the Los Angeles River to serve Boyle Heights. With the Los Angeles Lighting Company serving less than three thousand customers out of a total city population of about fifty-one thousand, Cline decided to reduce rates to attract more business, and shortly after taking control in 1889, he cut gas prices from $2.50 per thousand cubic feet to $2.25. A year later, he dropped the price to two dollars, and he continued to lower rates every two or three years. Even with these cuts, however, business did not boom.[1]

A major reason for the disappointing rate of Los Angeles Lighting's growth during the 1890s was the cutthroat competition among gas companies in southern California. Among others, T.S.C. Lowe and his son, Leon, reemerged as major rivals, having developed additional improved gas manufacturing processes. The new gas techniques and Los Angeles's increase in size led to the establishment of

Birdseye view of Los Angeles in 1894. The Aliso Street gas works (with smokestacks near Center Street) can be seen in the middle of the picture.

1889 | 1915

PACIFIC LIGHTING COMPANY MOVED INTO THE SOUTHERN CALIFORNIA UTILITY INDUSTRY AND BEGAN TO CONSOLIDATE GAS AND ELECTRIC SYSTEMS.

1889 | Pacific Lighting buys Los Angeles Gas Company and T.S.C. Lowe's early gas firms.

1890 | Pacific Lighting acquires Los Angeles Electric Company.

T.S.C. Lowe

Inventor, Gas Entrepreneur, and Balloonist.

Artist's conception of Lowe's airship.

One of the most important figures in the development of the gas industry in the United States was T.S.C. Lowe. A man with considerable drive, determination, and intelligence, Lowe — whose mottos were "experience is the best teacher" and "knowledge is power" — revolutionized gas manufacturing in the late 1800s by the invention of several improve-

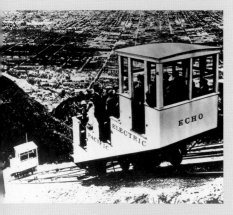

Mount Lowe Railway in the 1890s after it was purchased from Lowe by Henry Huntington.

ments in gas-making processes. In addition, Lowe was a major figure in the southern California gas industry due to his role in the creation of many gas companies. Lowe's diverse interests made him unique among gas entrepreneurs, and his background clearly demonstrated his many talents.

Thaddeus Sobieski Constantin Lowe — named by his mother after her three favorite characters in a popular novel of the day, *Thaddeus of Warsaw,*

by Jane Porter — was born in New Hampshire on August 20, 1832. In his teens, he moved to New York and became an apprentice to a traveling showman who dazzled audiences with feats of chemistry. When the entertainer died, Lowe inherited his equipment as well as his ersatz title of "Professor."

In addition to his activities as a showman, Lowe developed an interest in ballooning. In 1861, shortly after the Civil War had broken out, Lowe inadvertently flew a balloon from Cincinnati to a spot near the stateline between North and South Carolina where he was promptly arrested as a Union spy. Persuading his captors that he was not an agent for the North, Lowe was released. Shortly thereafter, at the invitation of President Abraham Lincoln, he hurried to Washington, D.C., to offer his services as a balloonist to the Union Army. Lincoln accepted Lowe's offer, and Lowe promptly organized the nation's first air corps, consisting of five balloons and 250 men. The corps made over three thousand flights to observe enemy troops and to direct artillery fire by telegraphed messages wired to the ground. Lowe's need for gas to inflate his balloons caused him to develop a hydrogen generator for making gas in the field, and after the Civil War had ended, he continued experiments on his device, leading to a string

of gas manufacturing patents. In 1882 Lowe sold some of his patents to United Gas Improvement Company in Philadelphia.

Poor health subsequently forced Lowe to move to California. The patent sale and money he had made from inventing an ice-making machine and equipment to refrigerate freight cars had made him a wealthy man, and he built a large home for his family on Orange Grove Boulevard in Pasadena. Ever inquisitive and acquisitive, Lowe became very involved in many diverse activities, including the construction of an opera house, the Mount Lowe inclined railway, two hotels, and an observatory on the top of Mount Lowe.

Lowe's prominence in his community and the affection that local citizens bore for him can best be seen in the fact that August 23, 1893, was

declared Professor Lowe Day in Pasadena. On that occasion, his many admirers honored him with a poem:
Praise God from whom all blessings flow.
And also praises to Professor Lowe.

Lowe's last years were spent trying to produce balloons to be navigated in the air like ships at sea; most of his designs were boat-like in shape. He died in 1913, three years after plans were made to transform the Raymond Avenue portion of the Pasadena Opera House block into a Lowe airship factory.[2]

Water-gas set patented September 5, 1875.

over fifty gas companies in the southern California area. Many of these firms were fly-by-night operations, created simply to cause problems and force well-established organizations to buy them out. As C.O.G. Miller commented many years later:

> Conditions in the utility business at that time were almost chaotic. Neither franchises, nor certificates of public convenience and necessity, nor any good intentions were needed in order to start gas or electric or water companies. Consequently, in almost every community the gas companies were subject to guerrilla attacks by new companies formed for the sole purpose of pirating the most profitable portion of the territory so as to create a nuisance value and sell out to the old company at an inflated price.[3]

The rivalry with electric companies was a parallel problem. While Los Angeles Lighting had absorbed some electrical works from Lowe Gas and Electric when it initially bought into the Los Angeles Basin, the bulk of the company's income derived from gas service. Nonetheless, competition from firms whose major focus was electricity was a serious problem for Los Angeles Lighting's gas operations. To overcome this attack on Los Angeles Lighting's revenues, Cline continued to reduce rates, and he ventured into new lines of business. First, Los Angeles Lighting began to import Australian and Welsh anthracite coals, English foundry coke, and Australian shale and then resold these fuels to other utility companies and local buyers. More importantly, however, Los Angeles Lighting diversified its gas production and distribution interests to include marketing gas appliances. It thus encouraged gas consumption for non-lighting purposes.

Despite the advantages that gas offered as a clean and efficient fuel, Cline found that promotion

Los Angeles Lighting's first home — from 1889 to 1891— in the basement of the Burdick Building, northeast corner of Second and Spring streets.

Bryson Building, northwest corner of Second and Spring streets, where Los Angeles Lighting had a gas appliance showroom in the early 1890s.

The Virtues of Gas

Testimonial for the Gas Stove.

I've cooked with onions, and I've cooked with garlic, but—Oh my!

The Los Angeles Gas Company frequently received letters praising its product, and the firm did not hesitate to use this correspondence in promotional literature. One such testimonial sent by a Los Angeles woman glowingly reported:

Gentlemen:

I take pleasure in offering you my testimonial for the gas cooking stove I have used for the past twelve months. I find it convenient in every respect, doing away with coal and all the dirty trash that accumulates. In every branch of cooking, baking, roasting, 'tis perfection, accomplished with less work and time, and always to a degree of high satisfaction. I could earnestly recommend it, and prefer it in every particular to coal or wood.[4]

FREE COOKING LESSONS

Held Every

WEDNESDAY AFTERNOON

At 2:30 o'clock

At **WOODMEN HALL**

Over Post Office

SOFT GINGERBREAD

1 cup butter, 1 cup molasses, 1 cup brown sugar, 1 cup boiling water, 1 teaspoon soda dissolved in boiling water, 1 tablespoon ginger, 1 teaspoon cinnamon, 2 eggs, from 4 to 5 cups flour, enough to make as thick as drop cake.

VEAL STEAK BROILED

Cut quite thick, place on hot broiler 1 inch below gas flame, turn once, and remove to hot platter when done, season with pepper and salt.

PASADENA CONSOLIDATED GAS CO.

Nov. 4, 1903

Advertisement by T.S.C. Lowe's Pasadena Consolidated Gas Company (purchased by Pacific Lighting in the early twentieth century) offered recipes to promote appliance sales.

A Hot Day but...
A Cool Dinner Hour If you use a Gas Range.

Gas as ....is **C**OOL
A Fuel **HEAP
CLEAN**

TRY ONE AND BE CONVINCED.

Sold at absolute cost for cash, or on installments if preferred.
Los Angeles Lighting Co.,
452 S. Broadway

Los Angeles Lighting Company advertisement, turn of the century.

of gas appliances was difficult because consumers had to be convinced that gas offered enough of an improvement over their existing wood and coal-burning appliances to warrant conversion. To persuade consumers to switch to gas, the company aggressively advertised its appliances. For example, an 1890 catalog for the firm's stoves claimed superiority over wood and coal appliances because gas created a steady and controlled fire. In addition, gas heated evenly and only where desired; one oven section could be left cool while another compartment was warmed. The company's advertising at one point even extolled gas stoves as preventives for the common cold. As the catalog explained, "half the unpleasantness of cooking [with wood or coal] is the overheating of the kitchen and the danger of catching cold after preparing a meal," presumably by entering a cooler room while still covered with kitchen-induced perspiration. Gas eliminated this risk by keeping the whole kitchen "cool and pleasant."[5]

Promotional literature also touted the benefits of other gas appliances. Some of these advertisements were frequently cloaked as home-help booklets, authored by women for women. They contained recipes as well as advice on the use of gas appliances. In addition to engravings of "modern" gas stoves, heaters, and water heaters, the booklets often featured items like hair-curling irons heated by gas flame. These curling irons could be warmed "in ten seconds, not blacking the iron in the slightest degree." The implied message was that gas-heated curling irons would not transfer soot to the hair. Other advantages offered by gas, according to the company's literature, were numerous: gas was cheaper than wood as a fuel; it was always ready to light instantly; it saved labor; gas heat could be controlled easily; meats cooked with gas retained their flavor; gas had "no possible danger of explosion"; gas was not paid for until used (unlike wood and coal which had to be purchased in advance); gas stoves and ovens required less maintenance than coal or wood stoves; and gas-fueled room heat was evenly distributed and contained no dust or dirt.[6]

Meanwhile, Los Angeles Lighting did not ignore the potential market for gas lights. The use of gas for illumination persisted in many buildings despite the competition from electricity. Gas was economical, the pipelines were already in place, and some people feared that the electric generating system might fail. Furthermore, the introduction of the Welsbach lamp in 1885, which C.O.G. Miller believed to be superior to other gas lamps, enabled gas companies to make what Miller called a "gallant fight" for the illumination market.[7] Underscoring this effort to remain competitive in the gas lighting business, Los Angeles Lighting Company printed on its monthly bills this rhetorical question: "Why use Electric Incandescent Light when you can Light your Premises with INCANDESCENT GAS LIGHTS for One Quarter the Cost?"[8]

Despite the expanded market for commercial energy, Los Angeles Lighting's business operations remained small during the 1890s. Less than one third of the space on only a single floor of Southern California Gas Company's South Flower Street headquarters in the 1980s would have comfortably accommodated the entire office force in 1891. Fewer than a half dozen people worked in the office. Only two individuals were assigned to reading meters and

Interior gas lighting at the Los Angeles Public Library around 1900.

In the late nineteenth century, servicemen often hand-carried meters to customers.

1892 | Los Angeles
oil discoveries.

1901 | Lowe and son perfect
method of manufacturing
gas from oil.

Above: Los Angeles Lighting
meter reader on his route,
turn of the century. Left:
Foreman J.B. Ginther's
timebook for 1903.

collecting payments, and they handled these duties on foot or by bicycle.[10]

Los Angeles Lighting's business may have been modest, but it was due to no fault of the company. Between 1890 and 1900, the highly competitive gas industry in southern California fell on hard times, especially during the national depression years of 1893 to 1897 — the worst economic crisis the country had experienced to that date. The rate of population increase slowed considerably, but even taking into account the diminished growth, the gas industry failed to keep pace. The immense cost of installing pipelines and building gas processing plants was difficult to overcome in an era of restricted financial resources, and competition made such investments risky propositions. Some small local gas companies could not withstand the intense rivalry with electricity and other gas suppliers, and they simply went out of business entirely. Others just barely hung on, hoping for better times. Still other firms tried to survive by becoming companies known in the industry as "Roman Riders" — firms that embraced both gas and electric utilities.[11]

The management of Pacific Lighting Company had decided early to pursue this latter strategy and to increase the firm's interest in providing electrical service. Shortly after Pacific Lighting became involved in the southern California gas business, in 1890 the firm had purchased a controlling interest in the Los Angeles Electric Company. Cline then assumed the presidency and management of the electric operations as well as that of Los Angeles Lighting. Pacific Lighting had also acquired other firms that either specialized in one type of energy production — such as San Bernardino's Electric

Light and Power Company — or that were dual utilities, like Ventura Gas and Electric Company.[12]

The Los Angeles Electric Company, like the gas firm, remained relatively small in the early 1890s. Initially, electricity — like gas — was used almost exclusively for illumination, and customers were billed on the basis of how many light fixtures they had, not on how much electricity was used. In 1893 Los Angeles Electric had only three main electrical circuits in the city. The first, the "store circuit," operated from one hour before sunset until 10:30 P.M. Two other circuits were turned off at 9:00 P.M. and at midnight, with the former providing service for homes and the latter for restaurants and saloons. Electric street lamps, like their gas counterparts, operated on an irregular schedule; they were lit only when the full moon did not provide enough light on its own.[13]

Just as gas firms tried to expand their operations by developing new markets, electric companies also sought additional ways to use their product. By 1895 electric fans, flatirons, curling irons, stoves, heating pads, and sewing machines were all available. With these appliances came the need to measure electric consumption

Los Angeles Lighting
employees at the Burdick
Building around 1890.

CALIFORNIA GAS AND COKE 1913
PASADENA GAS & ELEC.
PASADENA CONSOLIDATED GAS 1909

LOS ANGELES GAS AND ELECTRIC CORP.

LOS ANGELES GAS CO.
CONSUMERS' GAS, LIGHT
LOWE GAS & ELEC.
LOS ANGELES LIGHTING
LOS ANGELES ELECTRIC
LOS ANGELES GAS & ELEC. CO. 1909
INGLEWOOD GAS CO. 1912

Los Angeles Gas and Electric
family tree, 1908-1937.

Los Angeles Gas and Electric
horse-drawn wagon, turn
of the century.

William G. Kerckhoff

Hydroelectric Power Pioneer.

William G. Kerckhoff was born in Terre Haute, Indiana, on March 30, 1856. After a childhood in the Midwest, he visited California in 1875 on a camping trip. Kerckhoff was so taken with the state that he moved west three years later. His earliest business venture in California was the purchase of a lumber company, which constructed the first wooden wharfs at San Pedro. Kerckhoff also built a fleet of wooden commercial ships, and he moved into other endeavors by forming the Azusa Ice and Cold Storage Company to supply the Santa Fe Railroad with ice for chilling oranges to be shipped east. The ice company relied on water power, which led Kerckhoff and Allan C. Balch to organize the San Gabriel Power Company. Los Angeles received its first hydroelectric current from this firm in 1897.

Kerckhoff soon became involved in other hydroelectric organizations such as San Joaquin Light and Power Company, and his interest in harnessing water to generate electricity was enhanced by Henry Huntington's development of an electric streetcar system for Los Angeles. To provide current for the cars, Kerckhoff became one of the founders of Pacific Light and Power Company, which ultimately led in 1910 to the creation of Southern California Gas Company — at first one of Pacific Lighting's principal competitors and later one of its subsidiaries.

Aside from his business interests, Kerckhoff was prominent in San Francisco and Los Angeles community activities, and he was a generous benefactor to the California Institute of Technology at Pasadena and to the University of California, Los Angeles. Kerckhoff died in 1929.[14]

Electric streetcar at Broadway and Second streets, Los Angeles, 1905.

more accurately, and Los Angeles Electric gradually began to install meters. Nonetheless, as late as 1897 electricity was still so novel that one employee could read all the company's meters in less than a day.[15]

Like the situation in the gas industry, competition among electric firms throughout southern California was intense. Pacific Lighting's electric subsidiary in San Bernardino, for example, confronted two other electric companies even though the town had barely five thousand residents. Meanwhile, in Los Angeles, the electric business had its share of "pirates," who organized electric firms only to force older, more-established companies to buy them out. One such pirate, according to C.O.G. Miller, was C.R. Lloyd, who created "on paper and in his mind many opposition electric plants, all of which he has offered to consolidate with the Los Angeles Electric Company." Miller added that Los Angeles Electric had "never been able to see anything but 'cheek' in Lloyd's Los Angeles property."[16]

Despite the nuisance caused by pirates, Los Angeles Electric had serious competitors. Chief among them was Edison Electric Company, which was created in 1897 by the merger of two smaller firms, West Side Lighting (which supplied Los Angeles's city hall with free electricity to insure the company's favor) and Los Angeles Edison Electric Company. After its formation Edison Electric continued to bring smaller organizations into its system.[17]

Another significant competitor, Pacific Light and Power, was formed in 1902 by William G. Kerckhoff and Allan C. Balch — both of whom were heavily involved in developing hydroelectric power in the foothills of the Sierra Nevada through their San Joaquin Light and Power Company. Like

Edison Electric, Pacific Light and Power campaigned to consolidate electric properties throughout southern California. Both companies eventually entered the gas industry, thus offering competition to Pacific Lighting's gas and electric utility subsidiaries.[18]

Since parts of Pacific Light and Power and Edison Electric were eventually absorbed into Pacific Lighting Company's holdings, their backgrounds are significant to Pacific Lighting's history. This is particularly true because of important innovations they brought to the gas utility industry — changes that eventually came to benefit Pacific Lighting. These innovations included the use of underground natural gas on a large scale and the construction of a long-distance gas pipeline and compressor station to bring natural gas to the Los Angeles area.

The origins of Pacific Light and Power and Edison Electric and their roles as competitors to Pacific Lighting's subsidiaries stemmed from a second population boom that swept southern California between 1900 and 1915. This era of explosive growth was caused by a variety of factors. Oil discoveries throughout the southern part of the state triggered a rush to tap the black gold. In addition, Los Angeles boosterism lured thousands of tourists to the area seeking relaxation and the health benefits associated with the mild climate. Many visitors returned to take up permanent residence. Adding to the growth was Los Angeles's anti-union reputation — fostered by the *Los Angeles Times* — which kept labor costs down. The low pay scale attracted a substantial manufacturing base to the city.

Also contributing to Los Angeles's second boom was a natural disaster in another part of the state. Shortly after 5:00 A.M. on April 18, 1906,

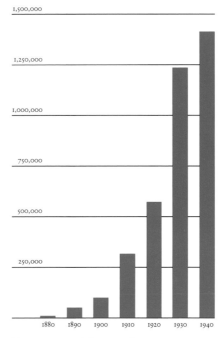

Enormous population growth of Los Angeles, 1880-1940.

La Fiesta de Los Angeles Parade, 1894, staged by civic organizations to attract tourists and settlers.

1902 | Oil-gas process implemented by Los Angeles Lighting Company.

1902 | Pacific Light and Power organized.

The Great Earthquake

C.O.G. Miller's Recollections of the 1906 San Francisco Earthquake.

We had been to the theatre Tuesday evening and retired very late. About 5:15 Wednesday morning [April 18, 1906] we were awakened from sound slumber by a severe and continued earthquake shock. . . . When the shock was over, I walked around and through the house . . . and noted there was little damage, fifty dollars would cover the loss of the contents. The only damage to the house was the falling of three out of four chimneys. I went back to bed again. A little later someone from across the street requested me to turn off the gas in the houses in the neighborhood where the fixtures had come down. . . .

I did not know anything about the fire until about

San Francisco in flames five hours after the great earthquake.

seven o'clock [A.M.] when Charles (our chauffeur) came up with the automobile and asked if we needed any assistance, saying that automobiles were badly needed downtown to take the wounded to the hospitals. I told him to do whatever he could for an hour or so and to come back at eight o'clock as we might need it for ourselves. . . . [To assess damages, I went downtown. I] left the motor at California and Mason streets and went down to the Savings Union Building [which housed Pacific Lighting's offices], where the only damage done was a little precipitation of plaster on the top floors. The first two or three floors seemed to be undisturbed. I spoke to several bankers on the sidewalk, and all expressed the opinion that

the Savings Union Building was in no danger from the fire, which then had reached the east side of Sansome Street two blocks away. Nevertheless, I went up to our offices on the fifth floor, took some papers out of my private safe and a list of the stockholders of the Pacific Lighting Company out of their safe. . . . [I then] started out again for the district near the fire to help carry women and children and their bundles to a place of safety. . . .

Thursday morning at 1:30 [A.M.] I was awakened . . . [and] told the fire extended to Bush and Polk streets. . . . I dressed and made another trip up to Lafayette Square and noted that the fire had not crossed Jones Street hill and decided it was perfectly safe not to make any move until morning. . . . [I was awakened

again at 4:00 A.M. and] made another trip up to the hill and noted that the fire was slowly extending west. The day before I had bought all the gasoline I could, getting it in quart bottles, gallon cans, and whatever we could lay our hands on [to use in the family automobile if an evacuation became necessary]. We were still very short, and it occurred to me that . . . [a neighbor] might have some in his stable, and at 5:30 [A.M.], we started out for his place in the automobile. We found him at his residence with a large wagon moving his furniture as he had been notified that the . . . residence opposite [his home] was to be dynamited at seven o'clock [to act as a fire break]. He had his machine full of gasoline and five gallons over and told me

Larkin and Fulton streets
with the ruins of city hall
on the left, April 18, 1906.

Looking west from the
intersection of California
and Market streets. Ruins
still smoldering on Friday,
April 20, 1906 — two days
after the quake.

he would let me have two gallons of it, and that he had declined everyone else. . . . [We
ascertained that the ferries
were running to Oakland and
then used the gasoline to deliver friends and relatives to
the docks.]

Upon going up to Lafa-
yette Square at six o'clock in
the evening and noting that
the fire had reached the east
side of Van Ness Avenue at

California Street and had gone
as far as Octavia at the southern part of the city, I returned
home and told Janet I thought
it would be a miracle if our
house was not burned within
twenty-four hours. . . . In the
afternoon between trips to
Lafayette Square, I cached all
of our silver and some of the
bronzes in the garden. When
we decided that we also would
go to Oakland, we dug up the
silver and bronzes, piled the
auto full, and with the cook
sitting in the front on the foot-
board and I standing on the
step, started for the ferry. We

caught the 8:20 ferry to
Oakland arriving at Fourteenth
and Union about 9:30 where
we all stayed overnight. . . .

On Saturday [after re-
turning to San Francisco to
rejoin relatives still there], I
made a trip through the banking district [to check on Pacific
Lighting's offices]. . . . I could
distinctly recognize in the
[fire-ravaged] debris at the
Savings Union [Building,
which the bankers had been
certain would never burn,] the
old-fashioned fireproof safe
that father bought some fifty
years ago. The safe was not
sprung; the only injury I could
see to it was the burning off of
the ornamental handle. . . .[19]

Looking west at destruction
along California Street. Note
St. Francis Hotel on extreme
left and Fairmont Hotel on
extreme right.

Oil Discoveries in Southern California.

The population boom of the 1880s in southern California brought an increased demand for fuel for domestic, commercial, and industrial use. About a million tons of coal were imported to California in 1886, increasing to over a million and a half tons in 1888. Most of this came through the port of San Francisco. Following the boom, a bitter contest began between those who advocated using coal for gas manufacturing and those who preferred T.S.C. Lowe's oil-gas process. Pacific Lighting Company relied solely on coal until the turn of the century, and Walter Cline was active in the Los Angeles "free harbor" fight of the 1890s to keep the transportation costs of this vital commodity low.

When major crude oil discoveries were made in southern California in the late 1880s and the early 1890s, Pacific Coast industrial development was stimulated. Between 1892 and 1897, twenty-three hundred wells were drilled in the Los Angeles area by over two hundred companies, and seventy-five million barrels of oil were extracted. The city placed restrictions on drilling within its limits thereafter, and by 1907 only a few new wells were sunk in Los Angeles.

Although state lawmakers were initially wary of the use of oil, the railroads shifted to it and away from coal as a fuel source. Gas manufacturing plants also made the change, and gas made from oil rapidly began to capture the heating and cooking market as well. By the turn of the century, the value of California oil as one of the state's greatest assets was well-established. Oil and its by-products had many uses: to manufacture gas for heating and cooking free of soot and ashes ("the housekeepers delight"); for paving and lighting streets; and for fuel for streetcars, locomotives, steamships, factories, machine shops, and other motor-driven equipment.[20]

Oil wells between First and Temple streets, Los Angeles, around 1900.

a massive earthquake on the San Andreas Fault rumbled through northern California. Thousands of sleeping San Franciscans were jolted from their beds; buildings were thrown off their foundations; brick structures collapsed; and gaping fissures opened in the earth. The earthquake was bad enough, but what followed made the quake look pale in comparison. Short-circuited electrical wires set off fires that burned block after block of the city's core. Volunteer fire fighters were no match for the firestorm because water mains had been shattered by the quake. By the time the fire burned itself out three days later, at least five hundred city blocks had been destroyed, including the city's main business district. Over 450 people lost their lives; 300,000 were left homeless; and damages were estimated to be $200 million.[21]

The destruction in northern California had the opposite effect on Los Angeles. Many panic-stricken San Francisco residents and businesses fled their city's ruins to the Los Angeles area, where homes and shops seemed to sprout overnight. The additional people placed more demands on the city's already overstressed utilities, which were just beginning to recover from the severe competition and the national depression of the 1890s.

Prompted by soaring population, gas manufacturing grew dramatically during the first decade of the twentieth century. The average daily production of Los Angeles Lighting Company was roughly a half million cubic feet in 1896, but less than a decade later it had jumped to a staggering four million cubic feet per day. Yet even with this nearly ten-fold increase, the company still could not keep pace with demand, much of which could be attributed to the firm's success in marketing gas appliances. As one long-time employee recalled, "it was during these early years that the growth of the territory began to give the growth of our gas plant a merry race, and sometimes in the winter cold spells we were seriously pressed."[22]

The population surge intensified competition once again, and Los Angeles Gas and Electric Company — formed in 1904 by the combination of Pacific Lighting's gas and electric utilities — found its system seriously strained. To discourage new entries into the energy market, the company extended service into recently settled parts of the city as fast as possible, but the expansion left the firm poorly equipped to supply gas during peak demand. Pressure in gas mains frequently fell off. To make matters worse, Los Angeles Gas and Electric accidentally introduced oil with a high sulphur content into its manufacturing process, and the resulting gas burned with a profound stench. While the scent problem was eventually remedied, the public's experience with short supplies and bad odors rekindled animosities and generated renewed complaints about the company's allegedly high prices. The firm faced a major public relations challenge.[23]

Los Angeles Gas and Electric's difficulties reached a crisis level in the winter of 1906-1907 when an unusually cold spell left many customers without heat, sometimes for days on end. "Gas Famine!" screamed newspaper headlines as the chilly days — both indoors and out — dragged on. The editors of the *Los Angeles Daily Times* knew precisely whom to blame for the shortages:

> The gas company throws up its hands. It is out of gas. It cannot supply the demand. It has been swamped. It acknowledges . . . [its fault] — which

Spring Street south from First Street, early 1900s.

Looking north up Spring Street from Third Street, 1903.

Advertisements from Los Angeles Gas and Electric's newspaper campaign to discredit City Gas Company, 1907.

City Gas Company men installing pipes, 1907.

is mighty cold comfort for its customers. It has had delays, accidents, hard luck, disappointments — and an utterly unexpected drain upon its resources due to the amazing growth of the population and the increased consumption of the popular fuel. When the gas company set about to encourage the use of gas stoves, it knew not what it was doing, eh?[24]

The shortages were embarrassing, but the company's reputation sank even lower when deaths were attributed to gas asphyxiation or carbon monoxide poisoning from poorly vented heaters using what little gas was available.[25]

By February 1907 the growing dissatisfaction with existing gas service and a national trend toward municipal reform movements led prominent Los Angeles business people — such as J.F. Sartori, who later became president of Security Pacific Bank, and John R. Haynes, a wealthy reformer and later president of Los Angeles's Board of Water and Power Commissioners — to band together to turn the public's displeasure with existing gas service to their financial advantage. After considerable discussion, the group organized City Gas Company as a competitor of Los Angeles Gas and Electric, hoping eventually to sell the new firm's works to the city for cost plus ten percent. City Gas, which its sponsors believed would act more responsively to consumer demands, quickly laid large feeder lines, and in March 1908 the firm began gas distribution from a plant located at Tenth Street and Santa Fe Avenue.[26]

Los Angeles Gas and Electric did not take this threat to its dominant position in the gas industry lightly. In an advertising brochure, the company noted that it had "made thirteen voluntary reductions in the price of gas" over the preceding seventeen

1906 | Los Angeles "gas famine," 1906-1907.

years leading to the 1907 rate of eighty cents per thousand cubic feet. The company also claimed that it was undertaking vast improvements to serve the burgeoning Los Angeles population. Among the changes were an increase in gas generating capacity from eleven million to twenty million cubic feet per day, the construction of a large gas holder capable of storing five million cubic feet, and the complete fireproofing of the company's electric works.[27]

These improvements were financed in part by changes relating to a 1907 reorganization of Pacific Lighting Company as Pacific Lighting Corporation. The rechartering allowed the firm to issue a new stock offering, a large portion of which was purchased by George Volkmann and August Schilling, who together operated the spice company bearing the latter's name. The Volkmann and Schilling families continued to have large holdings of Pacific Lighting's stock for decades thereafter, with grandsons of Volkmann and Schilling serving on the firm's board of directors as late as the 1980s.[28]

Simultaneous to Pacific Lighting's reorganization and its subsidiary's improvements, Los Angeles Gas and Electric fought to block City Gas Company's expansion efforts by all other means possible. Jumping on the reform movement bandwagon, Los Angeles Gas and Electric launched a newspaper advertisement blitz claiming that City Gas existed only on paper to benefit a so-called "bankers' syndicate" — syndicates and trusts being among the favorite targets of reformers of the day. When this tactic failed to stop consumers from signing up with City Gas, Los Angeles Gas and Electric went to court to obtain an injunction halting its rival's activities. As legal avenues were explored, extra-legal methods of

City Gas Company cartoon,
Los Angeles Record,
August 16, 1907.

A 1908 photograph of City Gas Company's plant at Tenth Street and Santa Fe Avenue.

1907 | City Gas Company formed to compete with Los Angeles Gas and Electric.

1907 | Pacific Lighting Company rechartered as Pacific Lighting Corporation.

44

Southern California Gas
Company survey gang,
Riverside, 1911.

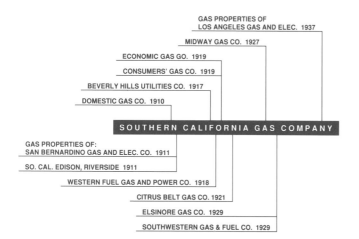

Southern California Gas
Company family tree,
1910-1937.

intimidation also came into play. Opposing maintenance and pipeline crews fought with pickhandles,
and each company surreptitiously removed its
opponent's meters. Eventually, however, City
Gas found it was no match for the older, more-
established Los Angeles Gas and Electric. Reluc-
tantly, the new firm sold its assets to Pacific Light
and Power, controlled by Kerckhoff and Balch, who
had positioned themselves to compete vigorously
for the lucrative southern California gas market.
Kerckhoff and Balch combined City Gas (renamed
Domestic Gas) with other gas holdings in 1910 to
form Southern California Gas Company, and this
consolidation emerged as one of Los Angeles Gas
and Electric's chief rivals.[29]

At about the same time, Edison Electric —
which had been reorganized as Southern California
Edison in 1909 — decided that the future belonged
to electricity, and to focus all of the firm's efforts on
that energy market, the company began to liquidate
its gas holdings throughout southern California.
C.S.S. Forney, a gas company entrepreneur, and
Ferdinand R. Bain, who had dabbled in a variety of
businesses in southern California and elsewhere, organized Southern Counties Gas Company of California in February 1911 to take over the gas networks
being sold by Southern California Edison. The new
firm initially purchased plants and distribution systems in Anaheim, Fullerton, Orange, Santa Ana,
and Whittier. Southern Counties Gas also absorbed
two companies headed by Forney that served
Arcadia, Azusa, Covina, Glendora, Monrovia,
and Sierra Madre.[30]

With the organization of Southern California
Gas and Southern Counties Gas, a substantial

1909 | Buena Vista Hills
"dry" gas field
discovered.

consolidation of public utilities had taken place. Even Los Angeles Gas and Electric had participated in the merger frenzy by purchasing T.S.C. Lowe's Pasadena Consolidated Gas in 1909.[31] This streamlined competitive situation forced Southern California Gas and Southern Counties Gas to investigate new technologies to expand their marketability. For the time being, however, Pacific Lighting was satisfied to let the newcomers gamble on untried gas technologies; its subsidiary, Los Angeles Gas and Electric, focused on improving service and recovering the associated costs.

The research in new gas technologies concentrated on making the natural gas found underground a viable fuel source. Initially, gas companies had shown little interest in piping natural gas into their systems. The gas found with crude oil drilling in the San Joaquin Valley, at Santa Maria, and in the Los Angeles Basin was casinghead gas (also called "wet" gas), which could not be made into a satisfactory fuel until technological innovations made this possible in 1903. Gas distribution companies also doubted that casinghead gas supplies were large enough to exploit even after a wet gas process was developed. The discovery of a huge natural gas field containing more desirable "dry" gas in the Buena Vista Hills near Taft, California, on June 16, 1909, changed everything. This gas was produced separately from oil and thus did not require the refining applied to casinghead gas. Moreover, the dry gas appeared to exist in huge quantities. Seeing a potential competitive edge, Kerckhoff and Balch's San Joaquin Light and Power Company became the first firm to convert its system from manufactured gas to dry natural gas piped in from the Buena Vista Hills.[32]

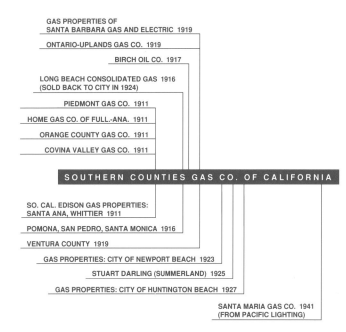

Southern Counties Gas Company family tree, 1911-1941.

Southern Counties Gas Company vehicle around 1915.

1910 | Southern California Gas Company formed.

1911 | Southern Counties Gas Company of California organized.

After San Joaquin Light and Power successfully switched its system — part of which served Bakersfield — to natural gas, Kerckhoff and Balch decided to bring natural gas into their Southern California Gas Company lines to better their competitive position in relation to Pacific Lighting's powerful subsidiary, Los Angeles Gas and Electric. To build the pipeline from the Buena Vista Hills to its Los Angeles distribution system, a distance of 112 miles, Kerckhoff and Balch met with John Martin, an organizer of northern California's Pacific Gas and Electric Company, and in November 1911 they incorporated Midway Gas Company as an affiliate of Southern California Gas. Southern California Gas raised the funds needed to build the pipeline by floating a bond issue, and it secured rights for additional gas wells to be drilled by another subsidiary, Northern Exploration Company.[33]

Construction on the Midway pipeline — one of the three longest pipelines in the nation at the time — began in April 1912. Substantial difficulties had to be overcome in hauling and installing the twelve-inch pipe over the mountains from the San Joaquin Valley to Glendale, where natural gas was to be introduced into the Southern California Gas Company mains. The terrain was extremely rugged. Roads were built to transport pipe and equipment, and because motor trucks were not capable of dealing with the demanding topography, wagons and horses had to be used. Other major problems confronted the project. Winter storms severely damaged construction, and the improper installation of rubber gaskets forced the reworking of several miles of pipeline. Despite the difficulties, the first natural gas reached Glendale in April 1913.[34]

Newhall Tunnel along Midway pipeline construction project.

A gas company truck, 1913. Such vehicles could not negotiate mountainous terrain on the Midway pipeline route, so horse-drawn wagons were used.

Midway pipeline construction through mountains.

Horse-drawn wagon used building the Midway pipeline.

While the pipeline was an engineering marvel of its day and a milestone in the history of southern California's gas industry, another innovative feature — a compressor station built at Taft by Midway Gas — was equally important. Whereas dry gas coming from the Buena Vista Hills was under tremendous natural pressure and provided its own impetus to flow to Los Angeles, there was a substantial volume of casinghead gas under lower pressure in the oil wells near Taft. This wet gas was simply being flared as a nuisance by oil companies even though processing was now theoretically possible. Including the casinghead gas in the Midway pipeline without increasing its compression, however, would have undermined one of the advantages offered by the dry gas field — its high pressure. Thus, to use the wet gas, in 1914 Midway Gas constructed the Taft compressor station — the first such facility west of the Rocky Mountains — which provided the necessary pressure.[35]

Other gas companies — including Pacific Lighting's subsidiary, Los Angeles Gas and Electric — cautiously watched the natural gas experiments. By the time the Midway pipeline was being constructed, Los Angeles had become one of the principal oil-producing areas in the state and yielded substantial quantities of casinghead gas, but it was not until the Midway pipeline and Taft compressor station proved successful that Los Angeles oil companies began to consider marketing their natural gas supplies. At first they had few buyers. Southern California Gas, with its heavy investment in the Midway pipeline, was in no position to invest further in pipelines to tap gas from Los Angeles oil fields. Los Angeles Gas and Electric viewed the

1912 | Midway pipeline construction begins.

whole proposition as too perilous (although it did buy natural gas from the Midway pipe and mixed this product with its own manufactured gas, creating what was known as "reformed" gas). Southern Counties Gas, on the other hand, was less timid. Franklin S. Wade, superintendent of operations for Southern Counties Gas (and later president of both that firm and Southern California Gas once the two companies had become Pacific Lighting subsidiaries), was so impressed by the success of the natural gas system at Bakersfield that in early 1914 he recommended that his firm introduce natural gas from the Olinda field a few miles north of Fullerton. This newly discovered field was estimated to be capable of producing 500,000 cubic feet of gas per day, a sizeable source of supply if it could be utilized. Tapping the oil fields, however, was a financially hazardous step because Southern Counties Gas bookkeepers projected that the greater burning efficiency of natural gas would cause less gas to be used and therefore contribute to diminished income.[36]

Despite the risk, Southern Counties Gas gambled that a shift to natural gas would ultimately pay for itself by stimulating increased consumer demand, and the company's officials decided to tie into the Olinda field. As expected, total revenues dropped precipitously to less than half of what they had been before the inclusion of natural gas. Yet within a short period, income rebounded as the demand for the new gas soared. The experiment proved so successful that Southern Counties Gas extended its pipelines to numerous oil and gas fields over the next few years. Eventually the company converted most of its system to natural gas except for a few areas where it bought supplies from Southern California Gas, which still relied on a mixture of natural and manufactured gas.[37]

By 1915 the utility industry in southern California was dominated by a handful of firms. Four major companies — Los Angeles Gas and Electric, Southern California Gas, Southern Counties Gas, and Southern California Edison — had consolidated the myriad small systems that had existed at the turn of the century into efficient, powerful, and competing organizations. They had done this through mergers, acquisitions, and a willingness to experiment with different fuel types and sources. Yet the years of unfettered growth had nearly come to an end. Coinciding with the consolidations was an enhanced public disillusionment with the activities of these seemingly uncontrollable utilities, and as Pacific Lighting started to make the final round of acquisitions, it became increasingly entangled in the fight over government regulation.

**International Gas
Congress display of
modern appliances, 1915.**

1913 | Midway pipeline completed bringing natural gas to Los Angeles from the San Joaquin Valley.

1914 | Southern Counties Gas Company begins use of Los Angeles Basin natural gas.

Regulation vs. Public Ownership

The Battle Joined.

IMPETUS FOR GOVERNMENT INVOLVEMENT in the Los Angeles utility business came from rapid urban development in the early years of the twentieth century a decade before the completion of the Midway pipeline. Los Angeles grew so quickly during this period that municipal services could not keep pace with demand, inevitably causing public displeasure with the utility companies. Like most major American cities at the turn of the century, Los Angeles was mired in machine politics that hindered civic progress. A national reform movement called "progressivism," which demanded more honest and efficient government, gained momentum. Agitation for change precipitated a crisis of public confidence in privately owned utilities, and citizens insisted upon direct government intervention. Two proposals emerged, one calling for government regulation of utilities and the other advocating municipal ownership. These twin issues of regulation and municipal ownership were central concerns to Pacific Lighting's management and the firm's subsidiaries throughout the first four decades of the twentieth century.

By 1905 public dissatisfaction with the high cost and inadequate gas service provided by Los Angeles Gas and Electric caused the Los Angeles City Council to consider a proposal to build a

The Los Angeles Gas and Electric Corporation building at 810 South Flower Street shortly after it was constructed in 1925.

1905 | 1937

BETWEEN 1906 AND 1936, ADVOCATES OF MUNICIPAL OWNERSHIP BATTLED WITH PACIFIC LIGHTING OVER ITS SUBSIDIARY'S ELECTRIC PROPERTIES, WHILE CALIFORNIA IMPOSED CONTROLS OVER PUBLIC UTILITIES.

1900 | Progressive reform era, 1900-1916.

1906 | Municipal Ownership Party formed in Los Angeles.

public gas works. The council also took firm steps to regulate gas rates. The following year, a Municipal Ownership Party was launched in Los Angeles with the operating premise that the city's political malaise was due to bribery of public officials by corporations seeking franchises. "The private ownership of public utilities is the cause of all political corruption," proclaimed Stanley B. Wilson, the Municipal Ownership Party's candidate for mayor, giving voice to one of the cardinal tenets of progressivism. Although the conservative *Los Angeles Times* derisively described the party's supporters as "dreamers, doctrinaires, professional agitators, and

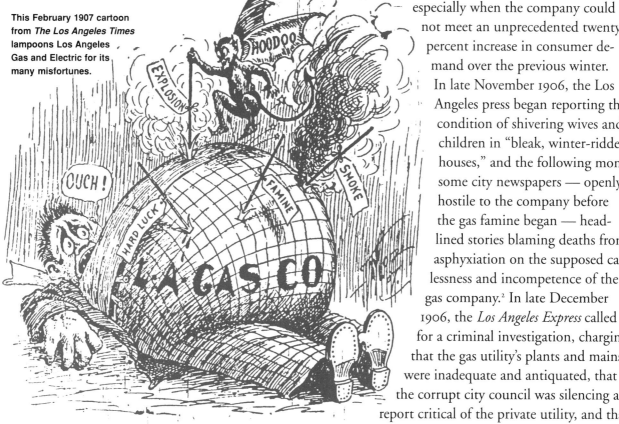

This February 1907 cartoon from *The Los Angeles Times* lampoons Los Angeles Gas and Electric for its many misfortunes.

reformers" drawn from the "army of discontent," the organization attracted many adherents. A large part of the new party's platform was attractive specifically to the working people of the city, but the elimination of political graft and the improvement of much-needed public services had a broader appeal. Many hoped that public ownership of water supply systems, railroads, and electric and gas utilities would bring cheaper rates and better service.[1]

Unfortunately for Pacific Lighting's subsidiary, the Los Angeles Gas and Electric Company, the gas famine during the winter of 1906-1907 gave added ammunition to the municipalists, especially when the company could not meet an unprecedented twenty percent increase in consumer demand over the previous winter. In late November 1906, the Los Angeles press began reporting the condition of shivering wives and children in "bleak, winter-ridden houses," and the following month some city newspapers — openly hostile to the company before the gas famine began — headlined stories blaming deaths from asphyxiation on the supposed carelessness and incompetence of the gas company.[2] In late December 1906, the *Los Angeles Express* called for a criminal investigation, charging that the gas utility's plants and mains were inadequate and antiquated, that the corrupt city council was silencing a report critical of the private utility, and that

1907 | City Gas Company formed to compete with Los Angeles Gas and Electric.

the company was making exorbitant profits for its stockholders — seventy cents on every thousand feet of eighty-five cent gas — rather than using "its funds to keep abreast of the city's growth and increasing demand." (While reports of profits were exaggerated, Pacific Lighting's stockholders were receiving a very good return on their investment. In 1908, for example, the firm advertised gas as "the favorite stock of the millionaire" and boasted that a fifty percent return was not too much for an investor to expect.)[3]

As newspapers fanned public anger, consumers became infuriated that their gas bills remained high in spite of the inadequate service. Responding to the call for government action to remedy the situation, the newly elected mayor, Arthur Harper — a Democrat sympathetic to the municipal ownership movement — criticized Los Angeles Gas and Electric for negligence, deception, and lack of foresight. Although the company's assistant secretary and future president, Addison B. Day, correctly identified the source of the crisis as "the amazing unparalleled growth of the city," an investigation was underway by mid-January 1907.[4]

By the end of the month, the experts enlisted to examine the gas works made their preliminary report totally exonerating Los Angeles Gas and Electric. The firm's equipment was modern and more than adequate to meet the city's needs, the experts determined, although they recommended that the city adopt an ordinance requiring a minimum pressure in the gas lines. Many residents were outraged and denounced the findings as a whitewash. The public was still hostile and houses remained cold when a gas explosion in a restaurant

Damage done by a gas explosion at the corner of Fifth and Crocker streets in 1909, two years after a similar disaster in a downtown restaurant caused public alarm over the safety of gas.

killed four people and injured fourteen. Although the company was again found innocent of negligence, this sensational event brought the real or imagined failings of Pacific Lighting's principal subsidiary even more into the public eye, and many people — including some who were friendly to the firm — seriously questioned the quality of gas service and the safety of the gas company's product.[5]

The mood of Los Angeles's utility customers did not improve when they learned of the prosecution of corrupt public officials in San Francisco. A key figure was Abraham Ruef, boss of that city's Union Labor Party, who served as a confidential attorney to various public utility corporations. Ruef was charged with receiving a twenty-thousand-dollar bribe from a Pacific Gas and Electric Company official in return for certain political favors with the city government. The well-publicized Ruef trial

In 1910 Southern California Gas
Company relied on immigrant
laborers — such as these workers
from India — for ditch digging.

persuaded many Los Angeles residents that their
own city utilities and political leaders were equally
corrupt, and this added fuel to the progressive
movement at the city and state government levels.[6]

Following the traumatic winter of 1906-1907,
which had done so much to blacken the reputation
of the utility corporations in Los Angeles, the issue
of municipal ownership found a broad political base
among "thousands of ordinary citizens uncommitted
to radicalism of any sort but dissatisfied with private
service," as historian Robert Fogelson has written.[7]
John R. Haynes, who eventually helped oversee Los
Angeles's municipal water and electric system as a
member of the Board of Water and Power Commissioners, was one of the discontented. Haynes was
convinced that the city government was in the hands
of a "corrupt minority." To counter the power of the
political machine, he founded the Direct Legislation
League, which introduced the initiative, recall, and
referendum to California and the nation. Like other

progressive reformers of the era, Haynes supported
civil service reform, nonpartisan elections, and
direct primaries, and he was sympathetic to the
principle of municipal utility ownership.

With the backing of people like Haynes, the
progressives waxed in strength and succeeded in
electing George Alexander as mayor of Los Angeles
in 1909 — and reelecting him in 1911 — as the
antimachine, Good Government Party candidate.[8]
Alexander's progressive administration quickly
moved forward to implement various reforms.
Shortly after Alexander's first election, the city advanced plans to develop hydroelectric power from
its Owens Valley Aqueduct — then under construction to bring new water supplies to Los Angeles —
and by a seven-to-one margin voters authorized
$3.5 million to finance hydroelectric generating
plants. At the same time, the city also established
a board of public utilities to bring the gas and electric companies under municipal regulatory control.
The progressive movement thus posed a threat to
Los Angeles Gas and Electric and other utilities in
the form of both government regulation and the
possibility of public ownership. The utility companies did not sit idly by as these proposals menaced
their hegemony. In an effort to protect their interests,
utility corporations offered to buy and market the
city's hydroelectric power from the Owens Valley
when it became available, but voters decisively
rejected this proposal in 1911.[9]

As the City of Los Angeles tightened its control over utility firms, the state government took
similar steps. As early as 1907 California Governor
James N. Gillett had urged that stricter regulatory
controls be adopted by the legislature, and two years

The social and industrial revolt that shook the City of Los Angeles in 1910-1911 had its roots in the 1890s, when Harrison Gray Otis, publisher of the *Los Angeles Times*, provoked that city's first serious labor conflict by refusing to compromise with members of the printers' union. The *Times* workers were protesting a twenty percent wage cut by staging a boycott, which ultimately proved to be unsuccessful. Otis was joined in his opposition to Los Angeles union activity by merchants, manufacturers, and other boosters, who were convinced that low wage levels would attract industry to Los Angeles, and together they kept organized labor from securing a foothold in the city. Thus, Los Angeles established itself as the citadel of the "open shop" just as the "closed shop" was becoming an accepted fact in San Francisco due to that city's powerful unions.

Despite stiff opposition from Otis and other civic leaders, a Union Labor Party was formed in Los Angeles in 1902, and although it was defeated in the municipal elections, the political strength of workers increased. Labor found a temporary ally in William

Randolph Hearst, the San Francisco newspaper publisher, when he established a rival newspaper in "Otistown."

Hostility in Los Angeles between pro- and anti-labor coalitions reached a peak when San Francisco union organizers lent their moral and financial support to the members of the Los Angeles metal trade unions, and fifteen hundred workers went on strike in early June 1910. Four months later while this strike — the largest the city had ever experienced — was still in progress, a pre-dawn explosion on October 1, 1910 destroyed the *Los Angeles Times* building. Twenty men died and seventeen were injured in the blast.

The utility companies as well as the other large employers were alarmed that similar bombing attacks might be made on their properties by "Red Socialists and the more than red IWW's [International Workers of the World]," as a Southern California Gas Company official later recalled. Several guns were purchased, and gas company employees guarded the firm's gas plant for three days and four nights

"on the lookout for bomb throwers and fire fiends who proposed, by taking matters into their own hands, to force submission to their plans of big pay for little or no work, under an anarchy of intimidation and compulsion."

The conservative *Times* and other big businesses joined forces with their foe, the Good Government Party, to defeat the Socialist Party candidate for mayor, Job Harriman, in the 1911 municipal election.

The *Times* explosion polarized the people of Los Angeles. While some agreed with the newspaper's charge that the blast was the "crime of the century," pro-labor sympathizers attributed it to a leaky gas main. Harrison Gray Otis feared that Los Angeles, like

Crowds of curious spectators gathered to stare at the wreckage of the *Times* building the day after the explosion.

San Francisco, would come under a pro-labor city administration when Job Harriman, the Socialist Party candidate for mayor, received more votes in the 1911 primary election than the Good Government Party incumbent, George Alexander. Otis had opposed progressives like Alexander during the early stages of the Los Angeles municipal reform movement, but he temporarily forgot his rancor against them and supported Alexander for reelection in order to defeat Harriman. Much to Otis's satisfaction, on the eve of the election, the Structural Iron Workers' Union secretary, John J. McNamara, and his brother James confessed to bombing the *Times* building. The McNamara brothers acknowledged that the bombing had been planned at the national headquarters of their union, thus discrediting and demoralizing the labor movement and perpetuating the open shop in Los Angeles for three more decades.[10]

Twenty thousand people watched as the first Owens Valley water reached the San Fernando Valley on November 5, 1913.

later the Wright Act widened the jurisdiction of the state's railroad commission to include gas and electric companies and oil pipelines. C.O.G. Miller, then president of the Pacific Coast Gas Association, had anticipated the state legislators' actions in 1908 when he strongly had advocated state regulation of utilities. In his presidential address to the organization, Miller had argued that "if a fair rate is fixed and protection is given the companies, they should welcome regulation," but he warned that city leaders were subject to local political pressures making it impossible for them to act impartially. Therefore, Miller had concluded, the jurisdiction over the gas industry should be given to a state commission, following the lead of other progressive states.[11]

Miller's hopes for state regulation were realized soon after Hiram Johnson — who had prosecuted Abraham Ruef in the famous San Francisco corruption trial — was elected governor of California in November 1910 with the support of progressive

Republicans, who demanded a spectrum of reforms including the creation of a state public utilities board. The progressives also won control of both houses of the state legislature, and they began to carry out their programs. Those appointed to the task of writing a bill to regulate utility companies obtained copies of similar laws in other states and toured the nation gathering information. Subsequently, the first draft of the proposed legislation was sent to the leading public utilities, railroads, and chambers of commerce for comment. The bill received little adverse criticism and was passed unanimously by both houses of the legislature.[12]

The Public Utilities Act of 1911 empowered the California Railroad Commission — later renamed the Public Utilities Commission (PUC) — to regulate rates, set standards of service and safety, enforce certain financial restrictions, and impose other restraints on utility operations. The law mandated that charges for utility service were to be reasonable and nondiscriminatory and that all utilities were to furnish information about their activities to the commission on demand. The commission had considerable power: it could make its own investigations, hold hearings, revoke licenses,

1911 | California Public
Utilities Act passed.

and seek judicial support if its rulings were defied. Procedures for filing grievances by the utility companies or consumers and methods for appeals to the courts were outlined. Although the commissioners were political appointees, which meant that policies of the regulatory agency would fluctuate from one gubernatorial administration to the next, the Public Utilities Act was, on the whole, an example of enlightened legislation.[13]

Utility companies seized on the Public Utilities Act as a means to forestall municipal ownership and local regulation. When Los Angeles continued to pass ordinances mandating lower gas rates, as it had been doing for a number of years, Southern California Gas Company — then one of Los Angeles Gas and Electric's main competitors — responded by obtaining a federal court order prohibiting the city from such action. Frustrated by this limitation on its powers, the city surrendered its power to fix gas rates to the California Railroad Commission in August 1915.[14] Formal jurisdiction under the commission began December 5, 1917.

The passage of the Public Utilities Act did not end the drive for municipalization of gas and electric systems, however. The progressives had expected municipal ownership of city services to receive such widespread public endorsement that the plan would be removed from partisan conflict. Instead, the controversial issue intensified political strife on the state and local levels. "The great interests which the private companies have at stake compel them to use all sorts of means to protect their interests," commented one observer. This statement succinctly described the continuing struggle in Los Angeles as Pacific Lighting's subsidiary and other gas

John R. Haynes (1853-1937), an important civic leader, was one of the chief advocates of municipal ownership of gas and electric utilities.

Ezra F. Scattergood (1871-1947) was a founder and first chief electrical engineer of the city-owned Los Angeles power system.

1913 | Owens Valley Aqueduct water reaches Los Angeles.

1916 | Discovery of large natural gas supply in Los Angeles Basin.

One of the sources of contention that embroiled Los Angeles Gas and Electric and the City of Los Angeles in prolonged litigation was the city's use of the firm's electric poles. The number of poles congested the Los Angeles skyline, as this 1924 photograph of Whittier Boulevard shows.

and electric firms fought to defend their properties from the advocates of municipal ownership.[15]

Pacific Lighting's two main political adversaries were John Haynes and Ezra F. Scattergood. Like Haynes, Scattergood was a reformer, and he was instrumental in the plan to develop hydroelectric power from the Owens Valley Aqueduct. He later served as chief engineer and general manager of the Los Angeles Bureau of Power and Light (established in 1911 and renamed the Department of Water and Power in 1925). Both Haynes and Scattergood were tireless crusaders for public ownership of electricity and gas distribution systems. Yet despite their persistent efforts to convince voters that privately held utilities could not deliver adequate service at reasonable rates, Los Angeles voters were reluctant to adopt municipal ownership because they were wary of attacking the institution of private property ownership. Moreover, they were opposed to incurring a heavy burden of municipal indebtedness.[16]

The beginning volley in the chronically acrimonious struggle between the Bureau of Power and Light and the utility companies began shortly after the city conceived its plan to develop hydroelectric power from the Owens Valley Aqueduct. With the new power source, Scattergood promised to cut electric bills by thirty-three percent if municipal ownership of Los Angeles's electric system was adopted. Faced with the prospect of competition from the city's proposed electric works as well as the possible condemnation of their properties, the privately owned electric companies — Los Angeles Gas and Electric, Pacific Light and Power, and Southern California Edison — made a strenuous effort to block the entire aqueduct project. For

example, according to Haynes Los Angeles Gas and Electric secretly financed two civil suits in 1914 in an attempt to discredit the quality of the Owens Valley water and thereby kill the entire project. Although unsuccessful, these court cases — and many other legal actions instigated and financed by Pacific Lighting's subsidiary and other utilities — helped obstruct municipal ownership for many years. The cases cost the taxpayers and utility consumers of Los Angeles many thousands of dollars in lawyers' fees over the next two decades.[17]

In addition to harassing the city with endless and costly litigation, the electric companies also openly fought proposed bond issues for financing development of the municipal electric system. With great effort, the utilities defeated a 1913 proposal to build a city distribution system by convincing voters that other less-costly alternatives to municipal ownership existed. Arguing that while some governmental regulation was necessary and beneficial, the utility companies contended it would be folly to let politicians run business. Despite the 1913 victory, the bond issue carried the following year, and the movement toward municipal ownership of the city's electric system proceeded under Haynes-Scattergood leadership.[18]

Having won an elective mandate to distribute hydroelectric power, the Los Angeles Bureau of Power and Light began construction of its own electric distribution system while simultaneously requesting that the state railroad commission appraise the electric properties of the utility companies for condemnation proceedings. Armed with the power from the Owens Valley Aqueduct, in 1917 the bureau — under Scattergood's direction — began

1917 | The United States enters World War I.

1922 | Los Angeles buys Southern California Edison's electric system within city limits.

This 1923 cartoon in *L.A. Gas Monthly*, a publication of Los Angeles Gas and Electic Corporation, shows city politicians' frustrations over their efforts to municipalize privately-owned utilities.

competition with the existing electric firms by stringing parallel lines down streets that already had power and by undercutting the private companies' rates. Negotiations over the fair prices for the electric properties of Southern California Edison (which had absorbed Pacific Light and Power) and Los Angeles Gas and Electric dragged on for months, and the latter finally withdrew from the talks in disgust. The city came to an agreement with Southern California Edison in 1919, and three years later the city bought Edison's works for $13.5 million, leaving the firm's system intact outside the city limits.[19]

In addition to the obstacles the city encountered securing taxpayer approval for bonds to build, expand, and acquire utility properties (which the private companies fought each step of the way), the city faced the even greater problem that hydroelectric power from the Owens Valley Aqueduct was inadequate to meet the growing energy demands of the city. While Scattergood and the Bureau of Power and Light had the will to bring all the utilities under public control, they lacked the energy supplies to do so. Los Angeles now owned Southern California Edison's distribution system within the city limits, but the bureau continued to rely heavily on Edison's steam generating plant to supplement Owens Valley Aqueduct power. This put the bureau at a competitive disadvantage with Los Angeles Gas and Electric because Edison charged the city high rates for electricity and because the downtown area served by Los Angeles Gas and Electric had a high density of use, thus keeping that firm's operating costs low. As a result, Scattergood's predicted drop of thirty-three percent in city electric rates failed to materialize.

With the battle for municipalization faring badly in the early 1920s, the possibility that Pacific Lighting's Los Angeles subsidiary might remain indefinitely in private hands so frustrated Haynes that at one point he made a spectacle of himself complaining to the city council about the high cost of gas for his twelve-room mansion. The *Los Angeles Times* — which had long supported the utility companies — gleefully reported the incident, commenting dryly that although Haynes's nearest neighbor was Los Angeles Gas and Electric's president, Walter Cline, Haynes nonetheless harbored such resentful thoughts about the company and its management "that he could cook by [his thoughts] in lieu of gas if he could get them under his skillet."[20]

As the *Times* report suggested, the pro- and antimunicipalization factions were equally matched throughout the 1920s, and the struggle temporarily reached a stalemate. While keeping the advocates of municipal ownership at bay, Los Angeles Gas and Electric had to concentrate its energies on expanding its services due to the explosive southern California growth. Among other improvements, the company built a new electric plant at Seal Beach and enlarged other substations at a cost of $10 million to accommodate the needs of the additional 114,000 electric consumers gained during the decade. The number of Los Angeles Gas and Electric's gas meters nearly doubled in the 1920s, and millions of dollars were spent to expand and improve gas service.

Despite the deadlock in the electric municipalization drive, municipal ownership continued to threaten the utility industry, including those firms with gas systems, and the managements of Los Angeles Gas and Electric, Southern California

Municipal utility districts promised rates at least twenty percent below those of privately owned utilities in order to win public support.

I hereby agree to purchase gas from the Central Counties Municipal Utility District, when formed, provided that the acquisition and/or construction of the gas system is financed by the sale of revenue bonds payable solely from income of the gas system, and that there can be no recourse on the taxpayers in case of insufficient gas revenue, and that the rates for gas shall be not less than 20% below existing gas rates within the area within the District.

Signed ....

Dated...   Address..

My gas bill for last month was $................

Los Angeles Gas and Electric's "L.A. Service" logo was first used around 1910.

Southern California Gas Company's logo was designed in the early 1920s.

Gas, and Southern Counties Gas realized that they would have to alter their policies in order to win greater public confidence in privately owned utilities. To achieve this goal and thus thwart future municipalization efforts, the gas firms began massive public relations campaigns. Training programs for employees were started, and no small amount of effort was expended to promote courteous service and employee loyalty. As part of this effort, a Southern California Gas official announced that although the utility industry's former goal had been profit, the highest aim now had become "winning . . . the confidence and esteem of the general public."[21] This same concern could be seen in the design of the companies' logos: "Dependable Service" was inscribed on the Southern California Gas Company's symbol, "L.A. Service" on that of Los Angeles Gas and Electric.

Like its subsidiary, Pacific Lighting itself also sought to improve public relations by selling Los Angeles Gas and Electric's securities to employees and to the public at large, thus bringing people into economic partnership with the utility industry. In late 1923, under Pacific Lighting direction Los Angeles Gas and Electric began offering an employee stock-purchase option, and within a short time a majority of permanent employees became shareholders. The stock sales gave the company credibility as a truly "public utility." Other gas firms across the nation also embraced the belief that "wholesome public relations is the most valuable asset which a public utility can possess." While serving as president of the American Gas Association in 1927, Alexander Macbeth, who had just been named president of Southern California Gas Company,

1922 | Swing-Johnson bill first introduced in Congress.

commented on the noticeable improvement in public relations that accompanied the widespread development of consumer utility stock ownership.[22]

The multifaceted program to improve the gas companies' public relations succeeded in redeeming the image of those utilities by the late 1920s, and to some extent this was responsible for temporarily cooled enthusiasm for gas system municipalization. Contributing to the favorable public climate was the general prosperity of the decade. The cost of living rose rapidly, yet gas prices remained nearly constant. Moreover, the failure of several attempts to municipalize gas utilities in communities near Los Angeles boosted the utility companies' morale. Publicly owned utilities in Avalon, Huntington Beach, Newport Beach, and Santa Clara had had difficulty in capitalizing expansion and modernization, and they had not produced anticipated rate reductions. This added to the public's dissatisfaction with municipally owned experiments, and by the mid-1920s, those cities had sold their utilities to private companies. San Francisco citizens simultaneously denied a bid to municipalize that city's utilities. The utility companies felt vindicated and relieved that municipal ownership was losing favor both nationally and within California. "Municipal ownership of a gas system does not work out in actual practice as satisfactorily and as favorably as the taxpayer is sometimes led to believe," one gas industry publication announced with ill-concealed satisfaction.[23]

While a sigh of relief had swept over the gas industry by the late 1920s, the specter of public ownership had continued to hang like a dark cloud over the electric utilities throughout the decade. A "California Water and Power" initiative, drafted

Between 1914 and 1927 the cost of utilities rose forty percent while the price of other necessities rose four times that amount.

by wealthy progressives, was placed on the state ballot first in 1922 and then again in 1924 and 1926 in attempts to institute state ownership and distribution of hydroelectric power. Hard-fought and expensive campaigns waged by the electric utility companies prevented the passage of these bills.[24]

Another more ominous threat came from the federal Swing-Johnson bill, first introduced in Congress in 1922 to finance the construction of Boulder Dam on the Colorado River. The dam would produce an enormous quantity of hydroelectric power, and the Los Angeles Bureau of Power and Light realized that if it could obtain some of this inexpensive energy, it could supplement its Owens Valley Aqueduct hydroelectric power. Securing Boulder Dam power would allow the bureau to fulfill its ambition to municipalize Los Angeles's electric system completely at a cost of $25 million. The bureau proposed to raise this money through a bond issue, which

Robert W. Miller

Comments on Holding Companies.

In 1931, while serving as executive vice-president of Pacific Lighting Corporation, Robert W. Miller — the eldest son of C.O.G. Miller — rose to the defense of the institution of the holding company, then under attack during one of the worst years of the Great Depression:

From all that we have heard about the holding company in the past six years, . . . the uninformed would conclude that holding companies were conceived in iniquity, dedicated to the malicious exploitations of our nation's natural resources and [as Pennsylvania Governor Gifford Pinchot] slanderously stated, backed by "the whole fabric of political corruption, the underworld, the protected racketeer and the criminal of high and low degree."

Public utility operating and holding companies are part

Robert W. Miller, 1935.

of the business fabric of our nation. Such accusations [by Governor Pinchot and others] . . . are nothing more than slander against the men of the public utility industry, who are not only superior businessmen, but men of high moral standards in the communities in which they live and in the activities of the federal government, in which many of them have held important positions of public trust. . . . It is unwise to disturb the vast investments of this industry, to embarrass the huge army of employees and to discourage their expansion programs which have certainly mitigated the distress of the present depression and may be a major cause towards the recovery of conditions in general if they are permitted to proceed with confidence and without harassment. . . .

There is nothing sinister or mysterious about the gas and electric industries' marvelous development nor in the huge investments which in many instances have been supplied by the

holding companies. . . . It was early realized by public utility managers that because of the huge capital investment required and the necessity of securing a sufficiently large volume of output to permit charges for the service which would be attractive to the public, it would be necessary in each locality to establish a centralization of control and concentration of sales territory [which] our economists more ably designate as a "monopoly." . . . The one early difficulty with which the light, power, and gas industries were confronted was financing, and this was probably more responsible than any other one thing for the development of the holding company. This problem of marketing securities . . . was insurmountable for the smaller and more remotely located utilities. . . . The holding company has . . . given the securities of its subsidiaries credit greater than was possible for those companies serving as individuals.

These financing organizations were invaluable to the industry. They made cheaper service charges long in advance

of what might otherwise have been possible. In this day when the worth of a known public utility stock is taken as a matter of course, we have lost sight of the great strength which this early movement gave to the industry. . . . [The] industry, with the help of these organizations, grew so rapidly that the early weaknesses of the business of the local operating companies were never realized by the general public. . . . These companies, which have so largely supplied the money for the development of this tremendous industry, have been called holding companies, but a better name would be "utility investment companies." . . .

The ambition of every farsighted utility executive has always been, and will continue to be, to furnish the best service at the lowest rate possible in conformity with a good credit standing for the operating and holding company. . . .[25]

would be approved by Los Angeles voters. When first placed on the ballot, this proposition — accompanied by another $24 million bond measure to fund the purchase of Los Angeles Gas and Electric — failed to pass. Sparing no expense, the private electric companies again succeeded in defeating this proposal in 1924 when it was presented to voters in what Haynes called "one of the bitterest campaigns in the history of Los Angeles." The utilities denounced the bond issue as "socialism" and as a "confiscation of private property," claiming that if the bill passed, it would likely bankrupt the city. After yet another hard-fought campaign, the city secured passage of a $16 million bond issue, assuring Los Angeles Gas and Electric that this money would not be used to acquire its lines. Los Angeles voters approved additional funds to enable the city to acquire Boulder Dam electric power in 1926.[26]

The political confrontation over the bond issues heightened the animosity between Los Angeles Gas and Electric and the proponents of municipalization. To discredit the city's claim that a publicly owned electric utility would provide cheaper rates to consumers, Los Angeles Gas and Electric voluntarily reduced electric rates in the late 1920s. This action served to embarrass the city and further polarized the pro- and antimunicipalization advocates.[27] The Haynes-Scattergood coalition sincerely believed that it was being placed on the defensive by a well-capitalized "power trust" because of the continuous flow of obstructive litigation and antibond-issue "propaganda." Pacific Lighting Corporation, on the other hand, had due cause to complain that the city was waging an offensive campaign to rob the firm of its private property.

The City of Los Angeles hoped to obtain Los Angeles Gas and Electric's two steam plants — the older one at Alameda Street built in the 1880s (above) and the more modern one at Seal Beach constructed in the mid-1920s (below). The photo above was taken around 1920, and the photo below around 1936 after the smokestack — knocked down during the 1933 Long Beach earthquake — was replaced.

1927 | City brings suit against Los Angeles Gas and Electric for using streets without a franchise.

1929 | Pacific Lighting acquires Southern California Gas Company.

Although Los Angeles Gas and Electric was able to duel the City of Los Angeles to a draw during the 1920s and to forestall appropriation of the private gas and electric properties by various legal and political maneuvers, the firm's "Achilles Heel" proved to be the franchise issue. Pacific Lighting's subsidiary had held a franchise for street lighting until it had expired in 1916, but the firm had nonetheless continued to use city streets for its transmission lines over the ensuing years. When city officials — angered over the utilities' opposition to its electric bond issues — brought suit in 1927 to restrain Los Angeles Gas and Electric from using the streets without a franchise, the company argued in court that the 1879 California Constitution exempted gas and electric utilities from municipal jurisdiction if they provided "gas light or illuminating light." According to company officials, this phrase gave the firm the privilege of providing complete service without city approval or consent. Los Angeles County Superior Court rendered a decision on the electric franchise on January 29, 1931, ruling that the company had no right to supply energy other than for illuminating purposes. In a related decision, the court again ruled against the company, requiring Los Angeles Gas and Electric to obtain a gas franchise. Both decisions were appealed to the California Supreme Court, and for the time being the company continued to enjoy free use of the streets for its gas and electric lines.[28]

As Los Angeles Gas and Electric awaited the Supreme Court's franchise rulings — which eventually upheld the lower court's decisions — the economic decline that had been triggered by the 1929 stock market crash began to play a role in the municipalization struggle. Utility companies again became vulnerable to political attacks by municipal ownership advocates, who claimed they could deliver gas and electric services at lower rates to anxious, cash-poor consumers. Pacific Lighting's officials felt their best defenses to keep community goodwill were to maintain excellent service, to stress maximum employee courtesy, to lower rates by economies of scale — now made easier by Pacific Lighting's acquisition of Southern Counties Gas in 1925 and Southern California Gas in 1929 — and to have frank and open dealings with the public. The firm's executives hoped that its subsidiaries' well-deserved, favorable reputations with the public, nurtured so carefully during the 1920s, would sustain them through the difficult years of the depression. As F.M. (Marion) Banks, general superintendent of Southern California Gas Company and later its chairman of the board, emphatically stated, "our guard is not propaganda, but service to the public."[29]

Despite such efforts by Pacific Lighting's subsidiaries and other utility firms, the balance of power between advocates of public and private control gradually shifted in favor of municipal ownership for two main reasons. First, the political climate of the depression years was, understandably, hostile to concentrations of corporate power. Secondly, and perhaps more importantly, those determined to municipalize the city's electric system had gained confidence from the Los Angeles voters' willingness to approve bond issues to acquire Boulder Dam hydroelectric power.

With this albeit limited public financial backing, in December 1929 Los Angeles officials had announced their resolution to buy the electric

properties held by Los Angeles Gas and Electric, thus taking control of all electric works within the city. Addison Day, president of the firm, respectfully replied that the company's electric properties were not for sale.[30] To thwart the city's plans for appropriating its electric investments and monopolizing the hydroelectric power from Boulder Dam, Los Angeles Gas and Electric — joined by Southern California Edison, which wanted to continue selling electricity to the city — attempted to influence the city council and thus temporarily stalled the city's efforts.[31] Yet after proponents of municipal ownership regained their dominant position in municipal politics in the early 1930s, the city signed long-term contracts with the federal government for a large share of Boulder Dam hydroelectric power. Subsequently, Los Angeles obtained a $22.8 million loan from the federal Reconstruction Finance Corporation — an agency created by President Herbert C. Hoover to offset the effects of the depression — to finance the construction of a transmission line from Boulder Dam to Los Angeles.

Although clearly on the defensive by 1933, Los Angeles Gas and Electric did not give up its electric properties without a struggle, as these generated approximately one-sixth of Pacific Lighting's gross revenues. Los Angeles Gas and Electric steadfastly refused to sell its properties, but with the sure knowledge that hydroelectric power would soon be available for use by the city, the company also adopted a new strategy for self-preservation. The firm began to maneuver to get a share of Boulder Dam power for itself to forestall a municipal monopoly over this source of electrical energy.

After the city's transmission line to bring Boulder Dam power to Los Angeles was finally under construction, Los Angeles Gas and Electric strengthened its bid to participate in the hydroelectric bonanza offered by the dam. In late 1933 the firm tried to obtain Boulder Dam power through the Southern Sierras Power Company, which was negotiating a contract with the federal government to give it the right to surplus power from the dam. Ezra Scattergood became aware of the proposed agreement, and in December 1933 he convinced Secretary of the Interior Harold Ickes to drop the Southern Sierras Power deal because it would have given that firm (and through it, Los Angeles Gas and Electric) one-sixth of the electricity already promised to the city at a price one third of that the city had contracted to pay.[32]

Angered by this latest ploy, the proponents of municipal ownership began to wield the best weapon they had against the utility companies: the public image of the typical corporation as a "customer-squeezing octopus" and utility executives as "robber barons." Unhappily, Pacific Lighting's financial success made such attacks by municipal ownership advocates credible. Pacific Lighting's utility companies had been cushioned from the worst economic aspects of the 1930s by excellent management, price stabilization by the railroad commission, and the constant demand for their services. Due to these factors, Pacific Lighting's dividends, though reduced, were not suspended during the depression years, and public clamor grew not only for lower utility rates but for higher corporate taxes. Moreover, businesses such as utilities in general had grown larger with the increasing number of mergers in the 1920s and 1930s. Many people understandably

feared this concentration of economic power, believing regulatory agencies to be ineffectual — a
situation far from the truth in California.[33] Nonetheless, politicians leapt to exploit the public's fears
by alluding to "power trusts," and the municipal
power advocates promoted this negative image to
help pass a bond issue to finance the purchase of the
electric system of Los Angeles Gas and Electric if the
firm could be persuaded to sell. The leverage needed
to force the sale lay in the gas franchise issue.

By 1934 it had become apparent that city
officials and other proponents of municipalization
would obstruct Los Angeles Gas and Electric's attempt to secure a gas franchise in order to force the
company to sell its electric properties to the city.
Such a strategy irked many area residents, and Los
Angeles Gas and Electric allies attacked the city for
its Machiavellian tactics, its politicking, and its in-
transigence over the franchise issue. One formidable
utility supporter was the *Los Angeles Times,* whose
coverage was highly sympathetic to the company.
For example, on July 21, 1934, the *Times* quoted Addison Day's charges that the city had refused "to
consent to the company's obtaining an electric franchise under any terms or conditions" and that the
city was obstructing the gas franchise in order to
"force the gas company to dispose of its electric
properties at less than the fair value thereof."[34] The
following month, the *Times* criticized the city for
"vicious politics" in its "gas grab" attempt:

> Through efficient management this corporation
> has met the rates of its tax-free rival, given better
> service, made substantial contributions to state
> and local taxes and made a profit besides. . . . It
> thus sets certain standards of efficiency which the
> Power Bureau does not like to have to meet.[35]

The "robber baron" image was
used to prevent Pacific Lighting's
subsidiary from obtaining a gas
franchise in the 1935 election.

While the *Times* generally supported Los
Angeles Gas and Electric, the cause for this particular invective against the city was an upcoming gas
franchise election. The long-awaited Supreme Court
decision on whether the California Constitution
exempted utilities from municipal jurisdiction had
finally been handed down, and it required the company to obtain a gas franchise before July 5, 1935.
Because wording for a new franchise proposed by
the city council was unacceptable to the firm, Los
Angeles Gas and Electric had succeeded in having a
more favorable franchise placed on the ballot by a
citizens' petition. This proposition, labeled Charter
Amendment 4-A, was presented to Los Angeles
voters in September 1934, and it met the city's stiff
opposition because it contained a number of provisions which the Haynes-Scattergood coalition believed were overly generous to the utility company.
If passed, the amendment would have given the

1929 | City announces it will
buy Los Angeles Gas
and Electric's electric
properties.

1932 | Franklin Delano
Roosevelt elected
president of the
United States.

A muckraking election brochure accused the gas utility of using underhanded tactics to persuade voters to pass Charter Amendment 1-A.

utility a thirty-five-year gas franchise, a very low tax rate on gross revenue, and a provision for a fair price based on "goodwill" should the city buy the gas properties in the future. The city, hoping to force the sale of the electric properties by opposing this gas franchise proposal, succeeded in defeating the 1934 amendment. A similarly worded amendment — this time called Proposition 1-A — was put on the ballot for April 1935.[36]

The vigorously contested April 1935 election was Pacific Lighting's final political battle in the long struggle with the advocates of municipal ownership. During the campaign, muckrakers revealed that an organization called the Municipal Affairs Committee, which had sponsored the franchise proposals in 1934 and 1935, was not a concerned citizens' group but rather represented primarily the interests of Pacific Lighting Corporation (in whose offices in San Francisco the amendments had been

drafted). In addition to this revelation, Pacific Lighting's large profits were repeatedly emphasized by those hostile to the franchise. It was "the same old wolf, the Los Angeles Gas Company again trying to get away with one of the biggest steals on record," claimed one newspaper.[37] An election brochure entitled "Dark History of the Los Angeles Gas Trust Brought To Light," urged a "no" vote on Proposition 1-A, "the San Francisco capitalists' nefarious scheme to raid and exploit the community." A classic piece of muckraking literature, this brochure "exposed" Los Angeles Gas and Electric and its "San Francisco masters" for their many allegedly underhanded legal and political tactics, concluding with a summary of the "extortionate" Los Angeles gas rates.[38]

Other election handbills exploited the "robber baron" image attributed to many large corporations with such headlines as "Financial Overlords of San Francisco Bleed Los Angeles." Former Pacific Lighting executive W. Morton (Mort) Jacobs recalled that on the front page of some of the political literature distributed throughout the city was

> a caricature of what was labeled a robber baron. He wore long tails; he had a stovepipe hat; he had diamond studs and a big fat cigar and a gold chain on which hung a little sign: "Gas Baron." He was out to rob the public. It was almost impossible to cope with politically.[39]

Not surprisingly, Los Angeles Gas and Electric's gas franchise went down to defeat. It was not until nearly six months later, however, that Pacific Lighting approved the sale of its electric properties to the city when the arrival of Boulder Dam electricity on October 23, 1936, made it clear that the city's cheap hydroelectric power would make competition impossible. In a special charter

1934 | Los Angeles Gas and Electric fails to obtain a gas franchise, 1934-1935.

1936 | Boulder Dam hydroelectric power reaches Los Angeles.

election on December 8, 1936, by a vote of two to one the people of Los Angeles gave their approval to the $46 million purchase. At the same time, they agreed to grant a gas franchise to Los Angeles Gas and Electric for thirty-five years. This deal had the full approval of the cities' key power-brokers, and in order to win voter consent, the city reminded voters that the settlement would include a payment of $505,000 for past use of the streets by the company, a $150,000 annual fee for subsequent street use, and the prospect of $3 million a year in revenues from the city's merged electric system. Most importantly, however, the city stressed that the settlement would bring an end to the costly litigation with the utility company.[40]

On January 18, 1937, the deed of ownership and the check for $46 million were exchanged. Ezra Scattergood was exultant, having finished as the winner in the battle that he had waged for twenty-five years. On the other hand, for Los Angeles Gas and Electric's president, Addison Day, the moment of the transfer was grim. "It was forced on us," Day said bitterly. "There was nothing we could do. It broke my heart."[41]

This was a Pyrrhic victory for the city, however. The price paid by the advocates of municipal ownership and the people of Los Angeles had been extremely high. The expenses of two and a half decades of litigation, numerous election campaigns, and a high rate of indebtedness from the bond issues all were to be lasting legacies of electric municipalization. And Pacific Lighting, in the end, retained its gas utility business in southern California. In this sense, the municipalists had only half succeeded in making city-owned utilities a reality.

The Municipal League's campaign literature during the December 1936 election urged Los Angeles voters to buy Los Angeles Gas and Electric's electric properties and also to approve a gas franchise for the company.

1937 | City buys electric properties of Los Angeles Gas and Electric, and company receives gas franchise.

The Future Belongs to Gas

Pacific Lighting Consolidates the Southern California Gas Distribution System.

ALTHOUGH IT EVENTUALLY LOST THE EPIC STRUGGLE over its electric properties to the City of Los Angeles, Pacific Lighting's achievements in the southern California gas market were no less than spectacular in the 1920s and 1930s. Pacific Lighting was a financially conservative firm in most respects, but it reorganized internal operations and adapted to changing conditions in order to meet the challenges of enormous growth, technological progress, and the problems of the depression years. The major accomplishment of the 1920s was Pacific Lighting's consolidation and integration of the southern California gas distribution system. In addition to its ownership of Los Angeles Gas and Electric, by the end of the 1920s Pacific Lighting had acquired controlling interests in the other major gas distribution systems in the region — those owned by Southern Counties Gas, Santa Maria Gas, and Southern California Gas. "The Pacific Lighting system has been operated with the idea of geographic and economic integration," C.O.G. Miller stated on August 24, 1936, the fiftieth anniversary of the formation of Pacific Lighting, and "it is in effect one large operating company."[1]

By the late 1930s, the firm's vast organization provided half the population of California with "as nearly perfect service as the

Gushing well from Bakersfield-Lakewood field during the oil boom years in southern California.

1914 | 1941

DURING THE FIRST FEW DECADES OF THE TWENTIETH CENTURY, PACIFIC LIGHTING CONSOLIDATED ITS GAS DISTRIBUTION SYSTEMS INTO THE LARGEST AND MOST EFFICIENT NATURAL GAS NETWORK IN THE NATION.

1914 | Southern Counties Gas provides service to Orange County.

1915 | First telephone call from New York to San Francisco.

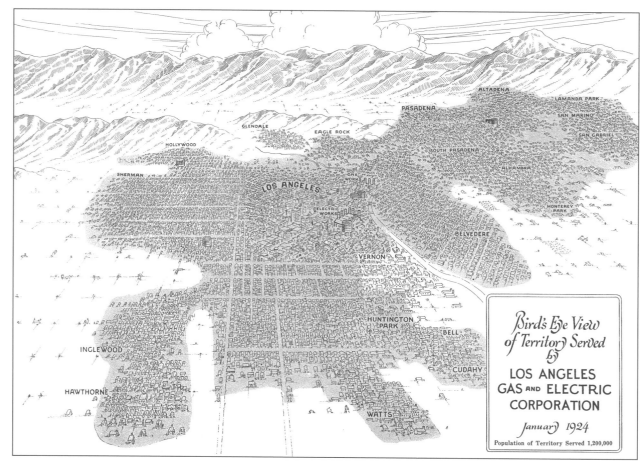

Bird's Eye View of Territory Served by LOS ANGELES GAS and ELECTRIC CORPORATION January 1924. Population of Territory Served 1,200,000

present state of technical advancement makes possible."[2] This impressive attainment did not occur overnight but was rather a difficult and gradual process induced by the conversion to natural gas service. This advance, in turn, was made possible by the ready availability of regional supplies of that fuel and technological improvements in the construction of high-pressure, long-distance pipelines.

The consolidation that had occurred among southern California gas and electric companies in the early twentieth century put the three major gas distribution companies — Los Angeles Gas and Electric, Southern California Gas, and Southern Counties Gas — in favorable positions to expand their service. From 1916 to 1925 the efforts of these rival firms were consumed in keeping up with the frantic rate of population growth in southern California. Capital expenditures ran into millions of dollars. Hundreds of miles of mains were installed; thousands of new meters were put into service; and

various system improvements were made. As the region grew, lines had to be continually extended, reinforced, and enlarged.

Under the leadership of Pacific Lighting's cofounder, Walter Cline, until the mid-1920s Los Angeles Gas and Electric expanded its business only within areas already served by its main pipelines in the older, downtown section of the city. This conservative approach was consistent with Pacific Lighting's long-standing policy of restricting its operations to those locations that could be reached from its existing gas manufacturing plants. The policy had served Los Angeles Gas and Electric Corporation well: gross earnings of the firm rose from $3 million in 1909 to nearly $13 million in 1923. Augmenting its supplies with natural gas imported through the Midway pipeline, Los Angeles Gas and Electric expanded its output of "reformed gas" — produced by mixing manufactured and natural gas — to double the company's daily sendout between 1920 and 1925. Serving about 152,000 households in 1920, the firm's gas system extended throughout Los Angeles itself and into about a dozen surrounding neighborhoods to reach 226,000 homes by 1930.[3]

Before Southern Counties Gas and Southern California Gas companies were acquired by Pacific Lighting (in 1925 and 1929 respectively), these organizations followed different paths of historical development which profoundly influenced the future of the parent firm. In addition to pioneering all-natural gas service to southern California consumers, Southern California Gas and Southern Counties Gas pursued more aggressive expansion policies than Los Angeles Gas and Electric, extending their lines into new territory as towns and cities sprang up in the area around Los Angeles.

Knowing that they could rely on the considerable resources of the utility empire controlled by William Kerckhoff and Allan Balch to help fund Southern California Gas Company initiatives, the firm's management consolidated service in San Bernardino and extended lines into Banning, Beaumont, Elsinore, Hemet, and San Jacinto, as well as the San Joaquin Valley. The company also provided service to Artesia, Burbank, Compton, Downey, and Glendale. In new boom towns such as Redondo Beach and Manhattan Beach, the population and number of gas meters tripled in the mid-1920s. In these and other growing areas, gas mains were laid prior to developments, thereby promoting real estate sales and increasing property values.

The number of cities and towns served by Southern California Gas quadrupled between 1921 and 1926, and the number of meters grew from

C.O.G. Miller, pictured here in the 1940s, long maintained an active role in the gas industry.

SANTA MARIA GAS CO. 1928
(TO SOUTHERN COUNTIES GAS 1941)

SOUTHERN COUNTIES GAS CO. 1925

LOS ANGELES GAS CO. 1889

PACIFIC LIGHTING CORPORATION

LOS ANGELES GAS & ELEC. 1904

INDUSTRIAL FUEL SUPPLY CO. 1925

SOUTHERN CALIFORNIA GAS CO. 1929

Principal acquisitions of Pacific Lighting Corporation, 1886-1941.

1920 | Oil and gas discoveries at Santa Fe Springs, Signal Hill, and Huntington Beach, 1920-1921.

This photograph of the Highland-LaBrea district of Los Angeles taken in June 1922 — when compared to the photo on the opposite page taken ten years later — vividly illustrates the rapid growth of the city.

50,000 in 1920 to 238,000 by the end of the decade. Plant investment rose from $10 million in 1920 to almost six times that amount by 1930, and annual gas output climbed from two billion to seventy-seven billion cubic feet. Challenging Los Angeles Gas and Electric's dominance, Southern California Gas served nearly half of Los Angeles and a variety of suburbs by the end of the 1920s.[4]

While Southern Counties Gas Company's expansion was not quite as spectacular as Southern California Gas Company's, the number of communities served by Southern Counties Gas doubled from 1916 to 1921 and tripled from 1921 to 1926. Southern Counties Gas had the strong financial backing of the prominent Chicago investors Charles G. Dawes (later vice-president of the United States under Calvin Coolidge) and his brother, Rufus,

who together had purchased the company in 1916. The firm had impressive holdings throughout Orange County as well as in parts of Los Angeles County, and by 1919 it had acquired gas properties in Montecito, Oxnard, Santa Barbara, Santa Paula, and Ventura. By 1929 Southern Counties Gas had extended its service to about seventy towns stretching from Laguna Beach to Santa Barbara. The number of meters had grown from 62,000 in 1920 to 148,000 in 1930, and plant investments had increased from about $6 million to $23 million.[5]

While the three gas companies extended gas service to thousands of new consumers throughout the growing southern California area in the first two decades of the twentieth century, they also led the nation in developing the domestic market for gas — for cooking as well as water and space heating. The gas companies increased domestic demand by encouraging consumers to use more gas appliances in the home, but they also sought commercial and industrial users.[6] Much of the increase in gas consumption in southern California in the 1920s can be attributed to this new field of gas service, which was

1925 | Pacific Lighting acquires Southern Counties Gas and Industrial Fuel Supply companies.

made possible by the pioneering efforts of Southern Counties Gas in introducing natural gas deliveries.

Southern Counties Gas moved into the new industrial market almost by accident. The firm took a considerable risk when it first introduced natural gas to some of its Orange County customers in 1914. Natural gas has twice the heating ability (measured in British Thermal Units or BTU's) as manufactured gas. As a result, domestic consumption and sales revenues dropped dramatically when natural gas service began, forcing Southern Counties Gas to find creative ways to utilize surplus gas and to pay for pipelines to oil and gas fields. With domestic customers using less gas to meet their energy needs, Southern Counties Gas sought potential industrial and commercial consumers to use excess gas supplies. First among these new customers were oil refineries and laundries, and eventually electric utilities began to employ natural gas to power steam-run generators. Like Southern Counties Gas, Southern California Gas likewise converted part of its delivery system to natural gas and faced the same challenges of developing new markets and financing pipelines.[7]

As both firms adapted to the changeover to natural gas service, they increasingly sought oil companies from which to buy their gas supplies. However, oil and gas producers were apprehensive about the threat of government regulation and were not eager to do business with gas distribution firms. On several occasions, the California Railroad Commission had indicated that provisions of the public utilities code might apply to oil companies selling gas for public distribution, but no formal ruling had been issued. Just the thought of such government intervention worried oil firms, and when Union Oil discovered a huge oil and natural gas field near Placentia in August 1919, it announced it would sell none of the casinghead gas to distributing companies. Union Oil had no intention of falling under state regulation for selling gas when oil pumping alone provided more than adequate income. One Union Oil executive informed Franklin Wade, then superintendent of operations at Southern Counties Gas, that Union Oil would let the gas flare forever rather than sell it to a public utility. Other large oil companies felt the same way.[8]

1925 | Testing lab for gas appliances established by the American Gas Association.

1926 | California Railroad Commission ruling requires changeover to natural gas.

Explosions and Asphyxiations

Public Concerns About the Safety of Gas.

One of the principal problems faced by Pacific Lighting's gas utilities in promoting their product during the first few decades of the twentieth century was the concern that manufactured gas and natural gas were not safe. This belief was fostered by accidental explosions, carbon monoxide poisonings, and asphyxiations. It took years of public education about how to use the fuel and gas appliances safely to overcome this public relations problem.

Most energy fuels — including manufactured gas and natural gas — are composed of hydrocarbons, which cause combustion when burned with oxygen. This chemical change creates energy, and if the reaction is controlled properly, it produces a regulated source of heat and light. Yet before safety standards were well developed, incorrectly installed appliances or damaged pipes sometimes allowed gas to accumulate in the presence of oxygen, and if a source of ignition was provided, an explosion occurred. In the 1920s, to help prevent explosions the gas companies introduced an odorizing agent to make

Radiant heaters were a hazard to public safety in the early years of the twentieth century.

known the presence of natural gas (which, unlike manufactured gas, in most cases has no characteristic smell of its own). Careful attention to appliance and equipment maintenance was also aimed at reducing the frequency of such catastrophes.

Aside from trying to curb explosions, Pacific Lighting's subsidiaries worked strenuously to overcome the notion that gas was toxic. Although carbon monoxide poisoning and asphyxiation were two separate but related problems, the general public frequently confused the two and attributed asphyxiations to the toxicity of gas.

Manufactured gas was produced from liquid or gaseous hydrocarbons — oil, for example — or carbonaceous solids, such as coal. These substances were reduced to combustible vapors in the manufacturing process by applying heat in an oxygen-poor environment. Absent oxygen, the vapors were then collected and stored in pipes or gas holders for later use as fuel. Manufactured gas was generally composed of methane, hydrogen, carbon dioxide, and carbon monoxide. The latter is extremely toxic, and in burning manufactured gas the carbon monoxide could be released if there was not enough oxygen available

to convert it into relatively benign carbon dioxide. Moreover, if oxygen levels were not high enough, additional carbon monoxide beyond that already inherent in manufactured gas could be formed from the burning methane. Thus, in poorly ventilated rooms where gas appliances were used, carbon monoxide could reach dangerous levels, causing severe illness or death by interfering with a number of critical physiological processes. Likewise, improperly vented appliances using manufactured gas could also lead to death by asphyxiation as oxygen supplies fell during combustion. Usually, accidental deaths were caused by a combination of asphyxiation and carbon monoxide poisoning.

Unlike manufactured gas, natural gas, which is nearly all methane, has no carbon monoxide component and is not inherently toxic. Yet it still could contribute to carbon monoxide poisonings and asphyxiations. Most such accidents — even after the introduction of natural gas — were caused by the use of old-fashioned, unventilated space heaters. Such heaters, if left burning in a closed room, could make oxygen fall to

dangerously low levels as it was used with methane in combustion. With an inadequate supply of oxygen, natural gas would produce carbon monoxide as a by-product of the burning process instead of carbon dioxide, and this could lead to simultaneous carbon monoxide poisoning and asphyxiation.

After many deaths had occurred in southern California during abnormally cold winters in the early part of the twentieth century, the gas industry and government took steps to protect the public from unsafe heating devices. Southern California gas firms lobbied legislators for restrictions on the use of space heaters and launched a campaign for better gas heating appliances — equipment that would heat an entire house and keep rooms properly ventilated. Aided by the widespread conversion to natural gas, eventually the gas industry began to overcome public fears that its product was poisonous or dangerously explosive. Yet only after central heating became commonplace and odorization helped reduce the number of explosions did such concerns become a part of the forgotten past.[9]

With oil firms refusing to provide any of their casinghead gas to gas distributing companies, Wade devised a plan to create a separate pipeline company to buy gas from the oil producers. This firm, in turn, could sell to the various gas distribution companies in southern California, thus moving the threat of regulation a full step away from the oil producers. The result was the incorporation of Industrial Fuel Supply Company, a subsidiary of Southern Counties Gas, on September 22, 1919. (Pacific Lighting later created Pacific Lighting Gas Supply Company in 1950 as an unregulated "non-utility" successor to Industrial Fuel Supply.) Wade's strategy satisfied the oil industry, and through this firm, Southern Counties Gas was able to negotiate a ten-year contract to purchase casinghead gas from Union Oil's Los Angeles Basin operations.[10]

The formation of Industrial Fuel Supply and other pipeline transmission companies resolved the problem of possible government regulation of the oil firms, and the extensive oil production in the Los Angeles area at Signal Hill and Huntington Beach in the early 1920s created an abundant supply of natural gas. With this encouragement, Southern Counties Gas continued to develop its natural gas distribution systems. By October 1923 the firm had seven local sources of supply: Brea-Olinda, Dominguez, Huntington Beach, Long Beach, Montebello, Richfield, and Santa Fe Springs. Following the lead of Southern Counties Gas, Southern California Gas Company tapped into gas supplies in the Los Angeles Basin oil fields as well.[11]

In committing themselves to natural gas service, Southern Counties Gas and Southern California Gas next confronted the difficult task of balancing expenditures and revenues by increasing the demand for surplus supplies. Because technology had not advanced to a point where the volume of casinghead gas reserves in active oil fields could be determined with accuracy, gas companies sustained high costs in laying expensive transmission lines to fields that they knew might produce gas for only a short term. Thus, the goal was to exploit gas — which was produced whether it was used or not as part of the oil pumping process — while it was available. Gas companies bid aggressively for industrial and commercial users, and they experimented with conversion burners in their own laboratories to facilitate the changeover from fuel oil or coal, on which most industrial users then relied for their energy needs. The cheap and abundant supply of natural gas was preferable to electricity for industrial and commercial users, especially after hydroelectric power development lagged in the 1920s.[12]

While both Southern California Gas and Southern Counties Gas worked to increase the number of their industrial and commercial customers, Southern Counties Gas also inaugurated intensive sales campaigns to augment domestic sales by promoting a variety of improved appliances; the success of these drives contributed to the need for better gas storage facilities. Since natural gas was less expensive, burned more efficiently, and was safer than manufactured gas, it was easier to market for home heating, and winter peak demands rose dramatically. Because of the need to store gas when it was available to meet seasonal demands, Southern Counties Gas Company engineers developed high-pressure holders. Unlike older types, the new holders were cylindrical in shape with hemispherical ends and

Anaheim holders being painted, 1928.

Southern Counties Gas holders in Orange, California, 1936.

An innovative design for gas storage: the hortonsphere, 1940.

could be placed either vertically or horizontally; these holders held large volumes of gas until it was needed.[13] This technological innovation — along with creative methods of balancing supply and demand — enabled Southern Counties Gas to utilize local gas supplies effectively to meet the needs of its southern California consumers.

While the abundance of casinghead gas in the early 1920s had prompted innovations such as high-pressure gas holders, by the middle of that decade fears grew that shortages would develop in the Los Angeles Basin since many oil companies continued to flare gas as an unwanted by-product of oil production. Because of the concern over possible shortages, Southern Counties Gas embarked on an ambitious project in 1925 to construct long-distance transmission lines from Ventura to bring more gas into the Los Angeles metropolitan area. This enterprise was economically feasible because of the tremendous size of the newly discovered gas reserves in deep zones of the Ventura oil fields and the growth of the Los Angeles market. The first of three transmission pipelines consisted of approximately seventy-seven miles of twelve-inch pipe and could deliver twenty-eight million cubic feet per day. Costing $1.5 million, the investment was well worth the money, for in 1928 the Ventura fields produced 185 million cubic feet of natural gas per day as well as 47,800 barrels of oil.[14]

Recognizing the significance of the Ventura pipeline project and the value of the Southern Counties Gas Company distribution system, Pacific Lighting acquired the firm in June 1925 from the Dawes brothers, who had decided to liquidate their holdings. After the transaction was consummated,

1929 | Gas Conservation Act limits flaring of casinghead gas by oil companies.

1929 | Pacific Lighting acquires Southern California Gas Company.

Pacific Lighting established the same relationship with its new subsidiary as it had maintained with Los Angeles Gas and Electric. From its San Francisco headquarters, Pacific Lighting's management exercised only broad policy decisions and provided considerable financial resources and related advice, while day-to-day operations for both subsidiaries were left in the hands of the utility companies' officers. Pacific Lighting's president, C.O.G. Miller, however, made frequent trips to Los Angeles to oversee the activities of the subsidiaries.

Pacific Lighting was favored with particularly capable leadership in its subsidiaries to carry out their work. Los Angeles Gas and Electric was managed by William Baurhyte, a former vice-president and general manager of the company who succeeded Walter Cline as president in 1924, although Cline retained the chairmanship of the board of directors. Unfortunately, Baurhyte served as president only briefly due to poor health, and he was succeeded by Addison Day in 1929, who was president until 1937.[15] When Southern Counties Gas joined the Pacific Lighting system, it was under the able leadership of President Ferdinand R. Bain and Franklin Wade — by then vice-president. Wade succeeded Bain as president and general manager in 1928. Not surprisingly, in this era of major growth and technological advances, many of these men had entrepreneurial skills or technical backgrounds.[16]

In the mid-1920s, both of Pacific Lighting's gas distribution subsidiaries were capably managed, yet their approaches to the gas business varied considerably. Although the acquisition of Southern Counties Gas Company gave Pacific Lighting access to extensive natural gas supplies, Los Angeles Gas

William Baurhyte, president, Los Angeles Gas and Electric, 1924-1929.

Addison B. Day, president, Los Angeles Gas and Electric, 1929-1937.

Ferdinand R. Bain, an organizer of Southern Counties Gas and its president until 1928.

Alexander B. Macbeth, president, Southern California Gas, 1927-1939.

Franklin S. Wade, president, Southern Counties Gas, 1928-1947. Wade also served as president of Southern California Gas from 1939 until 1950.

1930 | Southern Fuel Supply Company formed to construct pipeline from Kettleman Hills to Long Beach.

1931 | Empire State Building opened in New York City.

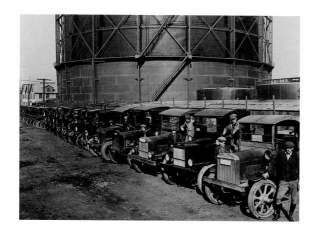

Fleet of Los Angeles Gas
and Electric service trucks in
front of a recently completed
holder at Eleventh Street and
Santa Fe Avenue.

With a capacity of fifteen
million cubic feet, Los Angeles
Gas and Electric's Ducommun
Street gas holder (constructed
in 1925) was the largest of this
new waterless type in the world.

and Electric's top officials pursued their traditionally conservative policies and were wary of converting their firm's system to all natural gas. Never having been fully satisfied that the supply of natural gas was sufficient to warrant a changeover from manufactured gas, the company's management believed it would be unwise to commit the firm and its customers to the uncertainties of natural gas, especially in light of previous gas shortages.

In addition to its fears of possible future shortages in natural gas supplies, Los Angeles Gas and Electric was understandably reluctant to abandon its substantial investment in its gas manufacturing plant and related equipment. The company also wanted to avoid the half-million-dollar expense of converting from a reformed to a natural gas system.[17] Another objection was the financial adjustment the company would have to make as the changeover occurred. Since natural gas had a much higher energy capacity, Los Angeles Gas and Electric officials knew that it would reduce consumer demand and corporate income because smaller volumes would be sold. Even shifting to reformed gas had caused this problem. In 1923, for example, the output of Los Angeles Gas and Electric had decreased markedly per meter when a reformed gas with a higher heating ability was delivered to consumers.[18]

Because Los Angeles Gas and Electric resisted the conversion to natural gas service, government agencies became involved. The City of Los Angeles brought suit against the firm to force the changeover. Nonetheless, the city's own board of public utilities found the company's arguments persuasive in 1924 and advised against the shift to all-natural gas service.[19] The issue was raised again in July 1925

1932 | Kettleman Hills
pipeline completed.

when Los Angeles Gas and Electric and Southern California Gas applied to the California Railroad Commission for rate relief due to rising costs for capital improvements and declining returns. At the hearings, many municipalities still being served by either manufactured or reformed gas made vigorous pleas for a change to straight natural gas, which was gaining wide acceptance as a more efficient and less dangerous fuel. Responding to consumer demand and ignoring the protests of Los Angeles Gas and Electric, in December 1926 the railroad commission not only refused a rate increase but also ordered that if Los Angeles Gas and Electric and Southern California Gas wanted to maintain existing prices, they would have to convert their entire systems to natural gas service.[20]

After the commission's order, Los Angeles Gas and Electric began the immense job of changing thousands of appliances to handle the higher BTU's provided by natural gas. The company's service department called upon thirty-five thousand

Top and bottom: Southern California Gas Company constructed two enormous new gas holders in the mid-1920s to accommodate consumer needs. Pictured above is the ten-million-cubic-foot waterless gas holder under construction at Slauson and Western avenues.

1933 | Long Beach earthquake causes $700,000 in losses for Los Angeles Gas and Electric.

1935 | Public Utilities Holding Company Act passed by Congress.

customers. Southern California Gas and Southern Counties Gas, both of which were already delivering natural gas to most of their customers, did not have such a huge task to perform. The companies were allowed to keep their gas manufacturing plants as backups, but by 1930 nearly all consumers were receiving straight natural gas.[21]

Despite the obstacles of converting Los Angeles Gas and Electric's system to natural gas, Pacific Lighting moved decisively to consolidate its southern California transmission and distribution network into an all-natural gas system. The purchase of Santa Maria Gas Company in 1928 added another source of natural gas to the Pacific Lighting system. With this acquisition, Pacific Lighting had access to

oil and gas fields in Ventura, the Santa Barbara area, and the Santa Maria Valley.[22]

Pacific Lighting's principal rival, Southern California Gas Company, was similarly consolidating its system. In late 1927 the California Railroad Commission permitted the firm to bring into its system Central Counties, Hanford, Midway, River Bend, and Valley Natural companies, forming a massive transmission and distribution network serving eighty-nine cities. The mergers prompted a reorganization of the companies, and in December 1927 several eastern and western investors joined to make Southern California Gas a large holding company. Although eastern financial interests, like Chase Security in New York, had a major share in the new corporation, it was agreed that the board of directors was to be controlled by local Los Angeles businessmen such as prominent attorney Stuart O'Melveny of the law firm O'Melveny and Myers.[23]

Scenic view of the Pacific Coast Highway between Ventura and Santa Barbara in the 1920s along the route of Southern Counties Gas Company's pipeline.

A little over a year after this reorganization, Pacific Lighting purchased Southern California Gas through an exchange of stock, thus taking over that firm's subsidiary gas operations. C.O.G. Miller observed that this transaction had been "long sought for by officials of both companies."[24] As an early company historian wrote, the acquisition of Southern California Gas gave Pacific Lighting

> new and valuable sources of gas supply, and an extensive distributing system which supplemented and completed the territory of the Pacific Lighting companies. . . . Vexatious questions of territory boundaries were thus eliminated and better balancing of sources of supply, storage and disposal of off-peak surpluses became possible.[25]

Pacific Lighting's purchase of Southern California Gas consolidated the major gas distribution and pipeline companies in southern California, and it made Pacific Lighting's system the largest in the country, serving over two hundred communities and nearly 800,000 households (representing approximately two million people). The four major gas firms — Southern Counties Gas, Southern California Gas, Los Angeles Gas and Electric, and Santa Maria Gas — became one giant, integrated system; gas was available to all through the several companies' existing facilities without expensive construction of new pipelines. With the exception of a few isolated settlements, every community within the 38,500 square miles of southern California territory (excluding San Diego County) received its gas service through this distribution network.[26]

The conversion to natural gas and the accompanying integration of the gas distribution network was a watershed in the history of Pacific Lighting Corporation. This transition had been made possible by prolific oil and gas field discoveries in the Los Angeles Basin, in Ventura and Santa Barbara counties, and in the San Joaquin Valley. With improved service, reasonable rates, adequate supplies, and vigorous sales campaigns, by the end of the 1920s the gas companies were able to make natural gas almost universally accepted for home heating in southern California as well as for cooking and water heating. California led the nation in natural gas consumption, and Los Angeles gas rates were lower than anywhere in the country.

Although gas prices were extremely reasonable, throughout the 1920s the gas utilities were embroiled in rate disputes with the California Railroad Commission. Because of the tremendous expenditures for capital improvements, the gas companies made repeated appeals to the commission for rate increases, which for the most part were denied. Even worse, after the all-natural gas system was mandated, the utilities were forced to make regular price reductions. In 1930, for example, the railroad commission ordered a nine percent rate cut, which Pacific Lighting fought unsuccessfully all the way to the U.S. Supreme Court. In addition, to recompense consumers for overpayment, the company had to pay $3.5 million in gas bill rebates in the early 1930s.[27]

The greater heating ability of straight natural gas initially brought reduced consumer usage as well as lower gas rates, and to augment their markets, Los Angeles Gas and Electric, Southern Counties Gas, and Southern California Gas set out with determination to attract more industrial customers. Learning from early efforts in this area by Southern Counties Gas, the search for such gas users became a major effort for Pacific Lighting's subsidiaries. As part of

Arc welder in front of a Los
Angeles home on West Fifth
Street, 1931.

Laying a twenty-two-inch pipe
in Sherman Oaks in the 1930s.

the campaign, the southern California gas distributing companies cooperatively maintained a Natural Gas Bureau in the late 1920s and early 1930s with exhibits of industrial gas appliances, and other promotions were developed. So fruitful were these efforts that Los Angeles Gas and Electric's president, Addison Day, remarked in 1931 that "in this territory, natural gas service is a domestic necessity, an industrial advantage, and a community asset."[28]

Industrial users were attracted by low rates with the contractual understanding that they would switch to other forms of energy when domestic consumption increased during the winter months. Gas companies were able to persuade commercial and industrial establishments that natural gas had many advantages as a fuel. Gas was more easily handled than coal or oil; it required no on-site storage space; it did not tie up capital in fuel inventories; it provided an even and easily controlled heat; and it left no residue. Moreover, steam-based electrical generators fueled by natural gas could be operated at one-third the cost of those run by oil. With this sales program, Pacific Lighting's subsidiaries created an industrial gas market to absorb surpluses during times of low demand. The "fine art" of gas management, as gas industry executives were learning, was "to develop consumption for off-peak periods of the day, of the month, of the year."[29]

Thus, the idea of a "firm" or "core" market evolved. Domestic, commercial, and some industrial users comprised the gas company's core market — the consumers who had a steady and primary service demand. To absorb surplus natural gas supplies, however, a "non-core" or "interruptible" market of industrial users came into being. These customers

1936 | U.S. Securities and Exchange
Commission exempts Pacific
Lighting from regulatory
restraints on diversification.

The Ventura oil fields provided about thirty percent of southern California's natural gas during the 1930s.

had very inexpensive rates and used backup oil supplies for energy when gas service was suspended during periods of peak demand by core users.

Having built up a steady and reliable market of domestic, commercial, and industrial consumers by the late 1920s, Pacific Lighting's subsidiaries became gravely concerned by the continuing depletion of casinghead gas reserves in Los Angeles Basin fields, which supplied seventy percent of their needs. While there had been a gas surplus in the early part of the decade, much of the gas had been burned off by flaring; as much as 162 billion cubic feet of casinghead gas were lost in 1929 alone because of this practice, and production fell dramatically thereafter due to continuing waste. (The value of natural gas in oil production initially was not appreciated by oil companies until they realized that gas helped lift oil to the surface and increased oil's fluidity. Even then not all oil companies used gas for oil production, and many continued to flare gas wastefully.)[30] Increasingly, natural gas reserves in more distant oil fields along the coast and in the San Joaquin Valley became vitally important to the gas

distributing companies and their customers, and there was an urgency to secure additional sources as well as to bring conservation policies into effect for future needs.

In 1929, as a result of general public concern and lobbying efforts by gas companies, the California legislature passed the Gas Conservation Act prohibiting the "unreasonable waste of natural gas," which, the legislators believed, was "opposed to the public interest." Due to such strengthening of the gas conservation laws in California, monthly waste was reduced from twenty-six billion cubic feet in February 1930 to a little under seven billion cubic feet in January 1931, according to the California Railroad Commission.[31]

Conservation practices went hand in hand with advancing technology to shape the natural gas industry during the 1920s and 1930s. Because locally-available natural gas reserves could not meet the

1936 | Los Angeles voters decide to purchase Los Angeles Gas and Electric's electric properties.

1937 | Merger of Southern California Gas and gas properties of Los Angeles Gas and Electric.

Kettleman Hills

California's Early Long-Distance Gas Pipelines.

In 1929 Pacific Gas and Electric Company completed a pipeline over two hundred miles long from Kettleman Hills (in Kings County, California) to San Francisco, an achievement made possible by major technological innovations in pipe-making and laying. The same year, Southern California Gas began building another long-distance pipeline to Los Angeles.

The project was a complex and logistical challenge. Southern California Gas maintained a field construction camp and office on the pipeline to supervise work, and they were moved as the project went forward. The field organization was composed of a superintendent and assistants,

an engineer, several foremen to oversee operations, and a crew of eighty men. Mechanical equipment consisted of three trenching machines (which dug a ditch thirty inches wide to an average depth of fifty inches), three cranes equipped for pipe manipulation, two backfillers, seven caterpillar tractors for moving welding equipment, and assorted painting machines. In addition, there were six trucks of various capacities. The field welding team was composed of ten experienced men, for whom a portable electric generating unit was provided. The new "Smith-weld" method was used, and the welding gang completed about 120 welds during a nine-hour work day.

Southern California Gas Company's Kettleman Hills pipeline was completed to Los Angeles in 1930, but because of continued depletion of the Los Angeles Basin oil and gas fields, the firm immediately decided it was necessary to construct an additional pipeline from Kettleman Hills to Long Beach. To oversee the project, Southern California Edison — which needed

natural gas for its Long Beach steam-run generating plant — and Pacific Lighting jointly formed Southern Fuel Supply Company. Constructed under the new organization's direction at a cost of $7 million, the twenty-six-inch pipeline increased the supply of gas to the Los Angeles metropolitan area by 130 million cubic feet per day. Edison and Pacific Lighting continued to own the pipeline jointly until 1938, when Pacific Lighting purchased the Edison interest and merged the property into Pacific Lighting's Industrial Fuel Supply system.[32]

All photos: Laying the twenty-six-inch pipeline from the Kettleman Hills to Long Beach, 1931.

demands of major metropolitan areas, the gas industry sought to advance pipeline technology in order to transmit gas greater distances to urban markets. The earliest pipelines, some of which were cast-iron, had been laid at the turn of the century and were inadequate in many respects. The Taft-Grapevine transmission line, for example, had to be unearthed in 1932 and its joints repaired. Improved acetylene welding techniques and advances in electrical welding averted similar problems for pipelines laid in the 1920s and later. In addition to improvements in pipelines, methods of fighting corrosion were developed and mechanized pipe-laying equipment expedited work formerly done by horses and men. These revolutionary innovations made it possible to undertake longer, more ambitious pipeline projects to tap more distant oil and gas fields.[33]

The technological developments had enabled northern California's Pacific Gas and Electric Company to complete a pipeline in 1929 from the San Francisco metropolitan area to the recently discovered, gas-rich reserves of Kettleman Hills in the San Joaquin Valley. Shortly thereafter, Pacific Lighting and Southern California Edison constructed a similar long-distance pipeline to bring Kettleman Hills gas to Long Beach to serve steam-run electric generating plants. The manufactured gas era finally drew to a close when Pacific Lighting completed its pipeline networks from the San Joaquin Valley and the coastal fields to its southern California market, and by 1931 the lion's share of the company's natural gas supplies came from these areas.[34]

In spite of poor business conditions during the Great Depression, Pacific Lighting suffered less than other utility firms. Pacific Lighting's survival

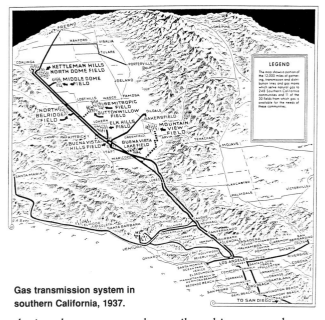

Gas transmission system in southern California, 1937.

during these years can be attributed in part to the company's adoption of the technological advances of the previous decade and in part to its active participation in national and regional gas industry organizations such as the American and the Pacific Coast Gas associations. These groups brought gas executives together to discuss common problems and developments. Pacific Lighting's executives played a leading role in these organizations. For example, they encouraged the gas industry to increase consumption by promoting gas appliance sales through advertising. Consequently, nationwide advertising campaigns were instituted stressing themes like "Modernize with Gas" and "Gas is the Modern Fuel." Attempting to counter the impression that gas supplies were limited and that gas appliances would have to be replaced with electric ones in a few years, cooperative advertising was extensive in the 1930s, and it targeted different types

1940 | California Railroad Commission refuses Pacific Lighting's request to merge Southern California Gas and Southern Counties Gas companies.

1941 | Pearl Harbor attacked.

Advertising in the 1930s

Increases in Competition for Appliance Customers.

During the 1930s it was well recognized that the "gas industry's most vital business . . . was the cooking load." Fighting off electric appliance competitors, Pacific Lighting and its subsidiaries aggressively promoted gas ranges and other gas appliances such as water heaters, home heating systems, and refrigerators. In the early 1930s $6 million was spent on advertising as part of an industry-wide, three-year program announced by the American Gas Association. The theme was that natural gas was modern, economical, and flexible.[35]

GAS

Simple Silent Saving

Booster stamps were used to sell the latest models of gas ranges in 1932. The clock-controlled range campaign appealed to the "modern" woman who desired more leisure time.

As the economy improved in the mid-1930s, the advertising focus shifted from an emphasis on the economical nature of gas appliances to their style.

Refreshing

BUY A NEW AUTOMATIC NATURAL GAS WATER HEATER

PLAY...

BATHE

and REST

Your

HOT WATER
Is Ready, Sir!

A number of advertisements were directed specifically at a male audience, stressing the comfort and convenience of hot water for bathing and shaving.

GAS REFRIGERATION
SILENT AS THE NIGHT

Most Economical Refrigeration for the Home

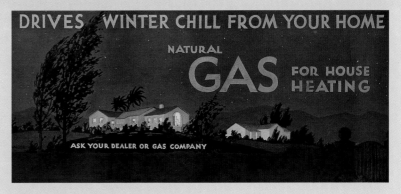

DRIVES WINTER CHILL FROM YOUR HOME

NATURAL

GAS FOR HOUSE HEATING

ASK YOUR DEALER OR GAS COMPANY

Natural Disasters

The 1933 Earthquakes and the 1938 Floods.

In March and again in October 1933, earthquakes shook southern California, causing considerable property damage and leaving many people homeless. According to estimates made in 1935 by Los Angeles Gas and Electric Company's auditor, the earthquakes — some of the worst in southern California's history — cost the company nearly $700,000 in lost income and damages, principally to its new Seal Beach electric plant. Although Pacific Lighting's gas customers suffered only minor disruptions in their service, neighboring gas systems were not as fortunate. For example, gas service to forty-six thousand people was entirely discontinued in Long Beach by the city's municipal gas department and was not fully restored for over two weeks.

The 1933 earthquake damage was minor compared to devastation wrought by the severe floods of 1938. On February 28, 1938, and again on March 2, 1938, huge rainstorms saturated the Los Angeles area. As much as twenty-eight inches of rain fell in some areas, turning normally dry streambeds into raging torrents. Bridges collapsed, roads became impassable, and a significant part of Pacific Lighting's gas pipeline system was damaged. The March storm was so bad that much of the supervisory staffs of Southern California Gas and Southern Counties Gas stayed on duty all night to direct repairs and maintenance activities. Thousands of gas customers lost their service due to damaged bridges and other wrecked pipe crossings. Despite deploying extra laborers, it took Pacific Lighting several days to restore service to most customers. However, because the firm had concentrated on integrating its gas subsidiaries' systems in the 1920s and 1930s, service remained uninterrupted for about ninety-five percent of Pacific Lighting's customers. Even in San Bernardino and Riverside counties, where flood damage was the greatest, consumers were without gas only for about forty-eight hours because Pacific Lighting summoned all available personnel into the field to repair damaged mains.[36]

Earthquake damage done to Southern Counties Gas Company's San Pedro office building in 1933.

of consumers through radio and magazine publicity. Billboards promoting gas appliances also appeared, and Pacific Lighting's subsidiaries even tried underwriting long-term appliance financing and subsidizing appliance manufacturers.[37]

So effective were the marketing campaigns that despite the Great Depression, gas appliance sales rose fifty percent in the early 1930s, provoking C.O.G. Miller's optimistic observation that the natural gas industry never had a brighter future:

> Gas has long since passed the time when its principal business is cooking and heating water in the home. It is adding new uses every day. In the home it is displacing all other fuels for house heating and in industry it is doing everything that fuel can do. There are today many thousands of new uses which were unknown fifteen years ago.[38]

While Pacific Lighting's triumph in building domestic gas demand was heartening, a shrinking base of industrial users during the depression years due to underpricing by other fuels was a cause for alarm. Pacific Lighting's subsidiaries offered very reasonable rates to industrial customers, but a great quantity of inexpensive low-grade oil — as cheap as ten to thirty cents per barrel — was dumped on the market in Los Angeles because oil producers had an oversupply due to their diminishing markets. In addition, the gas companies had to compete with inexpensive hydroelectric power brought in from Boulder Dam.[39]

Although Pacific Lighting fared better than most other utility businesses during the 1930s, the depression years were trying ones. The State of California increased taxes by nearly four percent, and like most other publicly held companies, Pacific Lighting's stock price plummeted.[40] To compound

matters, public opinion grew worse when several prominent but financially unstable holding companies in other states went bankrupt. The failure of one of the three largest holding companies in the nation, the Insull Group — which owned over one hundred utility firms from Maine to the Midwest as well as cotton and paper mills — left thousands of people without gas or electric service. Due to the public outcry, in 1935 Congress passed the Public Utilities Holding Company Act (PUHCA) to regulate holding companies and interstate commerce in gas and electricity. Yet because Pacific Lighting's business activities were geographically and functionally integrated and intrastate in nature, the firm obtained an exemption in 1936 from the U.S. Securities and Exchange Commission (SEC). Thus, Pacific Lighting was spared federal interference into its affairs under the terms of PUHCA.[41]

Despite the exemption, the year 1936 caused further difficult adjustments as the outcome of the Insull affair helped tip the scales so that Los Angeles Gas and Electric lost the battle to retain its electric properties and was forced to sell them to the City of Los Angeles. This sale precipitated the merger of Los Angeles Gas and Electric's gas system with that of the Southern California Gas Company on

"Enjoy Natural Gas Service For the 4 Big Jobs: Cooking, Water Heating, Refrigeration, House Heating." Southern California Home Show, 1939.

Electrolux gas refrigerators being unloaded at Southern California Gas Company, 1936.

May 13, 1937. While the California Railroad Commission approved this consolidation, in 1940 it denied a similar request to combine Southern Counties Gas with Southern California Gas on the ground that having two gas distribution firms in southern California — though owned by the same holding company — would promote healthy competition. The consolidation of Los Angeles Gas and Electric with Southern California Gas, while producing operational efficiency in the long run, was not accomplished easily because of differences in management philosophies, organizational and rate-schedule differences, and strong, inbred company loyalties.

The merger was partly responsible for major personnel reorganizations within Pacific Lighting and its subsidiaries. Many of the capable and experienced executives who had guided the companies through this era of phenomenal growth and startling change neared retirement age. Addison Day, president of Los Angeles Gas and Electric, became chairman of the "new" Southern California Gas Company's board of directors in 1937. Shortly thereafter, however, poor health forced him to retire. Alexander B. Macbeth — who had been with Southern California Gas since 1914 — continued as the firm's president and general manager until he retired in 1939 and was replaced by Franklin Wade, who also served as president at Southern Counties Gas. As part of the changing of the guard, LeRoy M. Edwards, formerly president of Industrial Fuel Supply, became vice-president at Pacific

Lighting and vice-president and general counsel of Southern Counties Gas. In addition, Robert W. Miller succeeded his father as president of Pacific Lighting in 1940, and Robert Hornby remained as vice-president, a post he had held since 1935.[42]

Despite these changes, from its small corporate offices in San Francisco Pacific Lighting maintained the same relationship with its southern California subsidiaries that had worked so effectively in the past. The major operating companies remaining after the 1937 merger — Southern California Gas, Southern Counties Gas, Santa Maria Gas, and Industrial Fuel Supply — operated on a daily basis more or less autonomously from the parent firm with Pacific Lighting directing major policy and financial decisions.

Having weathered the worst of the depression years, Pacific Lighting could look back with relief and pride at its tremendous achievements of the previous two decades. It had consolidated the largest, most modern, and most efficient natural gas distribution system in the nation. The firm now looked forward with confidence, having established conclusively that the future belonged to gas.

Some of the executives of the Pacific Lighting companies, 1939. From left to right: W.E. Houghton, T.J. Reynolds, H.L. Masser, C.O.G. Miller, A.B. Macbeth, R.W. Miller, L.M. Edwards, Wm. Moeller, Jr., and F.M. Banks.

Customer Satisfaction Is Employee Satisfaction

Management-Worker Relations.

HISTORICALLY, PACIFIC LIGHTING'S SUBSIDIARIES have enjoyed especially satisfactory relations between management and employees. Throughout the twentieth century, Pacific Lighting's utilities in southern California experienced constant growth, economic stability, and a remarkable continuity in managerial leadership. Employees and management worked cooperatively in the interests of maintaining good public relations and economic success, and in the process, they developed a strong sense of mutual interests. There was only one strike in the history of Pacific Lighting's utility subsidiaries because management was generally responsive to the needs of employees. Overall, during this era utility workers enjoyed higher wages, better benefits, and more job security than employees in most other large industries.

    Progressive personnel policies in the utility industry developed in response to several factors: the rapid growth in the ranks of workers after World War I, the on-going danger of municipal ownership, and the structural transformation of the utility business into a service industry. Privately held utilities throughout the state recognized that it was necessary to court community goodwill to maintain their franchise rights. A 1923 declaration by the president of

1914 | 1964

AS THE UTILITY BUSINESS WAS TRANSFORMED INTO A SERVICE INDUSTRY, THE NEED FOR GOOD PUBLIC RELATIONS CONTRIBUTED TO HARMONIOUS MANAGEMENT RELATIONS WITH EMPLOYEES.

1914 | Ford Motor Company raises basic wages from $2.40 for nine-hour day to $5.00 for eight-hour day.

1918 | World War I ends.

There was a strong fraternal feeling among Los Angeles Gas and Electric's Old Guard during the early decades of the twentieth century. Pictured here is the third annual Old Guard banquet, 1915.

The Early Days of Los Angeles Gas and Electric.

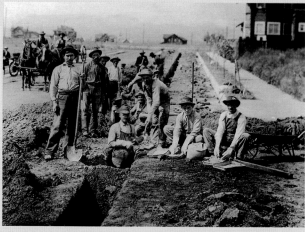

Workers laying pipe at a rate of fourteen hundred feet per day.

A member of the Old Guard remembered what work was like in the early days of Los Angeles Gas and Electric. When the firm was laying pipe to serve the city in the first few years of the twentieth century, digging was done by hand, and excavating forty feet of ditch three feet deep was considered a good day's work. Since the Los Angeles water table was higher than in later years, ditchdiggers frequently had to proceed by bailing with buckets. Several crews were needed to lay the regulation twelve-foot bell-and-spigot pipe, which was jointed with jute and lead. Since it took up

to forty-eight hours for the mixture to harden, checking for leaks was a time-consuming process. The gas pipes, once installed, needed frequent repair at joints, and storm damage, which happened often before Los Angeles had an effective flood control system, also meant more work. During one storm around 1910, for example, cast-iron pipe was broken; water and mud filled the low-pressure gas lines; and streams of muddy water squirted from gas cocks on the second stories of elegant homes in the Wilshire District. The periodic repairs created additional expenses, required

This meant that employees went to work at six o'clock in the morning and continued until six at night, Sundays and holidays included. Gasmakers sometimes even worked eighteen hours straight. Work was not only long but hard.

among the workers, and faithful employees were rewarded with one week's vacation per year and free turkeys on Christmas Day. At least some gas plant employees rebelled against this workload, and in 1914 — a year after a strike against northern California's Pacific Gas and Electric Company made it clear that such workloads were too severe — Los Angeles Gas and Electric workers' hours were reduced to nine hours per day.

Automobiles were a luxury at the turn of the century, and fitters and helpers had six horses and wagons for use to connect customers' meters. Thirteen strong draft horses and fourteen wagons were still being used by Los Angeles Gas and Electric Corporation as late as 1926, chiefly at the gas works to haul carbon briquets. Most animals, however, had been displaced by automobiles by 1914.[1]

Top: Gas leaks were a constant hazard faced by service crews. Bottom: Los Angeles Gas Company marketed carbon briquets, a by-product of the oil-gas process, at the turn of the century.

greater use of manpower, and caused customer irritation at the temporary interruptions in gas service.

"Six hour" days were in force at most gas plants.

In the days when coal was still being used for making gas, four men unloaded six cars of coal per day. The arduous work was lightened somewhat by the feeling of camaraderie northern California's Pacific Gas and Electric made this clear: "The aim of the company has been to win the public goodwill by deserving the public goodwill."[2]

Ten years earlier Pacific Gas and Electric had suffered a system-wide strike, and the lessons of this labor unrest were not lost on either that company's management or on C.O.G. Miller, who served on Pacific Gas and Electric's board of directors. Miller recognized that unhappy workers brought unwelcome publicity to utilities, and he believed that this negative image was to be carefully avoided. Because employees played a crucial role in shaping positive public relations in the service-oriented utility industry, under Miller's direction Pacific Lighting's subsidiaries launched a multifaceted campaign to improve employee-management relations and the companies' public images.

The managerial policies that Henry Ford had originally developed to deal with automobile plant workers in the early twentieth century set an example for other modern industrial leaders like

Miller to follow. According to Ford's thinking, if the owners of industry demonstrated a genuine concern for the well-being of their employees, the latter would respond with loyalty and high productivity. Ford, along with other high-ranking business leaders such as Herbert C. Hoover and Charles G. Dawes, encouraged industries to correct their own worst abuses to prevent a recurrence of the labor violence that had marked the turn of the century. Only such voluntary reforms coming from the private sector, Hoover warned, would avert government interference in business activities. Taking the lead, Ford put into effect various enlightened labor policies in his automobile plant. He treated workers better, paid them higher wages, and initiated pension programs and industrial safety measures. These changes had benefits beyond the workplace. Higher pay and increased productivity meant more people could afford cars, appliances, and other consumer goods, thus contributing to business prosperity and a sense of economic democracy.[3]

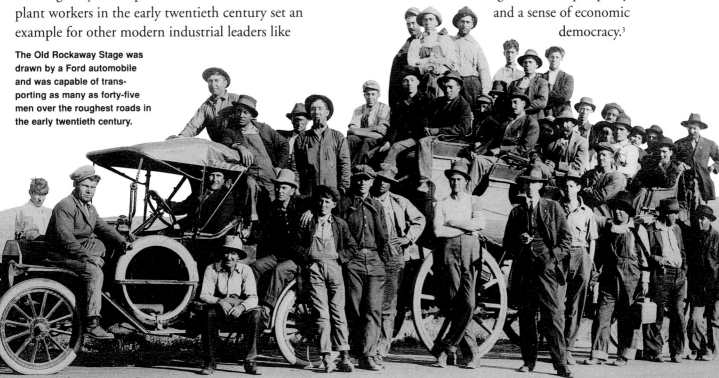

The Old Rockaway Stage was drawn by a Ford automobile and was capable of transporting as many as forty-five men over the roughest roads in the early twentieth century.

Workers producing meters in a factory, 1920s.

Cartoon from the *Saturday Evening Post*, 1924, illustrating the enviable situation of American workers in the 1920s.

At the end of World War I, there was a pressing need to implement similar improved personnel policies at Pacific Lighting's principal subsidiary, Los Angeles Gas and Electric. The company's rapid expansion following the war created many new positions, which the firm had difficulty filling with qualified workers. This personnel problem and the California Railroad Commission's General Order 58 of 1919 (which set standards of service for the gas industry) prompted the company's general manager, Addison Day — then president of the Pacific Coast Gas Association — to call for better training programs and other innovations:

> We must also, if we are to increase the permanency of our forces, make working conditions as nearly ideal as possible. We should see to it that proper ventilation, lighting, heating, lavatories, lockers, etc., are provided. Encourage active exercise; help to organize baseball or basketball teams, orchestras, and other social clubs. All of these will add to the welfare of employees and in turn reflect in a more efficient, stable, and loyal organization.[4]

Los Angeles Gas and Electric reaped the rewards from such reforms during the prosperous 1920s, a honeymoon era in employee-management relations throughout the country. Rarely have the interests of management and labor been so compatible and sympathetic or the spirit of cooperation and individual initiative so harmoniously blended. Contributing to this state of satisfaction was the prodigious national prosperity which rained like a "golden shower far and wide among all classes."[5] America appeared to have become a classless society as wages doubled, boosting the spending power of workers by twenty-five percent. Luxuries previously

1920 | Nineteenth amendment to the Constitution ratified giving women the right to vote.

affordable only by the rich — such as radios and automobiles — were now available to the masses due to assembly-line manufacturing, as developed by Henry Ford for the automobile. Utilities across the country experienced a period of unprecedented growth as reasonably priced gas and appliances became readily available. Material wealth was especially conspicuous in southern California, where natural gas was in abundant supply and the standard of living was among the highest in the nation. As the demand for gas increased, Pacific Lighting's Los Angeles subsidiary grew from a few dozen workers in the 1890s to thirty-five hundred employees by the 1920s.[6]

With this growth, the management of Los Angeles Gas and Electric sought to improve communication within the company in order to weld the growing ranks of employees into a united force. "Loyalty, cooperation, service — on this platform I stand," declared William Baurhyte on assuming the responsibilities of president of the firm in 1924. Since service and dependability were the images the utility sought to project to the general public, Los Angeles Gas and Electric wanted to develop these qualities in its personnel.[7]

One step toward enhancing communication and cultivating desirable traits in Los Angeles Gas and Electric workers had been taken as early as 1921 with the publication of the firm's first employee magazine, *The Bunch*. With its brotherly "hale-fellow-well-met" tone, this publication clearly reflected the values and experiences of the "Old Guard" — long-time employees — some of whom had been with the utility company since the 1890s. These workers believed in cooperation, loyalty, hard

Service crews' transportation changed over the years.

1921 | Los Angeles Gas and Electric's first employee magazine, *The Bunch*, published.

1923 | Employee stock-ownership plan introduced at Los Angeles Gas and Electric.

A. F. Lemunyon, Transmission, Taft, all set for a big day of fishing at Buena Vista Lake.

C. F. Smith, General Agent's, caught eight big swordfish on vacation at Guaymas, Mexico.

Muriel Snider, Customers, Riverside, got a nice sun tan on the beach at nearby Laguna.

...e Twoddle, Customers, ...le, and her camp site ...st Home pine trees.

Vacation Snaps

Babies

Babies of 1938

Suellen Hammond

...arie ...s

...nna Rae ...ones

J. H. Wallace, 3rd

Warren Roger Bartman

Babies of 1938

...Edward ...er

H. A. Dubbers, Transmission, Taft, with string of catfish caught in Buena Vista Lake.

R. F. Nelson, Customers, Los Angeles, snapped this beach scene on seashore vacation.

H. A. Harris, Sales, Compton, and family spent their vacation on a California ranch.

Minnie Krasselt, Customers, Riverside, and two friends at Crestline near Big Bear.

C. K. Graham, Customers, Banning, and family pose with nice catch of trout at Big Bear Lake.

work, and individual enterprise, and they had been rewarded by the firm for embracing such values as it grew. The Old Guard espoused the Rotary ideal — "he profits most who serves best" — as their motto. Many of the Old Guard were self-made men who had climbed the corporate ladder to positions of prominence, and they were somewhat astonished at the undreamed-of expansion and technological improvements they had witnessed during their careers with the utility company. They were genuinely dismayed and offended by the Los Angeles Bureau of Power and Light's characterization of their firm as a "power trust." To them, nothing could have been further from the truth. The Old Guard felt a bond toward one another and the company, which they hoped would be passed on to newer generations of employees through journals like *The Bunch* and later publications such as *L.A. Gas Monthly* and *L.A. Service Review*.[8] Like Los Angeles Gas and Electric, Southern California Gas — which became part of Pacific Lighting in 1929 — also sponsored a magazine for its employees to counteract the impersonality that had accompanied its corporate growth. The first issue of Southern California Gas Company's *Gas News* stated in 1924 that the journal's purpose was "to bring the employees closer together" in the hope that by learning about the progress of the company, workers would

1923 | First motion picture with sound produced.

"feel more and more that they are part of a big, living, straight-dealing fraternity."[9]

In addition to the newsletters and magazines, there were many programs that Pacific Lighting's subsidiaries instituted to strengthen employee relations. These included insurance and pension plans, employee and consumer stock-ownership programs, service award pins, vacation benefits, the introduction of safety equipment, and the inauguration of a safety-consciousness program. All of these progressive reforms to improve the condition of workers served to promote employee loyalty and satisfaction and were undertaken voluntarily by management with the anticipation that satisfied employees would help engender good public relations.

Employees appreciated these efforts, but it was the many social events sponsored and encouraged by management that won the hearts of the rank and file and nurtured long-lasting bonds of affection and commitment. These events served as an antidote to creeping anonymity, which increased as the utilities grew in size. There were Old Guard banquets and company-wide picnics, musical and theatrical events, and a wide variety of intramural sports competitions. Los Angeles Gas and Electric also inaugurated an employee association in 1926 as yet another means of building goodwill among workers. The new organization sponsored athletic, social, and educational activities primarily related to the gas and electric business, but some were of a more general interest. For example, more than six thousand people attended the association's first annual picnic. In addition to bathing-beauty parades, swimming, dancing, and tours of newly constructed facilities, baseball teams

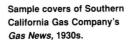

Sample covers of Southern California Gas Company's *Gas News,* 1930s.

1924 | First issue of Southern California Gas Company's *Gas News* is published.

Four thousand people attended Southern California Gas Company's annual picnic at the Santa Monica Pier in 1925.

Amateur theatrical presentation at Los Angeles Gas and Electric's Old Guard dinner, 1919.

contested for the W.B. Cline Perpetual Trophy, donated by Pacific Lighting's cofounder and chairman of Los Angeles Gas and Electric's board of directors. The employee association also developed health and accident insurance plans for its members.[10]

The cooperative and supportive spirit between management and employees in the 1920s was revealed in the goals for the forthcoming year announced at one of the early meetings of Los Angeles Gas and Electric's employee association: good fellowship among workers, self-help through the employee life insurance and disability funds, and the construction of an employee recreational center. *L.A. Service Review* reported that Addison Day rose at the banquet, and in keeping with management's generous support for employees, he "literally swept the gathering off its feet" by magnanimously offering corporate matching funds for building the employee center. The utility personnel were among the many workers enjoying the benefits of the era's economic abundance. As Los Angeles Gas and Electric's president, William Baurhyte, stated succinctly: "Never have people of all classes enjoyed more conveniences and comforts in the home, more freedom from drudgery, and the consequent increase of leisure time."[11]

1924 | William Baurhyte becomes president of Los Angeles Gas and Electric.

1925 | New Model "T" Ford sells for $260.

The company's active sponsorship of recreational activities complemented management's concern with the moral and mental health of its workers. Company publications not only carried a continual stream of newsy information about employees — promotions, deaths, marriages, births of children, vacation trips, and hobbies — but the journals also included inspirational and educational articles encouraging workers to strive for continual self-improvement. The Horatio Alger formula for success, widely accepted by many businesses, was held up for employees to emulate; the firm repeatedly advised that optimism, determination, honesty, loyalty, and hard work would be rewarded.

Through its employee magazines, Pacific Lighting's subsidiaries kept workers informed of significant developments in the utility business and even asked for advice on corporate problems. Employees enthusiastically responded to essay-writing and speaking contests — sponsored throughout the 1920s and 1930s — on subjects related to utility concerns. Topics included: "My Idea of Effective Goodwill Advertising for Los Angeles Gas and Electric," "Government Ownership of Utilities," and "What Can the Gas Companies Do To Still Further Popularize Gas Service?" In addition to cash awards,

Men's softball team, 1920s.

Los Angeles Gas and Electric's women's bowling team, 1927.

1926 | Southern California Gas Company employs 1,889 men and women.

1926 | Los Angeles Gas and Electric's employee association is formed.

Jésus Nuñez, José Nuñez, and Albert Mendez digging up Fourth Street near Main in preparation for extension of Southern California Gas Company's natural gas service, 1925.

Pacific Lighting's utilities published the best entries in employee publications, and winners were honored at department and industry meetings. Employees were thus invited to grapple with some of the most difficult problems facing the utility industry, and this strengthened the bond workers felt with management.

Adding to the feeling that employees made important contributions to the utility industry, executives implemented suggestions that came from servicemen and field workers regarding improvements in service or technology. During World War II, for example, Pacific Lighting's subsidiaries solicited employees' ideas about self-defense. In this and other ways, management confirmed the sense that they were in partnership with labor. By conveying a sincere regard for the opinions of the rank and file and by rewarding ability with promotions and recognition, Pacific Lighting's subsidiaries won the respect and loyalty of their employees.

Not only did the subsidiaries seek a bond with their workers, but they also were concerned for the general welfare of the community. Executives and other employees were encouraged to contribute to their communities by joining service clubs and otherwise involving themselves in civic affairs. "All those forty-six years I was with the company," one former employee later recalled, "I found that we basically were really good . . . citizens to the community. . . . [Utility personnel] worked hard and they played hard and they drank hard, but it was just a great group of guys who were good basic citizens; ones that put in a good day's work for a good day's pay." The standards of good citizenship and honorable behavior that pervaded the atmosphere of

Pacific Lighting's utility subsidiaries contributed to good morale. Employees felt pride and self-respect, and this was reinforced by the high esteem in which they were held in their communities. As the same former worker observed, "customer satisfaction is also employee satisfaction."[12]

The high moral standards and community service orientation — which simultaneously contributed to good public relations and promoted bonds of identification between employees and management — were achieved in large part by paternalistic management policies begun in the 1920s. Los Angeles Gas and Electric's concern for the character development of its workers was expressed in a variety of ways, but nowhere more graphically than in its 1925 employee manual. In this document, the company's role in guarding the morality of its workers and guiding their behavior was clearly revealed by the firm's regulations.

The rules for workers, which a half century later would have been deemed by many as unacceptable invasions of privacy, were typical of the nation's most progressive employers at the time, including Henry Ford. Employees were prohibited from gambling or doing "other things reflecting upon his [the worker's] character and bringing ill-repute to the corporation." Furthermore, participation in political activities was prohibited, and employees could not bring suit against anyone without obtaining permission from the heads of their departments. Workers had to secure the company's permission before they could circulate petitions or even raise funds to buy presents for other employees, and they were required to report any incidents of neglect of duties, fraud, or deception to their superiors.[13]

Both men and women performed clerical jobs in the 1920s as the number of such positions expanded.

In addition to personnel regulations, Los Angeles Gas and Electric's employee manual gave explicit guidelines for professional conduct, a concern directly related to good public relations. The "proper attitude toward complaining consumers," according to the booklet, was to "assume, in most cases, that there is simply a misunderstanding." Employees were to be business-like and respectful, and they were to bear in mind that they were salespeople "of service and goodwill." In a tactic aimed at disarming unhappy customers, employees were expected to express regret "that our consumers are displeased." A worker was not to blame other departments of the company for problems because

this would not only disparage fellow employees, but it also would reflect poorly on the worker himself for being part of an "incompetent organization." And, recognizing the power of regulatory agencies in shaping public relations, the employee manual advised workers to accord respect for the Public Utilities Commission since it existed "to guarantee fair treatment not only to the public but to the public utilities as well. . . ."[14]

Not surprisingly, the employee manual exalted democratic ideals in this era of widespread economic opportunity. Courteous and dependable service were to be extended to all persons in the community regardless of race, religion, or socio-economic status. This egalitarianism also extended to promotions for workers. A "qualified employee is practically certain of advancement," the handbook declared, because Los Angeles Gas and Electric was

1927 | Women's bowling team wins third place in the Pacific Coast Bowling Congress.

1928 | Herbert C. Hoover elected president of the United States.

growing rapidly and also because "the nature of the work is such that ability and achievement are quickly detected and readily estimated." Upward mobility was to be expected since many individuals with the company had risen from mechanics to executives.[15]

No better example of this advancement could be found than Los Angeles Gas and Electric's own Addison Day, who began his forty-four-year career with the firm in 1895 as a gas appliance salesman. A conscientious and hard-working employee, Day was rapidly promoted during the period of explosive utility growth in the first decades of the twentieth century, and he rose steadily between 1913 and 1928 from manager of operations to president and general manager. Pacific Lighting recognized and rewarded Day for his loyalty and ability, and by the end of his career in 1939, he had been elevated to chairman of the board of Southern California Gas.[16]

As Day's career confirmed, the southern California utility industry was remarkably democratic in its promotional practices for businesses of the time, and this contributed to good employee and public relations. As part of a trend toward egalitarianism, women became very visible and active in the southern California utility business by the mid-1920s. Although under Walter Cline's leadership Los Angeles Gas and Electric did not hire any women until 1924, Southern California Gas and Southern Counties Gas companies had started employing women as early as World War I, partly because of wartime labor shortages. Out of economic need and often a spirit of adventure, women entered this male-dominated industry, a change made possible by the introduction of labor-saving home appliances.

One of Southern Counties Gas Company's first female employees, Ethel Parks, in the Orange County office, 1914.

Exhibit in the Orange Show, San Bernardino, 1928.

1928 | Addison B. Day becomes president of Los Angeles Gas and Electric.

1932 | Uniform Pension and Benefit Plan put into effect at Los Angeles Gas and Electric.

"Cooking is Fun" poster from a 1939 *Los Angeles Times* advertisement.

In addition, organizational changes in the industry expanded the number of positions delegated to women, and many became secretaries, cashiers, and telephone operators. In an assessment of women's capabilities that was typical for the era, *Gas News* enthusiastically reported in 1928 that "because of their passion for detail, their patience, and their willingness to submerge their own opinions, women make ideal secretaries."[17]

Although more women were hired as time passed, the belief persisted that the "gas industry is a man's world." The managements of Pacific Lighting's subsidiaries, however, recognized the importance of understanding the "feminine viewpoint" because women purchased and operated most home appliances. Misapprehensions about gas use and its cost had made it clear that the utilities needed to put more emphasis on public education, and women were viewed as the logical people to carry out the duty. Executives increasingly appreciated the insights female employees provided into housewives' needs and preferences, and as a result, opportunities opened for some women in public relations and in "home service" sections of sales departments.[18]

Women's activities in the area of home service augmented the general public relations efforts of the Customer Service Department, which had been instituted in response to the California Railroad Commission's General Order 58. The order had been interpreted to mean that the gas utility companies' moral responsibility to customers included not only making sure that consumers were served without any gas leakage, but also that each appliance was using gas efficiently and safely. "The appliance is the key to service," one utility executive affirmed in 1929. "Therefore, it becomes the duty of the utility to itself and to its consumers to assume a responsibility toward the consumer's gas equipment."[19]

The intense company loyalty and the institution of the public relations efforts of the Customer Service Department facilitated aggressive gas marketing tactics. Beginning in the 1920s, Los Angeles Gas and Electric urged its employees to become enthusiastic boosters for gas use in their communities. "Every employee should be, in a

Demonstrations Promote Gas.

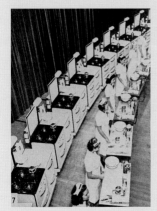

In order to promote gas appliance sales, the Pacific Coast Gas and American Gas associations encouraged gas distribution companies in the late 1920s to develop home service departments as adjuncts to their sales operations. The women hired to work in the home service departments were to serve as indispensable links in communicating the benefits of gas appliances to housewives.

Over three thousand women attended this three-day series of "All Gas" cooking classes in San Bernardino, 1935.

The many duties handled by the home service departments included presenting cooking demonstrations to large groups using gas ranges. These classes were an important part of the sales efforts of Pacific Lighting's subsidiaries, because they dispelled misconceptions and made gas appliances familiar to persons who had never owned them. For example, when Southern

Counties Gas home service representative Katie Rathbone demonstrated appliances to housewives in the 1920s, she kept a canary on stage to overcome some women's fears that gas was poisonous. Cooking classes were very popular and were sources of entertainment for women. In spite of inclement weather,

two thousand women attended the four-day South Bay Daily Breeze Cooking School in 1932, which featured displays of modern gas appliances. The theme was "A Cook's Tour — Royal Roads to Romance Via Kitchen Shelves."

Men also received gas cooking instruction, although for different reasons than women. Gladys B. Price, who served as Southern California Gas Company's home service supervisor from 1933 until her retirement in 1962, spent much of her time giving cooking demonstations to appliance servicemen and

salesmen, who needed to learn the art of cooking on gas appliances so they could answer housewives' questions. When Southern California Gas Company moved to new quarters at 810 South Flower Street in 1937, the home service department there was equipped with a model kitchen where servicemen were trained and recipes tested.

Like servicemen, home service representatives also visited customers in their homes. In late 1933 Price hired seven women — who like Price had college degrees in home economics — to train in home service for the regional offices. Among other things, these women were taught how to adjust thermostats, and they made home visits to each new appliance purchaser to instruct the owner on its use.

In addition to visiting appliance owners' homes and other duties, home service representatives also gave instructions in home economics classes at public schools and at Girl Scout meetings, and the representatives hosted dinners each year for home economics teachers. The home service departments also encouraged housewives to listen to weekly radio programs such as "Easier Housekeeping Hour," sponsored by the Pacific Coast Gas

Appliance exhibit at the Builders' Exposition, Shrine Auditorium, 1928.

Association, and "Woman's Magazine of the Air."

While the home service departments deserve some of the credit for boosting appliance sales during the 1930s and 1940s, they also performed an important public relations role in their communities. Throughout the depression and war years, the home service departments provided to their communities recipes and advice on nutritious and low-cost meal planning, thus helping those with little money to survive the economic and wartime crises.[20]

Local cake-baking champions testing modern gas ranges, 1939.

Personality Testing

The Humm-Wadsworth Temperament Test.

Developed by Guy W. Wadsworth, Jr., and Doncaster Humm, the Humm-Wadsworth Temperament Test was premised on the belief that behavior viewed by some people as abnormal was merely uncontrolled personal temperament found in the normal individual. According to this thesis, all persons could be labeled according to dominant clusters of traits, called components.

Most individuals within the range of what was considered "normal" also had components in categories called hysteroid, cycloid, schizoid, and epileptoid. A high degree of the "normal" component was a counterbalance, keeping the other components within socially acceptable limits.

The Humm-Wadsworth system thus placed employees into categories such as "normal-hysteroid" and "normal-cycloid." Normal-hysteroid people were often personally successful; their emphasis on self-interest focused their efforts on their own advancement. Normal-cycloid persons worked well with the public and had the ability to shift attention quickly, qualities useful in jobs such as sales, truck driving, and general advertising.

Additional categories defined other personality types. For example, "normal autistic" persons did not perform well in relation to the public but were satisfactory in routine jobs where long periods of isolated application were required. Such people made good bookkeepers, watchmen, and researchers. "Normal paranoid" subjects relished contention and made excellent lawyers and leaders of social and political movements. "Normal-epileptoid" persons were successful pushing projects to their completion without supervision and excelled at work requiring careful attention to detail; they made good foremen, superintendents, and skilled tradesmen.

When combined with an intelligence test, the Humm-Wadsworth Temperament Test was believed to be very successful in screening out unsuitable persons for employment and fitting acceptable employees into appropriate job categories. As late as 1967 one gas company employee described the Humm-Wadsworth test as "nationally recognized and widely used by large industries all over the country." Nonetheless, the test was abandoned in the 1960s when extensive studies proved its usefulness to be limited.[21]

Guy W. Wadsworth, Jr., chief executive officer of Southern Counties Gas Company from 1954 to 1969.

sense, a salesman of the corporation and its service," as the firm's employee manual reminded workers. Employees were encouraged to spot potential domestic and industrial customers, to advocate the purchase of company stock to their friends and neighbors, and to promote the use of gas appliances. In essence, the interests of the company were to be the interests of the employees.[22]

Every employee was thus enlisted to advertise and sell Los Angeles Gas and Electric's products and to be actively engaged in discovering new markets and methods of sales. This strategy also was extended to Pacific Lighting's other utility acquisitions, which pioneered many marketing techniques to compete with electric utilities. At a 1929 meeting of Southern California Gas workers, for example, the recommendation was made that all employees be instructed in sales so that every employee could "sell gas." A few years later, that subsidiary inaugurated a campaign whose slogan told the whole story: "Every Employee a Business Builder." Workers were expected to attend meetings to learn about the advantages of cooking with gas, entering "'with a will' into the spirit of this all-important program — as important to the employee himself as to his industry." Such thinking was characteristic of all Pacific Lighting's southern California utilities throughout the 1920s and 1930s.[23]

The cooperative efforts of management and employees in boosting gas appliance sales helped Pacific Lighting's subsidiaries weather the worst years of the Great Depression. Due to the increase in appliance sales and steady demand for gas, there were relatively few layoffs of utility workers, and most subsidiaries' employees considered themselves

fortunate to have employment. Job security contributed to company loyalty, but it was not the only
asset enjoyed by gas utility workers. Los Angeles Gas
and Electric put into effect its Uniform Pension and
Benefit Plan for all employees in September 1932,
and this added yet another reason why workers felt
a bond to the company. As Addison Day observed,
the idea that employers owed nothing to workers
belonged "in the dark ages of the industry."[24]

 Despite the pension and benefit plan and
the relative employment security, the economic
stresses of the depression years threatened to disrupt
the management-employee harmony that had
prevailed in the prosperous 1920s. To counter this
situation, the managements of Pacific Lighting's
southern California utility companies tried to spot
potential personnel problems by instituting pre-
employment intelligence and personality evaluation
tests. Beginning in the 1930s, the Humm-Wadsworth
Temperament Test was used system-wide in personnel hiring and evaluation. Developed by Southern
Counties Gas Company's personnel manager, Guy
W. Wadsworth, Jr. — who eventually became president of that firm — and his colleague Doncaster
Humm, this test was intended to screen out job
applicants with serious psychological disturbances
and to match particular personalities to appropriate

**Gas shop employees enthu-
siastically pledging themselves
to sell one share of company
stock, 1924.**

**Standard uniform for
servicemen, 1936.**

Serviceman, 1943.

1935 | Social Security Act
   passed by Congress.

1936 | Union recruitment
   begins.

The Evening Concert Series

The Gas Companies Sponsor a Classical Music Radio Program.

In early 1940 the two southern California gas companies considered sponsoring a nightly classical music radio program as a public relations and advertising strategy. The Evening Concert Series was to be based on an "Evening Concert" show sponsored by Pacific Gas and Electric Company in the San Francisco area. There were many advantages to this type of broadcasting. Audience loyalty to the San Francisco program and to a similar one in New York was high; there would be no "talent" costs because recordings would be used; the program would be flexible as to commercial content; it would attract affluent listeners; and it would give Pacific Lighting's subsidiaries a "classy" image. Gas company officials speculated that seventy-five hundred program guides would have to be printed weekly, costing the company $1,092 per year.

The Evening Concert Series began October 1, 1940, and was broadcast on AM (and later also on FM) stations nightly from 8:00 until 10:00 P.M. It carried only music "of the highest classical standard." Printed schedules were distributed at gas company offices, music departments of city and county schools, universities, public libraries, and personnel departments of major industries and businesses.

The program, which a company memo described as "one of the strongest public

relations activities we have," attracted a small but relatively influential audience. Not only did the gas companies receive favorable mail about the show, but sales and new gas hookups were directly traced to the commercial messages broadcast during the two-hour program. The broadcasts were "undoubtedly the most spontaneous association that the public or customers make with reference to the gas company," one executive observed. By 1953 the gas companies were distributing over fifty thousand schedules per week.

The Evening Concert Series earned a variety of awards, including being named by the Southern California Association for Better Radio and Television the most outstanding recorded musical program of local origination in 1950. The broadcasts also were honored by the Los Angeles District Federation of Women's Clubs as well as by the Tidings Radio Public Service. The Los Angeles County Board of Supervisors even commended the concert program in 1961. Despite the series' critical acclaim, it ended in 1989 when the carrier station changed ownership and subsequently altered its programming format.[25]

Well-known Los Angeles radio personality Thomas Cassidy was the "voice" of the Evening Concert Series from 1943 to 1987.

positions in order to increase worker productivity. According to Wadsworth, the purpose of the test was not to locate "super-applicants," but rather to find persons of general ability, who could "get along with people" and who dealt equally well with colleagues and superiors.[26]

In spite of such efforts to maintain employee-management harmony, the depression years caused a great deal of social dislocation and political turmoil which extended to the utility industry, and this began to undermine the good management-employee relations that had been created over the previous years. Added tensions were produced by Pacific Lighting's 1937 decision to merge the gas systems of Los Angeles Gas and Electric and Southern California Gas Company into one integrated utility after the former firm was forced to sell its electric properties to the City of Los Angeles. This merger of the gas utilities caused employee displacement, adjustment, and resentment. Those employed in the electric side of the business became city employees in the transfer of the electric properties. Gas utility workers, on the other hand, faced the possibility of losing their jobs as duplicate positions were eliminated. Although inevitably some positions were lost, the main source of unhappiness was the merger process itself. Job categories were redefined as was the hierarchy of authority. Persons with different approaches to business and intense loyalties to their respective companies were reorganized into newly created departments. Old loyalties died hard, and it was many years before employees accepted the changes.

While workers faced these difficult adjustments, union organization gained momentum in the nation during the 1930s, and several unions took root in Pacific Lighting's subsidiaries. The experience with unions varied from one Pacific Lighting firm to the other. Relations between Southern Counties Gas and its employees' union, the American Federation of Labor (AFL), for example, were fairly harmonious. Such was not the case at Southern California Gas, however.

One of the earliest unions at Southern California Gas was the Congress of Industrial Organizations (CIO), which was especially successful in recruiting members from the Central Division of the firm beginning in the mid-1930s. The company tried to counter union organization by issuing its "Statement of Minimum Wages and Other Working Conditions," which established a "floor under wages," or minimum pay level, but the firm's strategy did not dissuade union activists from seeking more members. In October 1937 — in another attempt to slow union growth — Southern California Gas President Alexander Macbeth wrote a letter to all workers discussing employer-employee relations and announcing management's neutrality regarding union organization. Nonetheless, representatives of the CIO — which had recruited less than a quarter of the 4,250 company employees — then appeared before management asking for official recognition as bargaining agents for all Southern California Gas workers. Negotiations between the CIO and the firm became increasingly difficult and acrimonious. Not only were the CIO union organizers considered radical by company executives, but the CIO leaders were very aggressive in pressing their demands, which quickly irritated the conservative managements of Southern California Gas and its parent company, Pacific Lighting.[27]

Safety programs lowered on-the-job accidents dramatically. Goggles saved this man's eye, 1940.

Samples of Evening Concert Series guides distributed by Pacific Lighting's gas subsidiaries.

Gas Company Benefits and Affirmative Action

Employee-Management and Customer Relations in the 1980s.

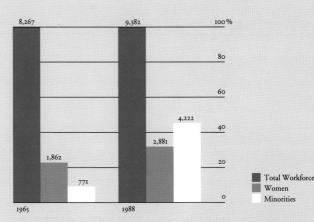

Percentages of women and minorities employed by Southern California Gas Company increased substantially after 1965 in response to affirmative action programs.

By the 1980s the bonds forged in the 1920s and 1930s between employees and management at Pacific Lighting's utility subsidiaries had evolved in ways that reflected the country's remarkable social changes during the intervening years. Yet the alterations — which included greater opportunities for women and minorities and enhanced employee benefits — continued to build on the premise that employee and customer satisfaction were interrelated.

During the first half of the twentieth century, women and minorities generally played lesser roles in working environments than white males, but by the 1980s major changes had occurred giving women and minorities greater opportunities in hiring and promotion. Encouraged in part by social protests during the 1960s and 1970s aimed at eliminating inequalities among ethnic, religious, and gender-based groups, federal and state legislation emerged compelling employers to end any practices in their hiring and promotional procedures that might result in discrimination. Affirmative action programs were mandated that would enable women and minorities to "catch up" with white males on the organizational charts of companies.

Recognizing that government policy, public sentiment, and the changing ethnic mix of the general population had a very important bearing on the success of their business, Pacific Lighting's utility subsidiaries made a significant commitment to affirmative action programs. Beginning in the 1960s, the firms developed programs to broaden opportunities for women and minorities, and the companies quickly became dedicated to achieving and maintaining a work force that was representative of the external labor market for the companies' service area — a standard established by the government's rules.

Examples of the commitment of Pacific Lighting's gas utilities to affirmative action are impressive. The number of employees in those firms grew from 8,267 in 1965 to 9,382 by the end of 1988. During that period, the number of women in the subsidiaries' work force increased from twenty-two percent to about thirty percent, making the firms' female representation almost identical to that for women in the available work force in southern California. Simultaneously, the gas utilities increased the number of minorities on the payroll from less than ten percent to nearly forty-five percent, exceeding the representation in the available work force. In addition,

the gas subsidiaries met or exceeded their goals for representation of women and minorities in management. Of the 2,312 management employees at Southern California Gas in 1988, over a quarter were female and a third were minorities.

The gas utilities also continued to offer a wide range of employee benefits. The pension, disability, and life insurance plans that had been started in 1932 were continued into the 1980s, with changes being made periodically after contractual negotiations with labor unions. In 1948, for example, medical insurance was added to employee benefits, and in 1971 this was supplemented by dental insurance. In addition, a retirement savings program was instituted in 1964.

As was true in the 1920s and 1930s, the maxim that "customer satisfaction is employee satisfaction" still was the case a half century later. With enhanced employee benefits and strong affirmative action programs reflecting

Southern California Gas Company's continuing concern for workers in a changing world, in 1989 the firm launched its "Glad to be of Service" program. The company stressed that this program was not merely an advertising tactic, but rather an effort to renew and strengthen the attention to customers' needs characteristic of past years. The plan was to extend this new version of the firm's "historically high level of service" many years into the future. Emphasis was placed on the important role employees played in interacting with customers. Thus, in many ways the heritage of the early decades of the twentieth century could be seen in employee-management relations and customer service many years later.[28]

With talks between Southern California Gas and the union disintegrating, the CIO applied to the National Labor Relations Board — Franklin Roosevelt's New Deal agency charged with overseeing union activities — for the right to represent all "production workers" at Southern California Gas. Management not only objected to this application because the CIO had the allegiance of just a minority of the gas utility's workers, but the company even denied that the National Labor Relations Board had jurisdiction over the firm since all the company's operations were within California and therefore did not constitute interstate commerce. The National Labor Relations Board ruled against the company, however, and granted CIO Local 132 recognition as the collective bargaining unit for the Central Division of Southern California Gas Company. Southern California Gas signed its first written contract with the CIO in June 1941.[29]

Union difficulties did not end with the official recognition of CIO Local 132. In the post-World War II anti-Communist hysteria, Congress passed the 1947 Taft-Hartley Act, requiring union officers to sign affidavits swearing they had no Communist affiliations. Southern California Gas — like other big businesses of the day — dutifully enforced this law, and when union leaders James L. Daugherty and L.R. Watterman refused to make such a pledge, they were fired and replaced by other union members who would. The new union leaders were less radical and willing to comply with the Taft-Hartley Act, and Southern California Gas Company found it easier to negotiate with them. Regardless of such problems with CIO Local 132, it did not remain the exclusive bargaining agent of Southern California

Union recruiters were active beginning in the late 1930s.

In 1947 the union demanded equal pay for women who performed the same jobs as men, and subsequently an equal-pay system was adopted.

A combination of high inflation and stiff rate regulation in the early 1950s made negotiations between management and labor difficult. There was a strike in 1953.

1941 | First union contract between the CIO and Southern California Gas Company.

1964 | New employee stock-purchase savings plan started.

Gas workers for long. Over the following years, nine other local unions were established, and eventually they joined forces to gain better representation through consolidated efforts.[30]

Prominent among early discussions between management and the unions were wage increases, the "closed shop," equal pay for women, and the use of seniority rather than merit as the basis for advancements. While the union fought for promotions based on seniority, management maintained that merit should be the guiding qualification for advancements, and to defuse the union position and insure fair play, the company instituted an employee rating system. Its aim was "to remove the charge of favoritism."[31] Aside from the rating system, various benefits were added due to union negotiations, including a medical plan, an employee loan policy, and an employee credit union. Pacific Lighting's

subsidiaries tried to reduce labor tensions further by initiating union-management committees to discuss operating problems. Such efforts by the utilities were partly successful in creating a working relationship with the unions, strengthening employee loyalty, and reducing personnel turnover. Nonetheless, as union activity grew, postwar increases in the cost of living drove workers to demand pay increases and support union goals, and by 1950 a majority of Southern California Gas workers were union members.[32]

While Pacific Lighting's subsidiaries generally met reasonable union demands, negotiations only broke down completely on one occasion. In 1953 CIO Utility Workers Union members sought a ten percent wage increase, while management countered with five percent. Finding this unacceptable, workers went on strike for several weeks. Due to

the conservative tone that dominated the early 1950s, the public had little sympathy for the union, especially since the gas company provided a vital community service. Because of this sentiment and because acts of sabotage committed during the strike were allegedly caused by union members, the strike was largely unsuccessful. Eventually, Southern California Gas and the workers reached an agreement essentially as first offered in which employees received a five percent wage increase.[33]

As this troubled era in employee-management relations at Southern California Gas Company drew to a close in the mid-1950s, a new period of post-war prosperity led to greater employee satisfaction. Because labor costs for the utility industry were relatively low compared to the annual investments in capital improvements and the costs associated with gas supplies, in the interest of harmony and good public relations, management met many union requests for improved benefits and higher wages. Long before other major industries, for example, Pacific Lighting's subsidiaries introduced alcohol treatment programs and maternity leave benefits as well as actively cooperated with government agencies to institute industrial safety measures.[34] Thus, Pacific Lighting's subsidiaries continued to support progressive personnel policies initiated in the 1920s, reviving the dormant familial spirit among its employees. The open dialogue between management and employees was the most significant legacy Pacific Lighting's subsidiaries left to the next generation of their workers.

Servicemen ready to begin work on a balmy southern California day in the early 1960s.

The War Years and Postwar Expansion

The Search for Gas Moves Beyond California's Borders.

THE BONDS OF LOYALTY AND COOPERATIVE SPIRIT that had developed between management and employees during the early decades of the twentieth century enabled Pacific Lighting to face the challenges generated by World War II and the postwar era. As the nation geared up for the war effort following the Japanese attack on Pearl Harbor on December 7, 1941, there was a pressing need for conservation of vital war products. In spite of a manpower shortage, Pacific Lighting contributed to the patriotic effort by channeling a steady flow of energy to defense manufacturers and by converting Southern California Gas Company's old Aliso Street gas works to the production of butadiene, a compound necessary to make synthetic rubber. Both during and after the war, the dramatic increase in the demand for natural gas stimulated a search for new sources of supply and better storage facilities. The defense industry attracted many new residents to southern California, and during the 1950s Pacific Lighting encountered conditions similar to those of the 1920s, with construction costs for extensions and improvements requiring huge capital expenditures. The gas utilities confronted skyrocketing demands from consumers — in part due to successful promotional campaigns. Simultaneously, management faced the unpleasant task of justifying

This mural advertising an Evening Concert Series opera appears to dramatize the forward march of the utility industry during and after World War II.

1941 | 1965

BETWEEN 1941 AND THE MID-1960s, PACIFIC LIGHTING FACED THE CHALLENGES OF WORLD WAR II AND THE BOOMING POSTWAR SOUTHERN CALIFORNIA ECONOMY.

1941 | The United States enters World War II.

1942 | Experiments demonstrate that butadiene can be manufactured at the Aliso Street gas plant.

Female gas company workers contributed to the war effort in many ways. This employee was a volunteer motor mechanic in the Women's Ambulance Corps.

During World War II, female gas company employees filled positions held by men who were in the armed forces.

rate increase requests to government regulators and the general public. By the end of the 1950s, however, Pacific Lighting — under the direction of Robert Miller and Robert Hornby — had overcome these difficulties. Moreover, the company could boast some of the lowest gas prices in the United States.

Pacific Lighting's subsidiaries began to feel wartime demands on their personnel even before Pearl Harbor. With tensions mounting around the world caused by the Japanese invasions of southeast Asian nations and Adolf Hitler's aggressions in Europe, the U.S. Congress passed the Selective Service Act of 1940 — the first peacetime conscription law in American history. The legislation called for 800,000 draftees between the ages of eighteen and thirty-five to join the armed forces, and Pacific Lighting's subsidiaries responded by making provisions for military service leaves of absence. The companies also established policies dealing with job security, pension and benefit plans, and seniority rights for employees returning from military duty. During 1940 and 1941, 160 employees were drafted from Pacific Lighting's subsidiaries, and the following year 642 went on military leave, including several women. By December 1944 the number of workers on military leave had risen to 992, and by the end of the war, slightly more than 1,200 Pacific Lighting employees had served their country. Twenty-four died while in uniform.[1]

While the preponderance of employees who ultimately served in the armed forces were, of course, men, women made substantial contributions to the war effort in other ways. As was the case in many war industries, women moved into positions formerly held by men at Pacific Lighting's

GAS makes **his** shells and weapons! *Use it wisely*

REN WICKS

subsidiaries. For example, women took over for gas company draftsmen; they completely dominated the messenger service; they became punch card operators; and they learned technical and mechanical skills. Some women's contributions to the war effort were more unusual. One member of the Customer Service Department spent her spare time learning auto mechanics in the Women's Ambulance Corps with other female volunteers. Such contributions, while gratefully appreciated by all, were occasionally met with benign amusement during an era of "traditional" gender roles. "Although it might be imagined that two hundred women would spend quite a bit of time discussing things far removed from motor mechanics, there was no feminine nonsense," an employee publication light-heartedly observed. "Each woman was anxious to contribute her energy to the war effort, and all stuck to their grimy, greasy jobs with hearty enthusiasm."[2]

To boost the morale of gas company workers who stayed behind while their colleagues went to war, Pacific Lighting and its subsidiaries used in-house publications to carry news about the war effort and employees in the service. For example, Southern California Gas Company's publication, *Gas News,* kept track of all staff who were serving in the armed forces. Almost every issue during World War II included photos and brief biographies of colleagues in uniform. *Gas News* editors encouraged workers still on their jobs in southern California to

Pacific Lighting's gas utilities launched a major advertising campaign to encourage wartime gas conservation.

LADY OF FASHION ~ *Spring 1943*

WOMEN NEEDED! TO REPLACE MEN IN OUR ESSENTIAL WAR INDUSTRIES

Robert W. Miller

Utilities Executive and Opera Patron.

Robert W. Miller, son of C.O.G. Miller, was president of Pacific Lighting from 1940 to 1956 and chairman of the board from 1956 to 1967. In addition, Miller sat on the board of directors of several giant corporations, including American Airlines, Standard Oil Company of California, Caterpillar Tractor Company, and Wells Fargo Bank. He was also a member of many prestigious social clubs in San Francisco, where he lived in Nob Hill's "jewel-box mansion" — a home well known for its distinctive architecture.

One of Miller's principal interests was the opera, and he became president of the San Francisco Opera Association in 1937. A tall, stern-looking gentleman, Miller was often seen at the opera in his top hat, cape, white tie, and tails — the picture of dignity and elegance. Miller brought to the opera association his shrewd business sense and sensitivity for what was good box office, and his quarter century of devotion ushered in a golden age for the San Francisco Opera in the 1950s under director Kurt Herbert Adler.

Miller was still serving as president of the San Francisco Opera Association when a labor crisis arose with the musicians' union in 1964. A union negotiator described Miller as one of the "toughest and firmest hard-rock

businessmen I've ever met." When an agreement could not be reached, the community was stunned by the possibility that the opera season might be canceled. "It's one of the penalties we pay for democracy," Miller commented. The opera season was eventually saved through the intervention of San Francisco's mayor.

San Francisco's "jewel-box mansion," Robert Miller's home.

San Francisco Chronicle columnist Herb Caen observed that Miller was one of the few people blessed with both class and style. According to Caen, Miller "never wavered from his particular, special view of life," and he conducted his life "without phoniness."[3]

Above: Robert W. Miller, 1950s.

correspond with those in the armed forces, and the publication welcomed returning servicemen and women by printing their pictures and noting their gas company departments. Pacific Lighting published a similar newsletter, *The Big Potato,* for its smaller work force in San Francisco.[4]

Aside from the individual roles played by employees of Pacific Lighting and its subsidiaries, the companies themselves also heavily supported the war effort. In addition to backing such wartime projects as blood drives, civil defense measures, Community Chest undertakings, government bond sales, and victory gardens, the firms helped conserve commodities in short supply. One important focus of conservation was natural gas, which the Pacific Lighting companies stressed in order that more of their product could be directed to war industries. For voluntary conservation, F.M. (Marion) Banks, vice-president of Southern California Gas and later its chairman, outlined a plan to conserve gas for cooking, water heaters, and room heating.[5] In case voluntary efforts were not enough, Pacific Lighting's subsidiaries developed procedures to cut back service to core, or "firm," customers when the demands of specific war industries dictated. As the gas companies explained to these consumers, "from now on, the No. 1 task of natural gas — is to speed war production!"[6] The gas companies also rigidly enforced shut-down requirements for interruptible, non-war businesses in order to direct energy supplies to defense production. Curtailments affected core and interruptible customers throughout the war, and the gas cutbacks regularly made front-page news in southern California.[7]

In addition to gas conservation, Pacific

Lighting and its subsidiaries helped to conserve other valuable resources, including rubber. Shortly after the beginning of World War II, the Japanese conquered the natural rubber-producing areas of southeast Asia, and the gas companies — like other businesses — urged their employees to help conserve this vital product. To stimulate the effort, the gas firms held a contest offering monetary rewards for the best rubber conservation suggestions. The companies also requested that employees ride bicycles to work in order to save wear on automobile tires, and *Gas News* published a detailed map of Los Angeles bus and streetcar routes, encouraging workers to use public transportation as an alternative to the automobile.[8]

Aside from advocating conservation of gas and other products, another major effort for Pacific Lighting and its subsidiaries during the war was manufacturing synthetic rubber. With the Japanese controlling rubber-producing parts of the world, the Allied armies desperately needed tires, and a search for a substitute for natural rubber became a top government priority. The country's leading scientists quickly determined that a synthetic rubber could be made from several chemicals, one of which was butadiene, a compound relatively easy to manufacture. With part of the solution at hand, the government explored possible sites for butadiene manufacturing facilities, and in southern California

Southern California Gas Company's butadiene manufacturing plant, 1944.

Early in World War II, employees were urged to ride bicycles to work to conserve automobile tires. Those who complied had their pictures and names published in *Gas News*.

F.M. (Marion) Banks, president of Southern California Gas Company, 1950-1967.

1944 | D-Day, June 6th.

1945 | World War II ends after atomic bombs are dropped on Japan.

The Skyway Program

The Plan to Aid Pilots.

World War II had an enormous impact on the development of the aircraft industry in southern California, and with the end of the conflict, the cooperation so carefully cultivated during the war between aeronautics firms and other companies continued to flourish. A good example was the creation of the Skyway Program to aid pilots. As originally conceived, there were to be several skyways, each marked by conspicuous landmarks easily visible from the air. Large arrows would be painted on the landmarks pointing directions, and navigational data also was to be provided. In addition, the winged symbol of the Skyway Program would be prominently displayed, much as transcontinental highways used shield emblems to mark their courses. Skyway Number One, which was planned between Los Angeles and Washington, D.C., was supported by the Los Angeles Chamber of Commerce,

various aeronautical groups, and private industries — including Pacific Lighting's subsidiaries. The gas companies cooperated with the plan by allowing the tops of their giant gas holders to be painted with Skyway information.

The gas companies' interest in the Skyway idea may have been stimulated in part by incidents such as one that occurred in the 1950s. A Southern California Gas retiree remembered that on a flight carrying company workers to Portland, Oregon, to help that city's utility firm make the shift from manufactured to natural gas, the copilot came back from the cockpit to ask for a road map to help determine the plane's location.[9]

Large gas holder directs pilots to Hollywood, 1947.

one location was Los Angeles Gas and Electric's old gas plant on Aliso Street, which had been closed since the company had switched to natural gas in 1927. Initial experiments in 1942 confirmed that the existing gas generators could be altered to produce butadiene, and within a short period of time Southern California Gas — which had inherited the Los Angeles Gas and Electric works when the two firms merged in 1937 — began nonprofit manufacturing under a government contract.[10]

Soon after butadiene production began, Los Angeles residents near the plant began to complain of burning eyes and choking throats, a concern reminiscent of the days when gas manufacturing took place next to the Los Angeles Plaza. The situation became worse when stinging clouds of haze — which came to be known as "smog" — drifted toward city hall and the mayor's office, and local government officials joined the chorus of criticism.[11] Although part of the smog problem was due to Los Angeles's growing number of automobiles, by August 1943 Mayor Fletcher Bowron had had enough, and he fired off an angry telegram to J.W. Livingston of the Rubber Reserve Company — a firm created by the federal government to coordinate synthetic rubber production:

> Complaints are widespread. Investigation shows actual health menace and fire hazard exist. Advised this is due to faulty construction and failure to take proper precaution as to release of gases, fumes, smudge, and smoke in populous downtown area. Unless we have assurance that immediate corrective steps are to be taken, we will be forced to take local action. We do not like to do anything to delay war production but feel slight consideration being given for health and welfare of people of this area.[12]

Livingston responded the next day. He informed the mayor that the Rubber Reserve Company had immediately authorized Southern California Gas to install new equipment "to completely eliminate the objectionable fumes" by enclosing the plant's outdoor cooling towers and that these changes would be "vigorously prosecuted." Livingston stressed, however, that synthetic rubber production in California was dependent "on the continued operation of this plant," and to be sure the facility remained functioning while the new equipment was installed, he personally visited southern California. After a complete examination of the plant, Livingston concluded that "while irritating to eyes and nostrils, . . . [the fumes] are not injurious to health."[13]

Despite Livingston's assurances, Southern California Gas Company executives estimated that it would take four months to make the necessary changes because special permits had to be secured to obtain rationed construction materials. In the meantime, smoggy days became an almost daily phenomenon. Complaints poured into the mayor's office and the city council, and after several brief plant closures brought on by especially severe smog episodes, the City of Los Angeles went to court in October 1943 asking for a preliminary injunction to halt the operations of the butadiene facility.[14]

The city's efforts to have the butadiene plant closed worried Southern California Gas officials and the federal government. In response, the government sent to Los Angeles Colonel Bradley Dewey, the official in charge of rubber manufacturing across the nation. Dewey appeared before the city council to make a plea to halt the court action, emphasizing

Los Angeles residents dramatizing their concern over smog.

that the facility was vital, and he observed that butadiene was used by rubber-manufacturing plants throughout southern California, including those operated by Dow Chemical, Goodyear Tire and Rubber, Shell Oil, and United States Rubber. If the butadiene plant were shut down, Dewey warned, production of synthetic rubber would cease in southern California, eliminating as many as six million tires per year from the war effort. Dewey was persuasive, and the city council withdrew its legal action after receiving assurances that enclosing the cooling towers would solve the smog problem. Despite the resolution of the suit, the plant remained controversial throughout the war years because smog did not completely disappear as automobile traffic increased.[15]

By the end of World War II, the butadiene plant had played a major role in the war industries of southern California. While it was the only such facility supplying rubber companies in the area and

1946 | PUC approves
Texas-to-California
Biggest Inch pipeline.

1946 | Construction
on Biggest Inch
pipeline begins.

128

**Demolition of Aliso
Street gas plant, 1947.**

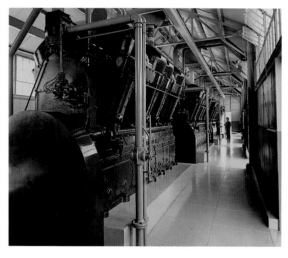

**Interior of compressor plant
at Goleta underground storage
facility, 1955.**

thus was responsible for the production of millions of tires, Los Angeles residents unjustly continued to blame the plant for smog even after the Los Angeles Smoke and Fume Commission pronounced the enclosed cooling towers free of any offensive emissions. Yet regardless of its cleaner operation, the butadiene plant was shut down in the summer of 1947 due to the postwar collapse of the synthetic rubber industry in southern California. The nosedive in the price of rubber, brought on by the liberation of southeast Asian nations at the close of the war and the discontinuation of government financial support, spelled the end of butadiene production. United States Rubber ceased its southern California operations in August 1947, and other firms began to scale back their synthetic rubber production. Even the development of the atomic bomb helped shape the demise of the Los Angeles butadiene plant since the federal government wanted rubber production spread around the country to make it less vulnerable to nuclear attack.[16]

The butadiene plant was one of Pacific Lighting's major contributions to the war effort, but it was not the only one made by the organization and its subsidiaries. The gas companies' primary purpose — the distribution of natural gas — continued to be the chief concern, especially since wartime demands dramatically increased gas consumption. The natural gas business skyrocketed during World War II. In 1941 defense industries boosted gas sales to four times the volume of 1930, and by 1945 consumption had increased by another 150 percent. Much of the demand came from electric companies, which turned to gas and oil-fueled steam-generating plants for new installations because hydroelectric

1947 | Butadiene manufacturing ends and Aliso Street gas plant is closed.

sites had become scarce and because energy could be produced more economically due to technological advances in improved generators. In addition to the needs of electric firms, Los Angeles had become one of the world's major aircraft manufacturing centers by the 1940s, and other industries such as shipbuilding, construction, and manufacturing all added to energy demands.[17]

Such economic expansion prompted Pacific Lighting to face the serious problem of finding adequate storage for gas to meet the extreme swings in the needs of wartime production. One possible solution appeared to be the utilization of a depleted gas field at Goleta, west of Santa Barbara. Pacific Lighting's subsidiaries projected that using the depleted gas field as a giant holder would allow a net deliverability increase of 164 million cubic feet of gas per day. With these figures as evidence, the companies secured permission from the War Production Board — which oversaw the distribution of materials needed by the war effort — to obtain the necessary construction supplies. At a cost of over $4 million, almost a hundred miles of pipeline eventually were built connecting the Goleta field with Pacific Lighting's Los Angeles distribution system; compressors also were added at Goleta for high-pressure injection. The new storage facility was the equivalent of a gas holder stretching across three hundred city blocks and towering four hundred feet tall, and it could sustain pressures of up to two thousand pounds per square inch.[18]

A second large underground storage endeavor launched by Pacific Lighting's subsidiaries during World War II was at Playa del Rey — only three miles from Pacific Lighting's transmission and

Playa del Rey underground storage cooling tower as it appeared in 1956.

Pacific Lighting eventually opened other underground storage facilities in southern California at Aliso Canyon, East Whittier, Honor Rancho, and Montebello (the latter shown above).

1947 | Marshall Plan providing reconstruction aid to Europe is passed by Congress.

1947 | Biggest Inch pipeline completed.

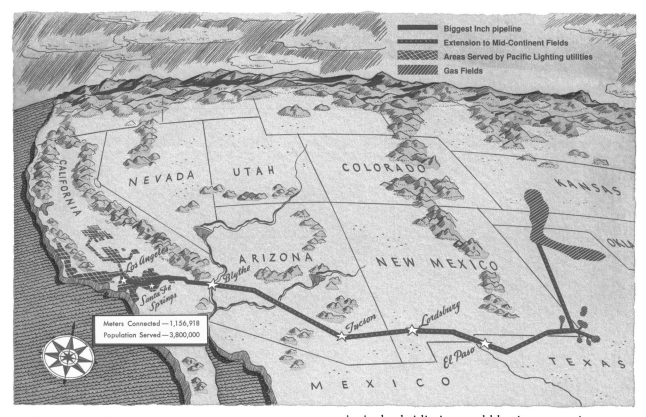

The following labels appear on the map:

Biggest Inch pipeline
Extension to Mid-Continent Fields
Areas Served by Pacific Lighting utilities
Gas Fields

CALIFORNIA
NEVADA
UTAH
COLORADO
KANSAS
ARIZONA
NEW MEXICO
OKLA
TEXAS
MEXICO

Los Angeles
Santa Fe Springs
Blythe
Tucson
Lordsburg
El Paso

Meters Connected — 1,156,918
Population Served — 3,800,000

The Biggest Inch pipeline, constructed in 1946-1947, brought gas supplies from Texas and eastern New Mexico to southern California.

distribution system. To test this field, Southern California Gas conducted experiments, and when these proved successful, the firm acquired the land with the aid of the federal government's wartime condemnation powers. The new storage facility, which was in operation by the end of 1942, provided about a hundred times the volume of the largest man-made gas holders; 120 million cubic feet of gas could be withdrawn daily whenever needed. Because of Playa del Rey's proximity to the Pacific Lighting gas distribution system, its storage facilities were used to meet daily demand fluctuations, while Goleta was used to adjust for seasonal variations.[19]

Although Pacific Lighting and its subsidiaries gave much attention to the butadiene plant and the development of storage at Playa del Rey and Goleta, other issues arose simultaneously that were just as compelling. As early as 1942, projections of gas supply and demand indicated that Pacific Lighting's

principal subsidiaries would begin to experience shortages within a few years if steps were not taken to find new supplies. The opening of the underground storage facilities had temporarily alleviated some problems brought on by peak demands, but the new storage had done nothing to augment total gas available for distribution. The problem stemmed from the fact that about ninety-five percent of all natural gas used in southern California was casinghead gas produced in conjunction with oil pumping. Southern California oil companies, which sold gas to Pacific Lighting's subsidiaries, had started to use large quantities of gas to repressurize oil wells, and this practice had reduced the gas supply available for distribution. With predictions that southern California's population would grow by twenty-five percent within a decade, Pacific Lighting's officials knew they had to find additional gas supplies. Estimates indicated that without more gas, peak requirements would outstrip supply as early as 1948.[20]

Franklin Wade, then president of both Southern California Gas and Southern Counties

1950 | F.M. (Marion) Banks becomes president of Southern California Gas.

1950 | U.S. sends troops to Korea.

Gas, found this situation alarming. Having witnessed first-hand the effects of the 1906-1907 gas famine, Wade was determined not to allow those circumstances to be repeated under his leadership. At his direction, the gas companies dispatched a procurement team to locate new gas sources in 1943. Initially, the team considered tapping the Rio Vista dry gas field in northern California, where Pacific Gas and Electric received a large portion of its supply. This option, however, was rejected because the pipeline to Los Angeles would have been expensive and because the limited volume of gas in that field did not warrant the cost.[21]

Having eliminated the Rio Vista area, the procurement team next began to examine out-of-state possibilities. A quick survey of non-California gas sources within economic reach of Los Angeles narrowed the search to the Hugoton-Panhandle dry gas fields in Kansas, Oklahoma, and Texas, and to the Permian Basin in western Texas and eastern New Mexico. Nearly all of the gas in the Permian Basin was casinghead gas and was being flared by oil companies since there were no local markets for it. After an analysis of the cost-effectiveness of bringing the gas to California, Pacific Lighting secured options to buy nearly 300 million cubic feet of gas per day and then sent engineers into the field to determine the most feasible route to Santa Fe Springs, California, where the gas could be fed into the Pacific Lighting distribution system. As part of the field work, Arthur F. Bridge, then vice-president of Southern Counties Gas Company, used air and ground reconnaissance to lay out a route for a pipeline to carry the gas across parts of New Mexico and Arizona to California.[22]

Arthur F. Bridge, president of Southern Counties Gas Company, 1947-1954.

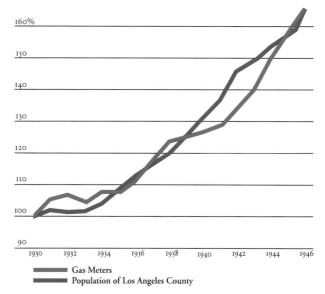

Gas Meters
Population of Los Angeles County

The percentage increase in the number of gas customers (meters) kept pace with the extraordinary growth of Los Angeles County's population during the 1930s and 1940s.

With options to purchase gas and a pipeline route laid out on paper, Bridge presented the plan to Pacific Lighting President Robert Miller, who was then on military leave serving as a lieutenant colonel in the U.S. Army Air Corps at Santa Ana, California. Miller was very enthusiastic when the proposal was outlined to him, but since his father had resumed the role of chief executive officer during his son's duties in the armed forces, the younger Miller deferred to his father's judgment. C.O.G. Miller strongly opposed Pacific Lighting becoming involved in out-of-state activities. He was reluctant to agree to the pipeline scheme for two reasons: potential federal regulation under the Public Utilities Holding Company Act and the large cost and risk of building the pipeline. He was, however, willing to undertake a joint venture with Pacific Gas and Electric, and while that firm showed some initial interest in the idea, it eventually declined to participate. For this reason, the pipeline to Texas was postponed in 1944.[23]

Although the plan to tap western Texas gas supplies was shelved for the time being, the idea remained alive as a possible long-term solution to mounting supply problems. By July 1945 a new proposal emerged whereby Pacific Lighting itself would not run a pipeline directly to the Texas oil and gas fields. Instead, after extensive negotiations, Pacific Lighting, its subsidiaries, and Pacific Gas and Electric contracted with El Paso Natural Gas Company — which was already involved in long-distance gas transmission — to build a pipeline. The line would vary between twenty-six and thirty inches in diameter — the largest such pipeline to date. It would begin at Eunice, New Mexico (where it would tap the

Permian Basin casinghead gas) and connect at Blythe, California, with a pipeline built by Pacific Lighting from Los Angeles. An extension would also be added to tap the Hugoton-Panhandle dry gas reserves. Gas company engineers estimated that the total pipeline, which would stretch over a thousand miles, would bring 175 million cubic feet of gas per day to southern California (with an additional 100 million cubic feet going to Pacific Gas and Electric). On days of extreme demand, the southern California allotment could be nearly doubled by extensive use of compressor stations, and thirteen were planned along the projected route. Pacific Lighting estimated the total cost at about $25 million.[24]

With El Paso Natural Gas planning to build the pipeline to the California state line, Pacific Lighting and its subsidiaries were to construct the remaining 215 miles from the Colorado River to Santa Fe Springs, thus decreasing the risk of federal regulation of Pacific Lighting's operations as a holding company by staying within the state's boundaries. Before the project could even begin, however, El Paso Natural Gas and Pacific Lighting had to secure permission from the Federal Power Commission, which oversaw all interstate pipelines. Moreover, Pacific Lighting also had to obtain approval from the California Public Utilities Commission for the pipeline's intrastate construction. The PUC held hearings on the California portion of the pipeline in December 1945, and with no opposition appearing, the commission gave its approval in August 1946.[25]

In Washington, D.C., the Federal Power Commission held its own hearings in February 1946 and granted approval the following May, concluding

1954 | Guy Wadsworth, Jr., becomes president of Southern Counties Gas Company.

1954 | U.S. Supreme Court rules in *Phillips Petroleum Co. vs. State of Wisconsin*, allowing federal regulation of interstate gas sales.

Chain-driven lorry used in
building the Biggest Inch, 1947.

Contractors inspect the
Biggest Inch, 1947.

that "there is a public need or demand for out-of-state natural gas in southern California, and that the economically feasible pipeline system proposed by the . . . qualified applicants will serve that need adequately and properly for the reasonably foreseeable future." Construction began in November 1946, and the pipeline was finished in October 1947. Gas began flowing to southern California the following month.[26]

The pipeline — dubbed the "Biggest Inch," a name derived from two smaller World War II petroleum pipelines called the "Big Inch" and the "Little Big Inch" — was one of the Southwest's engineering marvels, and it received wide coverage in the press. Public attention was well warranted because of the degree of difficulty faced by the companies' engineers and the sheer magnitude of the undertaking. For example, the pipeline crossed the mountainous Continental Divide as well as hundreds of miles of scorching desert. Technical problems abounded due to the demanding terrain. Construction crews found that the pipe's sixty-foot segments heated to such a degree in the desert sun that protective wrapping was easily damaged. To overcome this problem, workers whitewashed the pipe (which was naturally dark in color) to keep it cooler. Sophisticated engineering skills were employed to arc-weld all joints and then inspect them with gamma ray photography. In addition, reminiscent of the difficulties overcome in laying the Midway pipeline in 1912, some hillside stretches were so steep that trucks carrying supplies to construction sites had to be hauled up the slopes by bulldozers.[27]

Pacific Lighting viewed the effort as worth the labor and cost. The firm's officials boasted that when completed the Biggest Inch would be capable of supplying gas to the equivalent of every home and business in the combined cities of Akron, Des Moines, Indianapolis, and San Antonio. Pacific Lighting predicted that the pipeline at its ultimate capacity would deliver each day energy equal to almost fifty thousand barrels of oil, two hundred carloads of coal, or three times the electrical output of Boulder Dam. Moreover, Pacific Lighting calculated that construction would provide four million man-hours of work, much of it to local communities along the pipeline's route — a vital consideration with thousands of military men returning to civilian life.[28]

The completion of the Biggest Inch in 1947 was extremely fortuitous for the Pacific Lighting gas distribution system. While there had been predictions of a postwar population boom in southern California, no one had accurately foreseen its scope, and the growth rapidly became an explosion of newcomers. From Pacific Lighting's point of view, the population surge necessitated even more expansion of its gas distribution facilities, and the company made plans to double the Biggest Inch's capacity as soon as possible. By January 1949 El Paso Natural Gas had completed a new link to the Texas Panhandle, and the firm increased gas deliveries to

The last obstacles confronted by Biggest Inch construction crews were the rugged Chino Hills. In August 1947 one experienced worker declared this terrain to be the roughest he had ever encountered in his long career.

The Transwestern pipeline supplemented gas supplies carried by the Biggest Inch. This photo shows construction on the Transwestern pipeline in the early 1960s.

1956 | Robert Hornby becomes president of Pacific Lighting when Robert Miller is elevated to chairman of the board.

1958 | First U.S. satellite to go into orbit.

The Southern California Subsidiaries

Pacific Lighting's Relationship with its Subsidiaries.

In September 1958, *Gas News* interviewed Pacific Lighting's chairman of the board, Robert W. Miller, to provide employees of the firm's subsidiaries with more information on the parent holding company and its leadership. Miller explained in the discussion that Pacific Lighting deliberately held no interest in any companies except for Southern Counties Gas, Southern California Gas, and Pacific Lighting Gas Supply. "Our principal function, as we see it," Miller observed, "is to develop and to serve properly the needs of existing and future customers." He added that this goal had created such a huge demand for capital to serve the growing population of southern California that it would likely tax Pacific Lighting's credit for some time to come. This need to secure adequate funding for the subsidiaries' system improvements, Miller pointed out, was among the principal reasons that Pacific Lighting's headquarters remained in San Francisco. By keeping the company where it was born, it could obtain services from San Francisco's financial institutions easily.

Aside from acquiring capital for subsidiary expansion efforts, Miller stated that

there were other reasons why Pacific Lighting did not move to Los Angeles. Among them was his belief that the physical separation of Pacific Lighting from its affiliates allowed "greater independence of decision and action by the officers of both the subsidiaries and the parent company." Miller explained that "we at P.L. want to be informed, like to take part in the larger decisions of policy, but we believe that the way this system can best succeed is to preserve an autonomy in the separate companies."

Keeping Pacific Lighting in San Francisco, however, created a demanding travel schedule for the company's executives. A year after Miller's interview, the firm's president, Robert Hornby, pointed out that as a top Pacific Lighting executive, he was obligated to take an active role in overseeing the firm's Los Angeles subsidiaries. Hornby observed that during the previous twelve months he had made forty-two round-trips to his Los Angeles office — a grueling schedule for pre-jet aircraft days.[29]

300 million cubic feet per day. Even this proved to be insufficient, and over the next ten years Pacific Lighting and El Paso Natural Gas repeatedly added to the interstate pipelines until their combined capacities had grown to nearly two billion cubic feet per day. Within a decade Pacific Lighting had expanded the volume of its out-of-state delivery system eighteen times, including a new line paralleling the Biggest Inch operated by Transwestern Pipeline Company. Eventually, over ninety percent of all gas sold in southern California came from outside the state's borders.[30]

The additional gas supplies provided by the interstate pipelines, coupled with the increased holding capacities from the underground storage facilities, allowed the Pacific Lighting system to keep pace with the escalating energy needs of southern California. By the late 1950s Pacific Lighting's subsidiaries served over two million customers in the fourteen southern California counties. Since each "customer" represented a meter that provided gas to a household, the total number of people using Pacific Lighting gas was substantially higher than the actual meters indicated, probably by a factor of two or three times. The number of people served, therefore, was a relatively high percentage of the nearly nine million southern California residents.[31]

With the rapid development of the postwar years came changes in the management of Pacific Lighting and its subsidiaries. Franklin Wade retired in 1950 from Southern California Gas Company's active management and became chairman of the board. He was succeeded as president by Marion Banks. Guy Wadsworth was elevated to the position of president of Southern Counties Gas in 1954 when

Arthur Bridge retired from that post. At Pacific Lighting, Robert Hornby was named president in 1956 when Robert Miller, the chief executive officer, became chairman of the board, a title that had remained unused since C.O.G. Miller's death in 1952.[32]

The personnel changes had been fomented in part by the great expansion of the Pacific Lighting system in the postwar years, and the new management team had talents to match the changing times. Banks was an engineer with a strong marketing background, skills vital to Southern California Gas Company's prosperity in an era of major growth. Wadsworth, an expert in human resources, used his talent to bring into both Southern California Gas and Southern Counties Gas highly qualified executives and other employees. Hornby, with training in finance and management, provided essential coordination to the overall Pacific Lighting system.

With the prospect of continued expansion of its customer base and ample gas supplies, the Pacific Lighting companies aggressively promoted their product throughout the 1950s. Sales representatives called on architects, builders, homeowners, mechanical engineers, and restaurant operators to encourage gas use. In addition, salesmen offered incentives to real estate developers to install gas mains when new subdivisions were built; the gas companies' employees were awarded prizes for providing "leads" on possible new customers; weekly cooking classes using gas ranges were held in schools and community centers for Girl Scouts, Campfire Girls, and others; and home service representatives demonstrated "ideas to Mrs. Housewife which help her to appreciate that gas as a fuel saves her time, effort and money."[33]

Like gas use itself, gas appliances were promoted in a variety of ways. The Blue Flame dealership program, for example, awarded special status and economic incentives to appliance dealers who agreed to abide by the gas companies' high standards for appliance sales and service. The gas firms then advertised the Blue Flame program and distributed lists of recognized dealers, thus providing extra advertising for those businesses. Pacific Lighting's subsidiaries even marketed appliances themselves for many years, creating minor friction with non-company dealers. The extent of the gas appliance promotion campaign can be judged from the fact that one salesman made a special stop at the headquarters of the beer-making giant, Anheuser-Busch, on his way to a convention in the Midwest merely to persuade the firm's officials to install a gas range in the newly constructed company lounge at its southern California brewery. Regarding the thoroughness of the promotion efforts, a former gas sales director later recalled, "we covered that market completely, and I think [we] did a tremendous job on it."[34]

Pacific Lighting's utilities had so totally saturated the market by the end of the 1950s that ninety percent of all cooking ranges in southern California were gas fueled. Gas stove sales were about six times the national rate in comparison with electric ranges. Equally impressive, water heaters and home heating systems were both over ninety-eight percent gas operated.[35]

The success in marketing gas created a dilemma for Pacific Lighting and its subsidiaries. With such overwhelming percentages of gas appliances in use in southern California and with postwar industry relying on gas for much of its needs, company experts determined that on particularly cold days even the extensive storage facilities at Goleta, Playa del Rey, and elsewhere could not supply enough extra gas to meet peak home-heating requirements — always a priority for gas use. The solution lay in the expansion of the industrial curtailment procedures used so successfully prior to and during World War II. Under an extended version of this program, Pacific Lighting's subsidiaries offered industrial users very low rates in exchange for their willingness to switch to alternative energy sources when core uses peaked on cold winter days. With the establishment of several levels of priorities and a staggered gas price schedule, Pacific Lighting was able to meet virtually any demand placed on its system.[36]

Ironically, the success Pacific Lighting and its subsidiaries had experienced in capturing the southern California market during the 1950s placed the companies in the awkward position of concurrently petitioning the Public Utilities Commission for rate increases. To the consumer, this undoubtedly seemed odd, but to Pacific Lighting and its affiliates, rate hikes were imperative. The cost of operating the distribution system and related equipment had "risen fantastically since 1940," according to one Southern California Gas Company booklet prepared for public distribution. Capital expenditures per new customer, the firm noted, had climbed from one hundred dollars shortly before the war to nearly five hundred dollars a decade later.[37] As Robert Miller pointed out in his 1950 report to Pacific Lighting stockholders, "in the face of these rising costs, there will have to be further upward

rate adjustments to provide an adequate rate of return to the subsidiaries."[38]

While expenses for system improvements had climbed steadily, the price of purchasing gas also had continued to rise as oil companies in Texas began to exploit their gas production more fully and as gas utilities throughout the country began to vie for the Texas gas supplies. For these reasons, the cost of bringing gas into southern California had nearly doubled since the prewar years. The typical gas bill for the consumer, however, had climbed only fifteen percent during the same period.[39]

Under such circumstances, Pacific Lighting's subsidiaries had little choice but to seek a series of rate hikes throughout the 1950s. Needless to say, the price increases were highly unpopular with the general public, and the gas companies developed an extensive public relations campaign to combat the negative image associated with the rate hikes. To offset criticism, the firms were generous in their support of community programs and charities such as the Community Chest, the American Cancer Society, the Arthritis and Rheumatism Foundation, the Crippled Children Society, the Los Angeles Heart Association, the Red Cross, and the YMCA, among others.[40] Officials at Pacific Lighting's gas subsidiaries were so concerned about public perceptions of the rate-increase applications, that management published brochures for all employees so they could explain the need for higher prices to the general public. And, to demonstrate that customer satisfaction was a top priority, the gas companies strengthened their home services, frequently repairing gas appliances free of charge, although the cost of this improved service was built into the new gas rates.[41]

1960 | Southern California Edison and Tennessee Gas Transmission propose "Enchilada Inch" gas pipeline from Texas through Mexico to California.

1961 | First U.S. manned space flight.

| The PEMEX and Gulf Pacific Plans.

Part of the twenty-eight hundred pounds of paperwork generated by the Gulf Pacific FPC hearings, 1964.

Although Pacific Lighting had been successful in creating the largest natural gas distribution system in the world, the firm was not without competition. In the late 1950s and early 1960s other organizations proposed running long-distance pipelines to southern California to serve major industrial gas users. In 1960, for example, Southern California Edison contracted with Tennessee Gas Transmission Company and Petroleos Mexicanos (PEMEX) — Mexico's national oil and gas company — to construct a pipeline from Texas through northern Mexico to transport gas to southern California. This gas would then be sold directly to the electric company to fuel its steam generating plants. Edison claimed such a new pipeline would allow it to lower its rates. In addition, the electric company argued that the new pipeline would lessen smog in the Los Angeles Basin because the electric firm would not have to resort to fuel oil to power its generators when Pacific Lighting's system interrupted the electric utility's service to provide gas to core customers during winter months.

Marion Banks, president of Southern California Gas, decried Edison's plan. Banks was concerned that the loss of such a large interruptible gas user as the electric company would require Pacific Lighting's utilities to spend huge sums for additional facilities to meet the peak-day gas needs of non-interruptible consumers. For this reason, the gas company called the PEMEX pipeline "discriminatory, costly, unwise, unnecessary, [and] uneconomic."

In 1961 and 1962 the Federal Power Commission held hearings on the proposed project, dubbed the "Enchilada Inch." Pacific Lighting and its subsidiaries argued that the pipeline was an expensive duplication of facilities, and their reasoning was persuasive. The FPC staff announced its opposition in June 1962, stating that the project would result in "inferior use, high [gas] prices, [and] dubious smog help." With federal opposition clear, Southern California Edison and Tennessee Gas Transmission withdrew their applications in November 1962 and decided to revise their proposal.

Shortly thereafter, Gulf Pacific Pipeline Company — owned by Tennessee Gas Transmission, Humble Oil,

and others — outlined a plan to build a pipeline (all within the United States) to bring out-of-state gas supplies into southern California. Pacific Lighting's subsidiaries, El Paso Natural Gas Company, and Transwestern Pipeline Company vigorously opposed the Gulf Pacific proposal, contending that if Gulf Pacific's plan were authorized by the FPC, Pacific Lighting's customers would be faced with rate increases totaling well in excess of $200 million over a twenty-year period due to the firm's loss of large interruptible service contracts.

To counter the Gulf Pacific plan at the FPC hearings, Banks created a task force drawing on management and supporting personnel from Southern California Gas and Southern Counties Gas. The task force developed an alternative proposal, the Tailored Supply Plan, to meet the natural gas requirements of southern California — including the very large needs of the steam electric plants — without building additional pipelines.

Joseph Rensch, vice-president and director of Pacific Lighting Gas Supply and later president of Pacific Lighting Corporation, was the first witness at the FPC hearings in 1964. He described the Tailored Supply Plan as a way

of matching gas supplies to the requirements of all users by expanding the El Paso Natural Gas and Transwestern pipelines. "It's a cutting and fitting process," Rensch observed, and he argued that "the Gulf Pacific project would not only deprive southern California of low-cost tailored supplies available . . . from economic expansion of the Transwestern and El Paso systems but also would virtually remove the load-balancing value of interruptible steam plant sales." Later witnesses also testified that Pacific Lighting could provide ample gas at "very favorable prices" to Southern California Edison and other industrial users.

Hearings before the FPC extended over three years and resulted in more than twenty-five thousand pages of transcripts. In mid-1966 the FPC officially sanctioned Pacific Lighting's Tailored Supply Plan, stating that pollution from fuel oil itself was not a serious problem in Los Angeles at the time and that Pacific Lighting's Tailored Supply Plan would be substantially less expensive to implement than the Gulf Pacific proposal.[42]

Celebrities were frequently hired to advertise the advantages of gas appliances in the 1950s.

Many different types of gas appliances were promoted, as shown in this 1961 photo of a hair-dryer attachment for a gas clothes dryer.

Meanwhile to reassure investors, Pacific Lighting's new president, Robert Hornby, offered his firm's views of the price increases to stock analysts in 1959:

> Gas, I am sure you know, is a victim rather than a culprit in this era of inflation. Although the subsidiaries periodically find it necessary to apply for upward adjustments in rates, the price of gas to the customer since 1939 has gone up far less than other daily necessities. The food we eat costs 163% more than it did in 1939. But if, like most people in Los Angeles, you cook your food with gas, it costs you only 41% more to do so today. Meanwhile, in the Los Angeles area, over the same period, all consumer commodities — the necessities of life — have gone up 107%.[43]

Such assurances were necessary not just for general public relations, but more specifically because Pacific Lighting increasingly was turning to national financial markets to underwrite the huge cost of adding miles of new transmission lines, plants, storage facilities, and other capital improvements.[44]

Finally, after a decade of rate increases, Pacific Lighting's affiliates were able to reduce prices in the early part of the 1960s. A significant factor in the end to the rate hikes was the elimination of indefinite pricing provisions, which had required pipeline suppliers of Pacific Lighting and its affiliates to match the highest price paid to any producer in an area. Thus, an increase in price paid to one producer triggered similar increases to others, creating an upward price spiral. The Federal Power Commission mandated the end to these provisions in the early 1960s, allowing gas prices to stabilize.[45]

Another important event that eventually contributed to gas price stabilization in the 1960s was

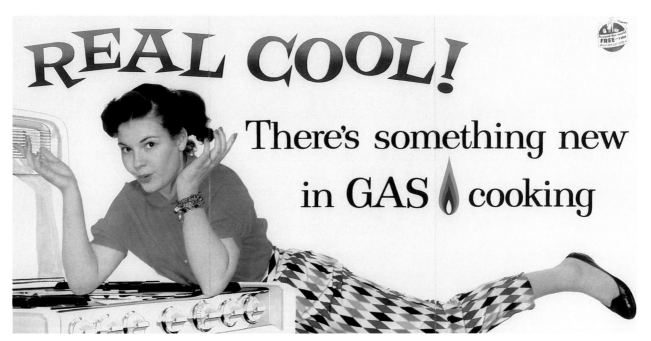

REAL COOL!

There's something new in GAS 🔥 cooking

the U.S. Supreme Court's precedent-setting 1954 ruling in *Phillips Petroleum Company vs. State of Wisconsin, et al.* In its decision, the court had held that the 1937 Natural Gas Act allowed federal officials to regulate prices of gas sold for interstate commerce and ultimate resale. Although the court had handed down this ruling in 1954, over the subsequent years complex pricing formulas had been established, helping to contribute to lower gas prices to customers by the early 1960s.[46]

The changes in gas production pricing, lower federal taxes, and Pacific Lighting's greater use of investment tax credits brought benefits to consumers. Thus, in the early 1960s when the Federal Power Commission approved deliveries of cheaper gas by El Paso Natural Gas Company, Pacific Lighting and its subsidiaries worked with the Public Utilities Commission to insure that these savings were passed

As part of the gas promotional efforts of the 1950s, advertising was aimed at young women.

on to customers in southern California. The company viewed this program as an integral part of its continuing effort to maintain good public relations. In 1965 consumers saw their sixth straight rate reduction, and gas utility prices in southern California dropped to among the lowest in the nation. Yet while Pacific Lighting had become the largest gas distributor in the world, the firm's phenomenal success in serving southern California energy markets created conditions which led to major changes in Pacific Lighting's overall business strategies beginning in the late 1960s.[47]

1963 | President John F. Kennedy is assassinated.

1964 | War on Poverty and Civil Rights Act are passed by Congress.

Whatever the Future Holds

The Search for New Gas Supplies and the Diversification Program.

IN THE TWO DECADES LEADING UP TO Pacific Lighting's one-hundredth anniversary in 1986 and in the years shortly thereafter, the company faced unprecedented challenges. Stimulated in part by the decline in surplus gas supplies in the 1960s and the severe oil and gas shortages of the 1970s, the firm embarked on a campaign to locate new sources of gas in order to continue providing southern California's consumers with the dependable service they had come to expect. Under the leadership of Paul Miller — who had become president of Pacific Lighting in 1968 and chairman of the board in 1972 — the company expanded its search for natural gas throughout North America, looking to places like the Rocky Mountains, the Canadian Arctic, and Alaska for additional reserves. Pacific Lighting also helped develop new technologies and examined such alternative methods of gas supply as liquefied natural gas brought from overseas and coal gasification. The latter process was planned to utilize vast coal deposits in the western part of the United States to manufacture gas comparable in quality to natural gas.

While searching for new gas supplies, the firm simultaneously broadened its corporate business strategy by diversifying into a few but highly different enterprises. Recognizing that the rate of growth

First Interstate World Center (middle), the tallest skyscraper west of Chicago, nearing completion in 1989. Pacific Enterprises planned to occupy part of the building as the firm's headquarters in 1990.

1965 | 1989

THROUGHOUT THE 1960s, 1970s, AND 1980s, PACIFIC LIGHTING EXPANDED ITS SEARCH FOR NEW GAS SOURCES, EXAMINED ALTERNATIVE GAS PRODUCTION TECHNIQUES, AND DIVERSIFIED ITS HOLDINGS.

1965 | Pacific Lighting Gas Supply becomes Pacific Lighting Service and Supply.

1967 | Robert W. Miller retires as Pacific Lighting's chairman of the board.

The development of adequate underground storage facilities such as at Aliso Canyon (below) made above-ground gas holders obsolete. The holders shown above near Los Angeles's city hall were torn down in the 1970s, saving Pacific Lighting's subsidiaries maintenance costs and improving views of the skyline.

in southern California had started to slow and that this would affect the future of the gas industry there, Pacific Lighting began establishing a revenue base beyond its traditional utility subsidiaries. Initially, new affiliates were gas related, such as early forays into gas-fueled energy plants to provide air conditioning for various commercial developments. Subsequently, however, Pacific Lighting branched into other economic endeavors — including real estate, agriculture, alternative energy projects, oil and gas exploration, and retailing — some of which the company sold when conditions warranted. By the late 1980s the combination of the diversification program and an improved gas supply situation placed the firm on solid ground to move forward during its second century of operation.

The changes in corporate policy were preceded by shifts in working arrangements between Pacific Lighting and its subsidiaries, thus providing the parent firm with greater control over its assets. Among other alterations, coordination between Southern California Gas and Southern Counties Gas was streamlined in 1965 by converting Pacific

1967 | Pacific Lighting moves its headquarters to Los Angeles.

Lighting Gas Supply Company into Pacific Lighting
Service and Supply and changing its relationship
with the other gas utilities. The new firm continued
to handle functions performed by the former supply
company, including contracting for California gas,
delivering part of the out-of-state gas supplies, and
operating underground storage projects. In addition,
Pacific Lighting Service and Supply also oversaw the
search for new gas sources and dealt with regulatory
matters, public relations efforts, and legal issues
for the entire Pacific Lighting system. W. Morton
(Mort) Jacobs, president of the old supply company,
headed the new organization.[1]

**Paul A. Miller — son of Robert
W. Miller and grandson of
C.O.G. Miller — became president of Pacific Lighting in
1968 and chairman of the
board in 1972.**

  Other shifts in how Pacific Lighting managed
its subsidiaries followed soon after the creation of
Pacific Lighting Service and Supply. In 1967 the par-
ent firm moved its corporate headquarters from San
Francisco to Los Angeles to expedite efficiency and
to establish a closer connection with the growing
Los Angeles business community. To reduce duplica-
tion, Pacific Lighting also sought approval from the
Public Utilities Commission to merge Southern
Counties Gas and Southern California Gas. While

1967 | One-hundredth
anniversary of gas
service in the Los
Angeles area.

1968 | Martin Luther
King, Jr., is
assassinated.

Southern California Gas Company's
Blue Flame logo on top of the firm's
South Flower Street headquarters
in Los Angeles in the 1970s. Pacific
Lighting's first Los Angeles offices
were also in this complex of buildings until the late 1980s.

this consolidation had been denied in 1940 due to that era's antipathy toward large corporations, in 1970 the PUC approved the request, and the twin gas subsidiaries were united as Southern California Gas Company. Under the leadership of Mort Jacobs — who had left his post at Pacific Lighting Service and Supply to become president of Southern California Gas in 1967 — and Southern California Gas Executive Vice-President Harvey A. Proctor, the merger was accomplished with a minimum of employee displacement.[2]

The search for gas supplies and the changes in organizational structure were anticipated to a large degree the previous decade. During the 1950s it had become increasingly apparent that the availability of gas in California was declining and that sooner or later Pacific Lighting's subsidiaries would have to augment their out-of-state gas purchases substantially.[3] Pacific Lighting had delayed the inevitability of seeking additional non-California gas supplies by offering improved contractual terms to California gas producers, by increasing gas deliveries from existing southwest suppliers, and by adding new underground storage facilities. None-theless, by the early 1960s the insatiable energy needs of southern California had overcome all of these efforts, and Pacific Lighting began to look for additional non-California sources.[4]

One of the earliest out-of-state proposals was the so-called Rock Springs project, which contemplated the construction of a pipeline from Wyoming to southern California. Pacific Lighting was interested in this source of gas because of its ability to deliver initially 200 million cubic feet per day (and up to 700 million cubic feet with expansions),

much of which would come through Rock Springs by an additional pipeline from the Permian Basin oil and gas fields in Texas and eastern New Mexico. Applications were filed with the Federal Power Commission in August 1958, and the following year Pacific Lighting President Robert Hornby speculated that if the FPC held hearings by January 1960, gas would be flowing through the Rock Springs pipeline as early as 1961. Despite Hornby's optimistic prediction, the FPC proceedings dragged on until 1962, and eventually opponents of the Rock Springs project — largely those who supported the PEMEX "Enchilada Inch" plan to pipe gas supplies through Mexico to southern California electric utilities — were successful in preventing government approval.[5]

The Rock Springs project was to be supplemented by a venture to bring natural gas into the United States from Alberta, Canada. While the expense in extending pipelines to Canada tended to diminish savings from the relatively low cost of that country's gas, fields around Alberta offered enormous quantities of new supplies that could be piped to southern California. To take advantage of this opportunity, Pacific Lighting contracted with El Paso Natural Gas to tap western Canada's gas fields. In January 1960 a Federal Power Commission examiner approved importing nearly 600 million cubic feet of natural gas per day from Alberta, but due to Pacific Lighting's inability to obtain government sanction for the Rock Springs undertaking, the Canadian supplement also was abandoned.[6]

The search for additional gas supplies in Canada and elsewhere continued into the 1970s, receiving extra impetus from the energy crises of that decade. While oil shortages appeared due to a

1968 | Paul A. Miller
becomes president of
Pacific Lighting.

1969 | First man sets
foot on the moon.

Robert A. Hornby

Gas Industry Mover and Shaker.

Known as a formidable force in the gas industry from the time he went to work for Southern California Gas until his retirement, Robert A. Hornby was one of the more colorful personalities in the business. Hornby was born in Kansas in 1900, and early in his life his family brought him first to Los Angeles and then to Berkeley where he studied engineering at the University of California. He worked briefly for Southern California Edison and the California Railroad Commission before joining Southern California Gas Company in 1925.

When Southern California Gas became a subsidiary of Pacific Lighting in 1929, it did not take long for Hornby to become recognized for his talents. According to company folklore, Hornby uncovered an embezzlement scheme in the gas company's purchasing department, and as a result, he was quickly promoted to controller in 1930. Later that year, Pacific Lighting Vice-President Robert Miller heard of Hornby's abilities and aggressive style and invited him to San Francisco to become Pacific Lighting's executive engineer. Hornby subsequently advanced to vice-president, executive vice-president, and finally to president in 1956.

As president, he played a central role in the addition of the Transwestern pipeline as a new Pacific Lighting out-of-state gas supplier, and he was instrumental in resisting the Gulf Pacific proposal. Hornby also helped to relocate Pacific Lighting's headquarters from San Francisco to Los Angeles in 1967. Aside from his duties at Pacific Lighting, Hornby also was very active in other firms and in his community.

Upon Robert Miller's retirement in 1967, Hornby became chief executive officer of Pacific Lighting for one year before he too retired. Long after leaving the firm in 1968, Hornby maintained an office at Southern California Gas from which he dispensed wisdom to those who followed him into the executive ranks. He continued to counsel his successors until he died in 1984 at the age of eighty-four. Typical of his wit and style, a few years before his death he wrote that "advancing years have not slowed down my pace, nor, evidently, have they caused senility or a diminished interest in the beauty that constitutes womanhood."[7]

Robert Hornby in the late 1950s.

decline in U.S. production and the actions of various oil-producing nations in curtailing supplies, gas shortages also developed, in part because of government pricing regulations. There had been warnings about the impending energy crises in the years before they occurred. The gas industry had been alerted to the possibility of shortages as early as 1968 by Mort Jacobs, who, as chairman of the American Gas Association, had predicted that supply problems were just over the horizon. He had offered a solution, however. Recognizing that federal price controls would ultimately lead to natural gas shortages, Jacobs had urged the government to reconsider its wellhead price regulatory policies.[8]

Jacobs's advice notwithstanding, by the 1970s natural gas shortages had become a reality for Pacific Lighting and other major distributors. Underscoring the problem, Transwestern Pipeline and El Paso Natural Gas each informed Pacific Lighting that they did not have enough reserves to provide additional gas supplies, and in 1972 these interstate pipeline firms even began to cut back deliveries through their systems. This, in turn, forced Pacific Lighting's subsidiaries to curtail much of their gas service to steam-run electric generating plants — such as those operated by Southern California Edison — in order to supply higher priority customers.[9]

As gas shortages became increasingly serious, Pacific Lighting and its subsidiaries quickly created teams to develop alternative gas supply projects. Investigating a multitude of potential new gas sources, these teams often competed among themselves as well as with other utilities. The California Public Utilities Commission supported Pacific Lighting's efforts and approved a new gas price schedule —

called the Gas Exploration and Development Adjustment (GEDA) — allowing Southern California Gas to offset approximately $40 million per year to finance possible gas supply projects.[10]

As part of the effort to find new gas supplies, in 1970 Pacific Lighting created a subsidiary, Pacific Lighting Gas Development Company, and the new firm contracted with Gulf Oil Canada, Ltd., to purchase large quantities of gas from undeveloped fields in Canada's Northwest Territories. A major long-distance pipeline under study from Canada and northern Alaska would have delivered this gas to American markets only in the Midwest and East, but Pacific Lighting Gas Development's agreement with Gulf Oil Canada — as well as a later accord to purchase gas reserves on Alaska's North Slope — helped, as a top Pacific Lighting executive later recalled, "to justify the company position that the proposed natural gas pipeline . . . [also] must provide for movement of natural gas to the West Coast."[11]

The northwestern part of Canada was not the only area of that country to be considered for gas supplies. The year after the Gulf Oil contract was signed, Pacific Lighting Gas Development

As Pacific Lighting began its search for new gas supplies, a 1971 earthquake complicated corporate plans by causing destruction in southern California (above) and making major repairs necessary (below).

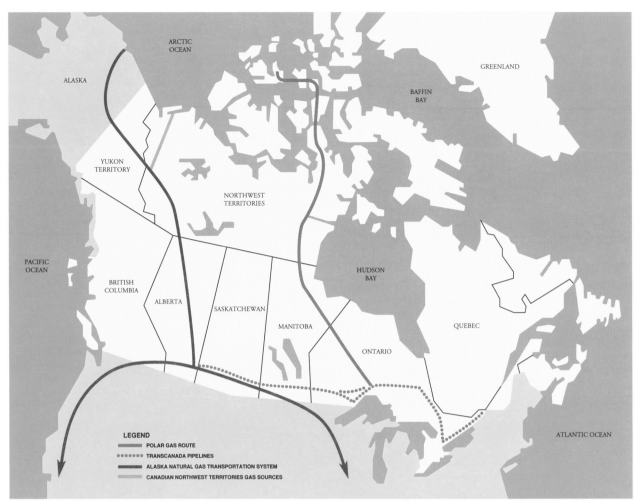

LEGEND

———— POLAR GAS ROUTE
●●●●●● TRANSCANADA PIPELINES
———— ALASKA NATURAL GAS TRANSPORTATION SYSTEM
———— CANADIAN NORTHWEST TERRITORIES GAS SOURCES

During the early 1970s, a variety of pipeline projects were contemplated to bring gas supplies from Alaska's North Slope, the Canadian Northwest Territories, and Canadian Arctic islands to markets in southern Canada and the United States.

joined forces with other firms in the Polar Gas Project — an immensely complicated scheme to transport natural gas from Canadian Arctic islands north of Hudson Bay. Building a pipeline from this distant source to southern markets meant facing a number of highly technical challenges, and extensive planning went into the venture. Nonetheless, the lessening of the gas crisis made the effort unnecessary.[12]

While the Canadian islands project was abandoned, other less complicated strategies to draw upon northern gas resources remained alive,

particularly in relation to Alaska. As early as 1969, Pacific Lighting and a consortium of other companies had begun studies of possible pipelines to tap newly discovered gas reserves in Alaska, and in 1976 Congress passed the Alaska Natural Gas Transportation Act, which established a procedure to select between competing pipeline proposals. The successful plan, called the Alaska Natural Gas Transportation System, originally contemplated the construction of a pipeline from Prudhoe Bay on the Arctic Ocean south across Alaska and through Alberta — where more gas fields would be tapped — to a point near Chicago. There the gas supplies would be distributed to various pipeline companies for use in the Midwest and East.[13]

While Pacific Lighting was quite interested in the undertaking, the direct line only to Chicago was clearly not in the firm's interests, and after

1970 | Southern California Gas and Southern Counties Gas companies are merged.

extensive negotiations, the project's other sponsors agreed to include a western as well as an eastern leg of the project. The western branch was to bring gas from a juncture with the main pipeline in Alberta south through Washington and Oregon for transportation through existing pipelines to southern California. Although the full Alaskan pipeline was not completed as late as 1989, the western branch from Alberta as far south as Oregon was built, and the eastern leg to the American Midwest also was constructed, both being used to transport surplus gas from Alberta's gas fields. The western leg fed Canadian gas to the Northwest Pipeline network, which, in turn, linked with the El Paso Natural Gas system, thus allowing 240 million cubic feet of gas per day to reach southern California from the Alberta fields. Although only partially completed, the Alaska Natural Gas Transportation System was one of the more significant activities in which Pacific Lighting was involved to tap additional out-of-state gas sources.[14]

At the same time that Pacific Lighting started to explore the possibility of importing new gas supplies by long-distance pipeline from Canada and Alaska, the firm also examined the feasibility of bringing gas from even more distant locations. With gas supplies abundant in a variety of overseas locations, as early as the 1950s Pacific Lighting considered the possibility of drawing upon some of these sources. Technical advances in the field of cryogenics made it possible to chill natural gas to extremely low temperatures, which turned the gas into a liquid. In this form the gas occupied considerably less space, allowing easier shipping and storage of large quantities. Since building long-distance pipelines across

Special equipment — such as this trencher used to cut through ice — had to be invented for the Polar Gas Project in the early 1970s.

Raymond W. Todd, vice-president of Southern California Gas Company (seated, right) and Ibnu Sutowa (seated, middle), of Pertamina — Indonesia's national oil and gas company — sign the 1973 contract to bring Indonesian LNG to California.

1970 | Pacific Lighting forms Pacific Lighting Gas Development Company.

1970 | Pacific Lighting acquires W.D. Fowler and Sons Corporation, a farming enterprise.

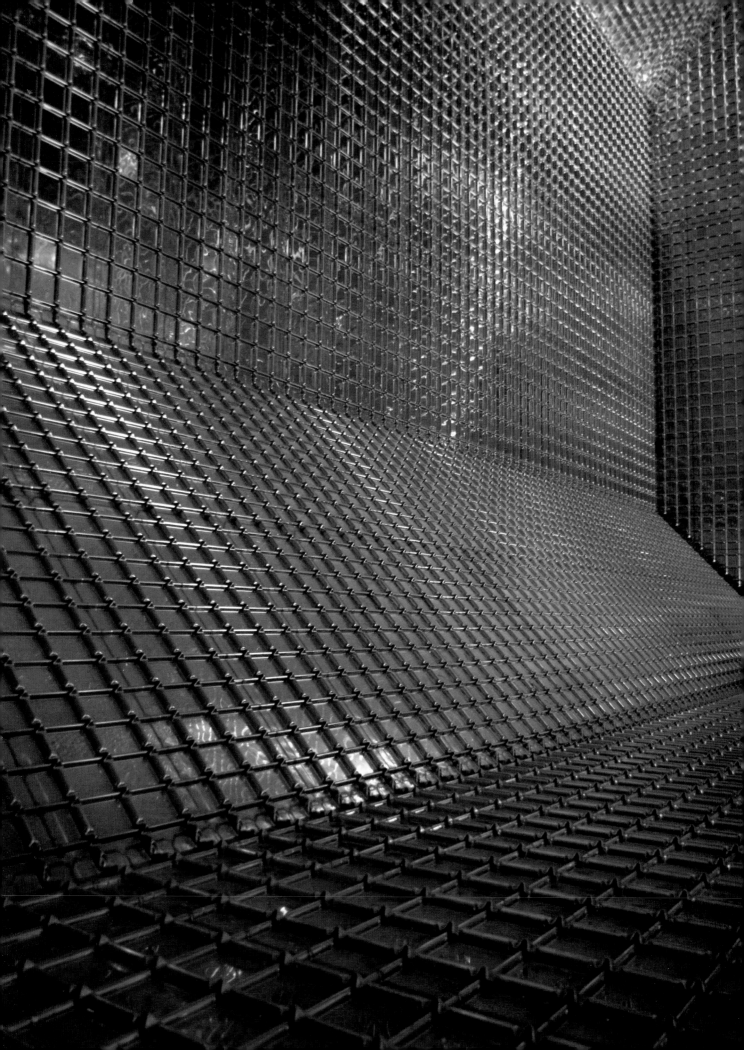

When chilled to -260 degrees Fahrenheit, natural gas liquefies and occupies one six-hundredth the space of its gaseous form. This 1976 photo shows the inside of the LNG tanks on the ship Ben Franklin.

deep-water ocean bottoms was not feasible, Pacific Lighting organizations and other utility firms proposed transporting liquefied natural gas — known in the industry as LNG — in oceangoing tankers and then reconstituting it into gaseous form where supplies were needed. As a coastal state, California was in an ideal position to import LNG from southern Alaska, Australia, Indonesia, Malaysia, and both Central and South America, and the amount of gas available from these locations was substantial. At the time LNG was first proposed, the overseas sources offered a supply of the fuel capable of lasting into the twenty-first century.[15]

Although there had been early LNG experiments in the 1950s and 1960s, the major stimulus to LNG research came from the oil and gas shortages of the 1970s. The energy crisis led Pacific Lighting and northern California's Pacific Gas and Electric to create joint subsidiaries such as Pacific Alaska LNG Company and Pacific Indonesia LNG Company to develop a viable liquefied natural gas program. These organizations signed contracts to purchase Alaskan and Indonesian gas and then sought permission from the Federal Power Commission to build LNG terminals along the southern California coast.[16]

LNG seemed like an idea particularly appropriate to help solve the energy shortages of the 1970s, and the California legislature passed a bill authorizing the Public Utilities Commission to issue a permit for a pioneer LNG plant within the state. With government approval in hand, Pacific Lighting and Pacific Gas and Electric initially considered three sites for LNG facilities, one at the Los Angeles harbor, the second near Oxnard, and the third at Little Cojo Bay, just east of Point Conception and

Joseph R. Rensch, president of Pacific Lighting, 1972-1986.

After Los Angeles harbor and Oxnard were eliminated as possible sites for LNG plants, Pacific Lighting received California's approval to build a facility at Little Cojo Bay near Point Conception. This artist's rendering shows the proposed plant.

1971 | Twenty-sixth amendment to the Constitution ratified lowering the voting age to eighteen.

1971 | Staff of SEC questions Pacific Lighting's exemption from 1935 Public Utilities Holding Company Act.

154

Preliminary excavation to build the LNG terminal at Little Cojo Bay drew the protests of Chumash Indians, who believed the area to be sacred.

about forty miles west of Santa Barbara. The Los Angeles harbor and Oxnard locations were soon eliminated due to safety concerns and their proximities to large population centers.[17]

The remaining site at Little Cojo Bay appeared to be ideal. Remote from urban areas, it became the focus of Pacific Lighting's efforts to construct an LNG terminal. Unfortunately for the company, however, the area was considered sacred by California's Chumash Indians, and beginning in May 1978, tribal members and their supporters occupied the location on several occasions in efforts to halt construction. The Chumash were determined to stop the project. One spiritual leader stated flatly that his tribe was not going to allow the utility companies to build at Little Cojo Bay, and he added defiantly that if necessary he would put his "life on the

line." Pacific Lighting executives charged that the protest was actually motivated and funded by non-Indian opponents to the LNG project who feared the facility would undermine property values. The confrontation remained a standoff for months. Eventually, in early 1979 Western LNG Terminal Associates — the firm building the facility — obtained a court order ending the disruptions, and preliminary construction work went forward.[18]

The Chumash Indians and their supporters were not the only opponents of the LNG terminal at Little Cojo Bay. In the late 1970s, the site also drew objections from environmentalists, who contended that a breakwater would have to be built to protect the LNG facility and that this would prevent replenishment of sand on nearby beaches. To make matters worse, critics pointed to an earthquake fault running close to the site and argued that wind, wave, and fog conditions raised other safety considerations. Eventually, adversaries suggested that perhaps the best solution would be for Western LNG to build its terminal offshore. Even this proposal did not quell objections because by the late 1970s — with federal pricing policies starting to change and with the oil and gas crisis abating — some southern Californians began to question whether the LNG plant was necessary at all.[19]

Meanwhile, executives such as Joseph R. Rensch, who had become Pacific Lighting's president in 1972 when Paul Miller was named chairman of the board, and Harvey Proctor, by this time chairman of Southern California Gas, aggressively defended the LNG plans in the media and in regulatory proceedings. In a 1977 interview with newsman Mike Wallace on the television program "60

1972 | Pacific Lighting forms Pacific Lighting Coal Gasification Company.

1972 | Paul A. Miller becomes Pacific Lighting's chairman of the board.

The Great Plains Coal Gasification Plant near Beulah, North Dakota. In 1982 Pacific Lighting bought a ten percent interest in this project for $60 million, which the company held until 1985.

Minutes," Rensch — a respected leader in the natural gas industry — argued that if new supplies were not found, southern California's economy would suffer severely due to the region's heavy reliance on natural gas for its energy needs. "The two LNG projects [gas from Alaska and Indonesia] are the only ones we can get in here in time to avert the chaos I've been talking about," Rensch stated. Affirming that LNG was entirely safe, he added:

> Right from the beginning I personally had to be convinced that our terminal was safe or it was not going to be built. I would never allow it to be built otherwise. I've got to sleep nights.[20]

The Public Utilities Commission supported Rensch's opinion. After completing studies that the agency deemed "the most detailed scientific investigation in its history," the PUC declared in 1979:

> We are convinced that the seismic criteria and safety recommendations we have required Western Terminal to adopt would result in the construction of a terminal that is consistent with public health, safety, and welfare. Thus, we confirm our previous findings that Little Cojo Bay is California's LNG terminal site.[21]

While the location of the LNG facility was a major concern at the time, the issue eventually became moot in the early 1980s due to the easing of natural gas shortages. With increasing supplies of new gas accessible by pipelines, Pacific Lighting decided in 1983 that it was best to shelve the LNG venture until needed in the future. Opponents such as the Sierra Club cheered the decision, calling the project's demise a "major victory for environmentalists, . . . a stinging defeat for the California legislature, . . . an embarrassment to the state's

Artist's conception of Pacific Lighting's proposed New Mexico coal gasification plant, around 1975.

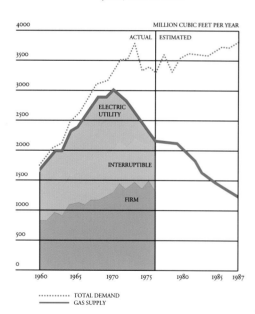

This chart shows the shortage of gas forecast in 1976, and it illustrates why Pacific Lighting saw a need for alternative gas supply projects.

public utilities, . . . [and] welcome news for California ratepayers."[22] The Public Utilities Commission, however, was more sympathetic to Pacific Lighting's efforts to assure an adequate gas supply for southern California, and the agency allowed the firm to recover part of the LNG project's costs.[23]

While the LNG episode was going forward, Pacific Lighting was also engaged in plans to develop coal gasification as an additional means of augmenting supplies. Like the early LNG experiments, studies of this new gas source had taken place in the 1950s, financed in part by one of Pacific Lighting's subsidiaries. The process for making gas from coal had advanced considerably since the first days of the gas industry in southern California, and the modern product — which was nearly all methane — did not contain carbon monoxide, thus rendering it nontoxic. Vast deposits of coal existed in Colorado, New Mexico, Utah, and Wyoming, and although initial cost projections indicated that making gas from these sources would be more expensive than natural gas, Pacific Lighting's officials believed that more technological improvements would bring prices down.[24]

To further the investigation into coal gasification, in 1971 Pacific Lighting joined with two other major energy companies, Texas Eastern Transmission Corporation and Utah International, Incorporated, to examine the feasibility of constructing a coal gasification plant near existing gas supply lines in northwestern New Mexico. About a year later Pacific Lighting created a new subsidiary, Pacific Lighting Coal Gasification Company, to participate in implementing the project, and within a few weeks, the new firm filed an application with the

1973 | Arab oil embargo.

Federal Power Commission to construct a $250 million coal gasification plant. Joseph Rensch predicted that the facility could be in operation by late 1975.[25]

Aware of the possibility of protests by environmentalists that the coal gasification program would be detrimental to the local ecology, Pacific Lighting and its partners went to great lengths to counter any negative impact on the desert Southwest. In addition to specifying the expenditure of $40 million on environmental equipment, the companies assured concerned parties that "current plans meet all state and federal standards for air and water pollution, noise abatement, and strip mining reclamation." To minimize air pollution, filters and wash towers would be used, and through such means emissions would be kept extremely low. Moreover, once coal was extracted from the earth, the partners planned to restore the surface and seed it with grasses.[26]

Pacific Lighting and its associates also tried to satisfy Native American concerns since the plan called for the gasification plant to be on land leased from the Navajo Indians. The firms held extensive talks with tribal leaders to secure the right to build the facility on the Navajo reservation, and the companies pledged that the majority of construction workers hired would be Navajos — a significant consideration in light of the reservation's high unemployment rate. Nonetheless, in February 1978 the Navajos rejected locating the plant on their reservation.[27] Undaunted, Pacific Lighting's officials decided to explore other coal gasification projects, but like the LNG efforts and the plans to tap Arctic gas supplies, the coal gasification efforts were eventually tabled due to a changed energy picture.

In 1980 Southern California Gas Company received President Jimmy Carter's White House Conservation Award for the firm's active involvement in energy conservation. Shown here is Los Angeles Mayor Tom Bradley (left) presenting the award to gas company President Robert M. McIntyre.

As part of its conservation efforts in the 1970s, Southern California Gas Company created this mobile conservation center to demonstrate effective energy management techniques.

1974 | President Richard M. Nixon resigns. Gerald R. Ford becomes president of the United States.

1975 | Pacific Lighting Exploration Company purchases interest in oil and gas properties in Dutch North Sea.

During the gas shortages of the 1970s, Pacific Lighting and its subsidiaries launched a major advertising campaign to conserve energy.

Not only did Pacific Lighting and its subsidiaries devote a considerable amount of time and effort in the 1970s to searching for alternative gas sources and developing new technologies, but the firms also took active roles in keeping the public informed about the long-term outlook for gas supplies. Believing that federal officials were convinced government policy ought to encourage electric and nuclear power due to apparently diminishing gas supplies, Pacific Lighting and its subsidiaries reassured the public that the firms were making strenuous efforts to obtain additional gas supplies. These new sources, the companies advertised, would solve the shortages when combined with appropriate conservation techniques. Reinforcing the advertising program, Southern California Gas vigorously promoted gas-efficient appliances and provided incentives to consumers to install solar energy systems and insulation. As Robert M. McIntyre — chairman of Southern California Gas from 1986 to 1988 — recalled, "the marketing effort changed completely, and it was really a situation where we were, in effect, encouraging conservation in terms of more efficient use of gas rather than the past traditional benefit of trying to get people to use more and more gas."[28]

Although conservation and new gas supplies helped to eliminate some of the gas shortages by the end of the 1970s, ironically, the easing of the energy crisis stemmed largely from events outside Pacific Lighting's purview. The firm and its subsidiaries had worked assiduously to locate new gas sources, but ultimately it was government action that ended the gas shortages. As Paul Miller later commented:

1976 | Congress passes Alaska Natural Gas Transportation Act.

There are lessons to be learned from these efforts to solve the gas supply situation. Like wars, crises often stimulate enormous efforts to resolve them, but like wars, the solutions to crises frequently cannot be predicted. Unfortunately, many of our efforts in dealing with the gas shortages, while required at the time, turned out to be wasted when the government finally solved the crisis for us by long-needed actions entirely beyond our control.[29]

The federal action to which Miller referred was the passage of the Natural Gas Policy Act of 1978. The catalyst to this law lay in events two years earlier. In the winter of 1976-1977 many parts of the eastern United States had experienced record-breaking and prolonged cold weather. This placed tremendous strains on national gas pipelines to provide sufficient fuel for home and office heating, and the operating pressure in certain eastern distribution systems could not be maintained at necessary levels. Fortunately, although the East was very cold, western states were having an unusually mild winter, and gas companies serving that part of the country — including Pacific Lighting's subsidiaries — were able to divert large quantities of gas to eastern cities such as Buffalo, New York, and Philadelphia. These events clearly demonstrated to Congress that something needed to be done to solve the gas shortages, and the result was the Natural Gas Policy Act providing exploration incentives and allowing partial price deregulation for newly discovered gas. Pacific Lighting had strongly endorsed this critical piece of legislation, and Harvey Proctor and Joseph Rensch had worked tirelessly for its passage.

Full federal price deregulation did not occur until 1989. This change and new directives issued by the California Public Utilities Commission relating

Southern California Gas Company chief executives, 1967-1989. Clockwise from top left: John C. Abram, W. Morton (Mort) Jacobs, Robert M. McIntyre, Harvey A. Proctor, and Harry P. Letton, Jr.

1976 | Cold winters and gas shortages strike East Coast and Midwest.

1977 | Cabinet-level Department of Energy created.

A Pacific Lighting Exploration Company well, Alberta, Canada, 1969. This firm originally was founded in 1960 as Pacific Natural Gas Exploration Company and was one of the earliest Pacific Lighting subsidiaries created as part of the diversification program.

to state deregulation became major concerns of executives such as Richard D. Farman — Robert McIntyre's successor as chairman of Southern California Gas — who grappled with the resulting alterations in the gas utility industry. Yet partial deregulation a decade earlier brought its own changes, one of which was higher prices to consumers. There were many factors contributing to higher rates — including soaring exploration costs, reduced consumer demand due to successful conservation efforts, higher employee wages, more stringent pipeline safety rules, and the general inflationary spiral of the 1970s. The most important reason for higher gas prices, however, was more expensive gas at the wellhead. This, in turn, was caused by the first stages of gas deregulation under the provisions of the Natural Gas Policy Act.[30]

To counter the public's displeasure with the increased rates, Pacific Lighting's subsidiaries intensified their public relations efforts. By the early 1980s, Southern California Gas — then under the leadership of John C. Abram, McIntyre's predecessor as chairman and chief executive officer — had initiated Operation Cope to have the firm's employees join forces with its customers in seeking solutions to escalating gas prices. With customer "high-bill" complaints having risen a thousand percent since the previous decade, the program included workshops to help employees become more effective in meeting customers' needs. In 1983 the Customer Support Program was added to provide consumers with information on the reasons for increased gas bills, and in a phrase reminiscent of the 1950s, the program also aimed "to emphasize the company's commitment to providing consumers with a high

1978 | Pacific Lighting acquires Pacific Offshore Pipeline Company to obtain gas from oil and gas wells at sea.

level of service." The company used television commercials, radio announcements, brochures, speeches, posters, and news releases to educate the public about such services as low-interest financing and rebates for home weatherization, free energy-saving audits, partial-payment plans, appliance adjustments, safety reminders, and a conservation hotline.[31]

The gas shortages and the rate hikes of the 1970s underscored what some Pacific Lighting top officials had believed for a number of years — that in order for the firm to balance the ups and downs of the gas utility business, diversification into other industries ultimately would be necessary. Executives such as Paul Miller, Mort Jacobs, and Joseph Rensch recognized that growth in the utility business was generally restricted to the rate of population increase, and by the beginning of the 1970s the rate of new arrivals in southern California — while still substantial — had slowed to about two percent per year. Moreover, as the PEMEX and Gulf Pacific proposals had indicated, competition in the gas business might eventually become a reality. Thus, diversification was not optional for Pacific Lighting; it was a necessity.[32]

Miller, Jacobs, and Rensch had been proponents of diversification as early as the 1960s, but Pacific Lighting Chairman of the Board Robert Miller and President Robert Hornby had been reluctant to move away from the firm's utility core. Paul Miller later speculated that his father and Hornby probably believed greater diversification would not serve the firm's best interest. "In any case," the younger Miller recalled, diversification "didn't particularly swing at the start."[33]

There's a better way to keep cool!

Buy Gas Air Conditioning—the finest made. Phone *now* for a free estimate and you'll enjoy these important advantages:

- Up to 7 year financing with interest as low as 5%
- Installation with no down payment
- Special discount rates on gas used for air conditioning from May through October
- Fully automatic heating-cooling system through the house
- Dependable units (heating-cooling cycle has no rotating parts to wear out, break down)
- Operating costs at least 30% less than comparable equipment

**Phone
for a free estimate on
Gas Air Conditioning**

Advertisement for gas air conditioning, 1962. Gas-fueled cooling was seen as an effective way to increase gas use during summer months when heating demands were low.

1978 | Congress passes Natural Gas Policy Act allowing partial gas price deregulation.

1979 | Three Mile Island nuclear reactor accident.

Roof-top view of a cooling tower outlet, Central Plants' facility at Bunker Hill, 1980s.

Exterior of Central Plants' air conditioning facility at Bunker Hill in downtown Los Angeles, 1970.

Even though Paul Miller's predecessors had been hesitant about diversification, Pacific Lighting had actually started to move in that direction before Robert Miller's retirement, albeit in a limited manner and in lines of business closely linked to the oil and gas industries. Recognizing the growing popularity of air conditioning, Pacific Lighting and its subsidiaries had started to promote gas-fueled cooling systems in the early 1960s because summer air conditioning fueled by gas could help balance the heavy winter demand for gas used in heating. Initially, Pacific Lighting's subsidiaries championed air conditioning by showing model homes equipped with gas units, and the companies also offered attractive warranties and service plans to entice homeowners to install gas cooling systems.[34]

Pacific Lighting quickly supplemented the home cooling venture by a more aggressive effort to provide gas air conditioning to large buildings such as office complexes, hotels, and shopping malls. To cool these structures, Pacific Lighting planned to build, operate, and maintain gas-fueled central air conditioning plants. The firm formed a new non-utility subsidiary, Uni-Plant Corporation, in 1963 to oversee this operation, and Uni-Plant's first central air conditioning system was installed at Douglas Aircraft Company's space center at Huntington Beach. A second subsidiary, Central Plants, Incorporated, was created the same year to handle air conditioning projects for groups of customers or buildings, including Century City, the Bunker Hill redevelopment project in downtown Los Angeles, and a Santa Fe Springs industrial complex.[35]

The theoretical premise that gas air conditioning could compete successfully with electric

1979 | Pacific Lighting sells agricultural subsidiaries, 1979-1980.

cooling systems may have seemed compelling, but Pacific Lighting saw few returns from its Uni-Plant and Central Plant subsidiaries for many years. A significant reason for the poor showing was that gas air conditioning plants and their related service pipelines were more expensive to install than electric cooling systems. Moreover, some of the gas systems were predicated partly on customers' growth, and at least one major Central Plant consumer, Century City, did not expand as fast as had been anticipated. "It was a losing proposition," remembered Charles T. Dierker, who headed the gas-fueled cooling efforts. "We lost money every year." Only after years had passed did the air conditioning subsidiaries become profitable, and then only when most of the smaller plants had been sold.[36]

Undaunted by such temporary setbacks, Paul Miller greatly expanded the diversification program beyond the gas business upon Robert Miller's retirement as chairman of the board in 1967. Under the younger Miller's direction, in 1969 Pacific Lighting acquired Blackfield Hawaii Corporation, a developer of resort facilities, apartments, and condominiums. As the firm's name suggested, most of its activities were in Hawaii.[37] Blackfield's operations were soon supplemented by other real estate additions to the Pacific Lighting system. The same year that Blackfield was acquired, Pacific Lighting's directors approved a plan to purchase Dunn Properties Corporation of Santa Ana, California, and Fredricks Development Corporation of Fullerton. Dunn developed and leased industrial and commercial buildings in Los Angeles and Orange counties, and it had branched into such fields as recreational vehicles, motels, mobile home parks, and modular

Grand Circle Commercentre, built by Dunn Properties Corporation in Corona, California.

Charles T. Dierker, who headed Pacific Lighting's commercial gas air conditioning, alternative energy, and real estate ventures.

1983 | Southern California Gas institutes Customer Support Program.

1983 | Organization of Petroleum Exporting Countries (OPEC) lowers oil prices.

164

A Southern California Gas Company employee installs solar panels on the roof of an Orange County apartment building as part of the firm's SAGE program in the mid-1970s.

Pacific Lighting branched into alternative energy as part of its diversification program. This photograph shows a geothermal power plant near Mammoth Lakes, California, in the 1980s.

housing. Fredricks was one of the nation's leading builders of multi-family housing, constructing more than two thousand units per year. The company built apartment complexes in Orange County, and it had plans for additional projects in Texas and Georgia. Pacific Lighting made its last large acquisition in the real estate field in 1984 with the purchase of the Presley Companies, which specialized in residential construction.[38]

Pacific Lighting remained in the real estate industry until the late 1980s because the firm was reasonably comfortable with land development and related activities. Moreover, Paul Miller noted that "our [gas utility] business was closely allied to the growth of housing development." Nonetheless, in 1987 Pacific Lighting sold its real estate enterprises at a profit. A principal reason for the change of heart was that land development complicated Pacific Lighting's other diversification plans, which required the capital tied up in the real estate ventures. In addition, the financial community viewed the real estate investments unfavorably, and although the company believed those subsidiaries to be solid investments with the potential for significant earnings, Pacific Lighting's officials decided that they "could do better . . . getting into something else."[39]

As the real estate enterprises were evolving, Pacific Lighting also moved into agriculture. In 1970 the firm acquired W.D. Fowler and Sons Corporation, a farm management operation in Tulare County, California. Fowler packed and shipped almost a million boxes of citrus fruit per year, and the company managed orange, lemon, avocado, and other orchards for absentee owners. Fowler also provided Pacific Lighting with a stake in about

1984 | Pacific Lighting acquires the Presley Companies.

Gas-dispatching center at Spence Street, Los Angeles, in the 1970s.

seven hundred acres of pistachio nut trees, which *Gas News* humorously dubbed "the only vertically integrated pistachio nut business in the United States" because Fowler also shipped and sold this crop. In addition to Fowler, Pacific Lighting bought Blue Goose Growers, Incorporated, a much larger organization that owned six farm management companies, twelve packing houses, and over ten thousand acres in Arizona, California, Florida, and Maryland. Although these ventures into agribusiness returned positive income quickly, Pacific Lighting's management came to believe that the profits were not enough to warrant staying in this field of business, and the firm sold its agricultural investments in 1979 and 1980.[40]

At about the same time that Pacific Lighting was moving into agribusiness and real estate development, it also was broadening its operating base by diversifying into alternative energy. In the early 1970s, Southern California Gas launched two major solar energy research projects, Solar Assisted Gas Energy (SAGE) and the Minimum Energy Dwelling (MED). For the SAGE program, the gas company worked with the National Science Foundation, California Institute of Technology's Jet Propulsion

Laboratory, and the Federal Energy Administration to install a solar water heating system with a gas backup in an existing apartment complex in El Toro, California. A second project involved placing a similar system in a new apartment building under construction. The purpose of the SAGE projects was to examine the long-term commercial feasibility of solar energy. As the SAGE experiments were underway, the MED project produced two homes in Mission Viejo, California, each having a wide range of energy conservation features, including solar systems.[41]

Solar energy was not Pacific Lighting's only foray into alternative energy. The company also examined other undertakings such as landfill gas fields, wood-fueled power plants, dual-fuel energy systems for fleet vehicles, fuel cells, and geothermal energy projects. Yet while the relatively high oil and gas prices of the 1970s made alternative energy ventures appear to be attractive additions to Pacific Lighting's diversification program, when energy prices later fell, these endeavors became less

1986 | Major accident at Soviet Union's Chernobyl nuclear power plant.

In 1982 Pacific Offshore Pipeline Company, a Pacific Lighting subsidiary, installed the deepest underwater gas pipeline at that time connecting Exxon's Platform Hondo in the Santa Barbara Channel to Pacific Lighting's onshore gas treatment plant.

Pacific Lighting acquired Pacific Offshore Pipeline Company in 1978 to bring gas in from wells at sea, such as those drilled from Exxon's Platform Hondo in the Santa Barbara Channel.

In 1988, shortly after Pacific Lighting became Pacific Enterprises, the company acquired Sabine Corporation, a firm engaged in oil and gas exploration.

appealing. Nonetheless, the expertise gained by the alternative energy experiments prepared Pacific Lighting to reenter these fields at a future date should the need arise.[42]

Almost simultaneous with the ventures into agriculture, real estate, and alternative energy, Pacific Lighting had begun to increase its interests in oil and gas exploration and development. In 1975 Pacific Lighting Exploration Company — which had originally been formed in 1960 as Pacific Natural Gas Exploration Company — purchased an interest in drilling activities sponsored by several firms in the Dutch North Sea. While Pacific Lighting's subsidiary took part in this effort only as an investor and left the actual drilling to other companies, after almost ten years of searching, a considerable amount of gas was located.[43]

Even before the European exploration had borne fruit, however, Pacific Lighting began considering other oil and gas exploration activities. Because Pacific Lighting and Pacific Lighting Exploration Company already had some experience in gas production and transmission, the parent firm's management felt comfortable moving more broadly into the exploration and production end of the business, and after the success in the Dutch North Sea, Pacific Lighting began to search for other oil and gas exploration and development opportunities.[44]

Pacific Lighting's major expansion into oil and gas exploration began with the 1983 acquisition of Terra Resources, a unit of Farmland Industries, Incorporated. Terra's oil and gas properties were located in eighteen states with producing areas in Alabama, Louisiana, Texas, and Wyoming. Five years after the Terra addition, Pacific Lighting

168

Principal executives of Pacific Enterprises' subsidiaries in the late 1980s. Clockwise from top left: Richard G. Eils, president of Thrifty Corporation; Richard D. Farman, chairman of the board of Southern California Gas Company; Harry L. Lepape, chairman of the board of Pacific Enterprises Oil Company; Leonard H. Straus, chairman of the board of Thrifty Corporation; and Jonel C. Hill, president of Southern California Gas Company.

purchased Sabine Corporation, a Dallas, Texas, exploration firm. Pacific Lighting was attracted to Sabine by that company's established oil and gas reserves and by a large portfolio of mineral rights in Kansas, Oklahoma, and Texas, which Pacific Lighting's management believed would provide years of future production possibilities. By the end of the 1980s, the ventures into oil and gas exploration had proven highly successful even in the face of depressed oil and gas prices, producing over eleven percent of the parent firm's operating income after taxes. "We knew what we were doing, and we knew we could operate efficiently," remarked Harry L. Lepape, chairman of the board and chief executive officer of Pacific Enterprises Oil Company, a subsidiary formed in 1988 to oversee all oil and gas development activities. "Our performance has been excellent," he concluded.[45]

Although the diversification efforts were broadening Pacific Lighting's revenue base in the 1970s and 1980s, the moves into new fields were not without difficulty. One problem that emerged early in the program involved federal regulation. Because of the unusual situation of a utility holding company acquiring non-utility subsidiaries, in 1971 the staff of the Securities and Exchange Commission (SEC) questioned Pacific Lighting's exemption from the 1935 Public Utility Holding Company Act. Although Pacific Lighting had obtained the exemption in 1936 because its activities at the time were all linked to intrastate gas distribution, the commission's staff argued that the company's expansion into such fields as land development, industrial park leasing, and agribusiness was detrimental to the public interest. The SEC

1986 | One-hundredth anniversary of the founding of Pacific Lighting.

SOUTHERN CALIFORNIA gas **COMPANY**

PACIFIC ENTERPRISES OIL COMPANY

THRIFTY CORPORATION

Logos of Pacific Enterprises'
three principal subsidiaries in
the late 1980s.

believed the issue needed to be resolved before matters got "out of hand."[46]

Pacific Lighting — supported by other utility holding companies — countered that because of rate regulations, inadequate gas resources, and increased production costs, the firm had to diversify into unregulated areas to provide adequate returns to shareholders. Pacific Lighting claimed its diversification program was a financial success, but the SEC staff would not accept success as a defense. "One fundamental, overriding purpose" of the Public Utility Holding Company Act, the SEC staff stated in its review, was "to restrict utility holding companies to the utility business." The SEC staff believed the farming venture to be speculative, and the staff contended that such enterprises were not in the interests of consumers or shareholders — parties the agency was responsible to protect.[47]

Despite the SEC staff's initial concerns, in January 1973 the commission decided on a split vote

not to revoke the 1936 exemption. Nonetheless, the issue was not dead, and it resurfaced almost two decades later. In the 1980s, with holding companies elsewhere in the nation acquiring non-utility subsidiaries, the SEC started a larger investigation into the question of whether any utility holding company ought to be allowed to diversify. As late as 1989, however, this issue remained unresolved.[48]

Aside from the SEC investigations, the diversification program also caused concern among other groups. As the policy accelerated in the 1980s, some investors and financial analysts believed Pacific Lighting was moving in too many directions too quickly, and within the firm's own gas subsidiary, some employees thought that the value of their stock-based retirement savings funds was being undermined by new stock issues authorized to acquire subsidiaries. Regardless of these concerns and the SEC investigations, Pacific Lighting's management continued to diversify with the resolute

1986 | Pacific Lighting
acquires Thrifty
Corporation.

1987 | Pacific Lighting sells
real estate ventures.

Thrifty Corporation

Profile of a Pacific Lighting Subsidiary.

Although at first glance, Thrifty Corporation — with its strong emphasis on the Los Angeles retail industry — and Pacific Lighting might appear to be an unlikely pairing, on closer examination the two companies reveal many similarities. Both enjoyed the benefits brought by decades of rapid southern California expansion; both prospered under the direction of managements that took advantage of opportunities when they appeared and changed business tactics when situations warranted; and both enjoyed good relations with their employees and with the general public. Such similarities undoubtedly were significant factors in Pacific Lighting's friendly offer in 1986 to purchase Thrifty and that company's decision to accept the bid.

Like Pacific Lighting Corporation, Thrifty's roots in southern California extend back many years. Founded in Los Angeles in 1919 by two brothers, Harry and Robert Borun, and their brother-in-law, Norman Levin, the business was originally named Borun Brothers. The firm specialized in wholesale drug

Thrifty was founded in 1919 as Borun Brothers, a wholesale drug and sundry supplier. By 1934 Thrifty had seventeen stores in Los Angeles.

and sundry sales to retailers. The booming 1920s in southern California created an excellent business climate, and, as Pacific Lighting experienced in the utility industry, Thrifty found the retail sector to be economically sound. The decade following the stock market crash of 1929, however, brought major restructuring

In 1989, with 575 locations Thrifty was the most prevalent drugstore chain on the West Coast.

to both firms as they adjusted to changing economic, social, and political values. While Pacific Lighting lost its electric properties to the City of Los Angeles due to rising antipathy toward large corporations,

Borun Brothers also underwent dramatic changes. When it appeared that the main retail outlets of Borun Brothers were having financial difficulties, thus limiting the firm's wholesale business, the company created its own stores and in 1929 opened the first Thrifty Cut Rate Drug Store at 412 South Broadway in downtown Los Angeles. By the end of 1934, seventeen Thrifty stores were in operation, and the following year Thrifty Drug Stores Company, Incorporated, was formed. The new firm took over the stores and all of the capital stock of Borun Brothers and continued to operate that company as a

subsidiary. Thrifty stores were relatively small, conforming to the corner market concept prevalent during the era, and they originally featured rough pine counters for displaying a limited array of merchandise. Highly advertised "loss-leaders" attracted customers. This approach to retailing proved successful for several decades.

After World War II, Thrifty — like Pacific Lighting's subsidiaries — underwent major changes once again. The tremendous growth in southern California during the postwar years had important ramifications for Thrifty. The small neighborhood stores that had served the company so well since the late 1920s were obsolete in an era when subdivision after subdivision marched across the southern California landscape, and by the early 1950s Thrifty's profits had dropped precipitously. As Pacific Lighting had been forced to implement new gas storage and supply schemes to serve the growing population, Thrifty also innovated to accommodate the flood of newcomers. Under the leadership of Leonard H. Straus, significant changes in the company's operations took place. Straus — who in 1941 had married Dorothy Borun, the daughter of Robert Borun — had

joined Thrifty in 1945. He assumed general responsibility for the company's operations in 1953 and became president and chief executive officer in 1957. Under his direction, larger stores were introduced carrying broader merchandising lines, and a vigorous store expansion program was instituted. Like Pacific Lighting's new gas mains, Thrifty stores appeared seemingly overnight in subdivisions still under construction, and wide-ranging promotional efforts were augmented to attract new customers.

To improve the firm's name recognition, community involvement was stressed by top management, and Thrifty implemented a corporate strategy based on the importance of harmonious management-employee relations. Thrifty's salaried employees were motivated with bonuses, stock options, and a profit-sharing plan to encourage maximum efforts on behalf of the firm, while union negotiations with the company looked after the interests of hourly workers. Personnel policies instituted by Straus were so successful that by the mid-1950s Thrifty formalized them in a code of personnel administration, and the firm received a commendation from the State of California for advanced practices in the

field of human relations. All of these innovations turned Thrifty around from the slump of the early 1950s, and the company flourished throughout the following decades.

Like Pacific Lighting, Thrifty had to adjust to the changing economy of the late 1960s and early 1970s. With rising inflation prompting greater competition among discount retailers, Thrifty once again changed direction to stay ahead of its rivals. In the mid-1970s, Thrifty became more aggressive in its merchandising approach and eliminated "low-end" promotional items in favor of a "total discount" retailing policy. Massive displays of brand name merchandise were combined with the revitalization of existing stores to attract more customers, and the results were dramatic increases in same-store sales.

The successful marketing changes, community efforts, and good management-employee relations created — as within the Pacific Lighting system — a feeling of camaraderie or family spirit, and this sentiment made Thrifty's management unwilling to consider selling the firm to any organization. By 1975 the company had developed a retailing

network with over five hundred stores that functioned efficiently and profitably, and its employees were rewarded for their loyalty and devotion. Thrifty's top executives like Straus, who had become chairman of the board in 1979, and President Richard G. Eils knew

Thrifty Corporation's principal subsidiaries in the late 1980s.

that while they were obligated by their responsibilities to stockholders to consider any take-over offers, they nonetheless wished to avoid a buy-out to maintain the management philosophy that had led to the successful operation created over the years.

Early Thrifty stores were small and featured only a limited array of merchandise.

Despite the fact that management contolled over fifty percent of Thrifty's outstanding stock, by the mid-1980s the firm had decided to develop a list of compatible companies to which they could turn in the event a hostile take-over offer was submitted. Concurrently, in May 1986 Pacific Lighting's chairman of the board of directors, Paul Miller, broached the possibility of acquiring Thrifty with Leonard Straus. While Thrifty was reluctant, the potential for a hostile take-over was growing daily, and Thrifty finally agreed to the idea. Thrifty's concurrence was in part based on the knowledge of Pacific Lighting's generally good relations with its subsidiaries' operating managements. The merger process took place very rapidly after shareholders of both firms voted approval. On August 6, 1986, Thrifty became Pacific Lighting's second largest operating company.[49]

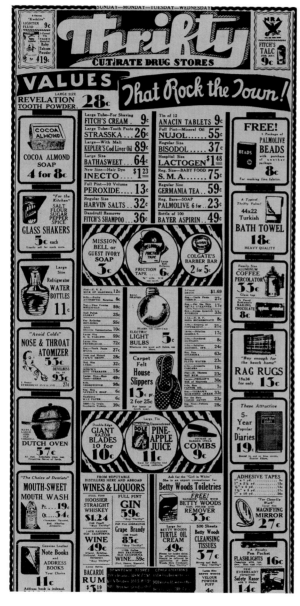

Thrifty originally relied on "loss-leaders" to attract customers, as this 1930s advertisement attests.

conviction that although the gas utility was to remain the central enterprise, part of the company's future prosperity was tied to investments in other lines of business.[50]

As Pacific Lighting broadened in its diversification efforts in the 1980s, it became increasingly clear that the company needed additional expertise in managing the program. With Paul Miller and Joseph Rensch facing retirement by the end of the decade, Pacific Lighting took steps to expand the scope of its management's business experience, and in 1984 the firm hired James R. Ukropina as executive vice-president and general counsel. Ukropina left a similar position at Santa Fe International Corporation, and prior to his affiliation with that company, he had been a partner in the Los Angeles law firm of O'Melveny and Myers. Over the years he had developed extensive experience in mergers, acquisitions, and corporate finance.[51]

Ukropina's addition to top management contributed to another major effort in the diversification program — the move into retailing. With the memory of the oil and gas shortages of the 1970s still fresh, Pacific Lighting's top officials fully understood the potential volatility of the energy field, and to "add a fourth leg to the stool" — as several executives characterized it at the time — management examined a number of other possible endeavors, including financial institutions, publishing houses, cable television franchises, and construction firms. After considerable deliberation, however, Ukropina and Pacific Lighting Executive Vice-President Lloyd A. Levitin successfully proposed a move into retailing. As a result, in mid-1986 the firm acquired Thrifty Corporation, a Los Angeles-based chain

Northern California Earthquake of 1989

Southern California Gas Company Helps Restore Service.

On Tuesday, October 17, 1989, at 5:04 P.M., a massive earthquake rocked the San Francisco Bay area. Registering 7.1 on the open-ended Richter scale, the quake — the largest since the temblor that had destroyed much of San Francisco in 1906 — shook northern California for fifteen long seconds before finally subsiding. By the time the earth stopped convulsing, over fifty people had been killed; nearly four thousand were injured; and at least twelve thousand were left homeless. Property damage was extensive. Part of the upper deck of the San Francisco-Oakland Bay Bridge had fallen onto the lower roadway, closing that vital artery between two of the region's largest cities for over a month; a large section of the Nimitz Freeway in downtown Oakland had collapsed, crushing scores of automobiles; much of the Marina District in San Francisco was reduced to rubble; and thousands of buildings throughout the area were severely damaged.

In addition to the dramatic destruction flashed by television cameras around the

Above: A Southern California Gas Company employee uses a flame ionization unit (commonly called a "leak-detector") to search for broken gas lines under the rubble.

world, the earthquake also had a major impact on utility service in northern California. A large proportion of homes and businesses lost electric service, and gas pipelines in many locations were fractured by the lengthy shaking. Adding to the damage caused by the quake itself, thousands of gas customers — contrary to the long-standing advice of California's utility companies — rushed to turn off gas valves even before determining whether their home pipelines or appliances were damaged or leaking gas. The combination of the earthquake's destruction and the many needlessly closed home gas lines created a utility nightmare for Pacific Gas and Electric (PG & E), the firm providing both gas and electric service in northern California. Fortunately, however, PG & E did not have to face this crisis alone.

As early as the 1950s, PG & E — like Southern California Gas and the state's other major gas supply firm, San Diego Gas and Electric — had anticipated that a national emergency or a natural disaster might someday create the need to call on other utility companies for aid. A mutual assistance agreement had been considered by the state's gas utilities as early as the 1950s in response to "Cold War" concerns over civil defense,

and by 1965 an accord was in place (which was updated in the 1980s) allowing any one of the corporate signers to call on the others for help in the event of a natural disaster or other emergency.

Although the mutual assistance agreement initially took effect in the mid-1960s,

Meters and home appliances were checked for damage or gas leaks.

the 1989 northern California earthquake was the first time the accord was actually implemented. Within minutes of the end of the quake, PG & E officials contacted Southern California Gas Company, requesting help under the terms of the mutual assistance agreement. At first, PG & E only asked that Southern California Gas monitor the large transmission inter-tie lines connecting the two companies' systems, but the

morning after the quake — when the full dimensions of the disaster had become better known — PG & E appealed for additional help. Southern California Gas immediately responded by sending over two hundred employees to the quake-ravaged area. Deployed into task forces on the

San Francisco Peninsula, in Oakland and the East Bay, and in hard-hit communities south of San Francisco such as Watsonville, Santa Cruz, Los Gatos, and San Jose, Southern California Gas workers helped survey underground pipes for leaks and assisted in restoring service to over forty thousand homes and businesses. By the time Southern California Gas Company crews left the area, they had helped restore service to more gas utility customers than had been affected by any other California natural disaster.[52]

Top management team of
Pacific Enterprises as the
1980s ended. Clockwise from
top left: James R. Ukropina,
chairman of the board; Willis
B. Wood, Jr., president; and
Lloyd A. Levitin, executive
vice-president.

owning over five hundred Thrifty discount drug-stores, twenty-seven Thrifty Jr. drugstores, and eighty-nine Big 5 Sporting Goods stores.[53]

Thrifty offered a number of attractions to Pacific Lighting, a central one of which was the Los Angeles market. As Ukropina, one of the principal architects behind the choice of Thrifty as a retail acquisition, explained later, "I think most experts think . . . southern California is the best retail market in the world." In fact, as Pacific Lighting's officials knew, the southern California market had been so favorable that Thrifty's earnings had increased nearly every year for over three decades, and its sales had grown annually for more than a half century. Also attractive to Pacific Lighting were Thrifty's top executives — headed by Chairman of the Board Leonard H. Straus and President Richard G. Eils — whom Pacific Lighting intended to leave in place due to their expertise in the retail world. An added benefit was that Thrifty, which had been resisting take-over bids for years, now considered Pacific Lighting a viable suitor because Pacific Lighting's top management pledged to leave most of Thrifty's business and employee policies intact.[54]

The Thrifty acquisition laid the groundwork for other moves into the retailing world. Within two years after joining Pacific Lighting, Thrifty — with Pacific Lighting's financial backing — purchased several sporting goods retailers in Colorado and the Midwest, including Gart Bros. Sporting Goods Company; Michigan Sporting Goods Distributors, Incorporated; and Dave Cook Sporting Goods. When combined with Thrifty's eighty-nine Big 5 stores, these new additions made Pacific Lighting the second largest sporting goods retailer in the

Artist's rendition of the Gas Company Center (foreground) and to its left, the First Interstate World Center. Plans to construct the Gas Company Center at Fifth Street and Grand Avenue were announced in 1987. Completion was expected by 1991.

Pacific **Enterprises**

United States. In addition, Thrifty acquired over a hundred Pay 'n Save drugstores and thirty-seven Bi-Mart general merchandise stores in the Pacific Northwest. These additions solidified Pacific Lighting's position through its Thrifty subsidiary as the leading drugstore chain retailer in the western United States.[55]

The bold moves into retailing and the growing size of Pacific Lighting's investments in oil and gas exploration made it abundantly clear that the company was no longer solely in the gas distribution business. Therefore, on February 16, 1988, the firm changed its name to Pacific Enterprises in order to reflect its diversification program more accurately. The new designation symbolically set the stage for Pacific Enterprises to grow into its second century of operation.[56]

1989 | Paul A. Miller retires as Pacific Lighting's chairman of the board of directors.

Conclusion

THE GROWTH OF PACIFIC ENTERPRISES from a small venture — then called Pacific Lighting — to the major diversified organization that it had become by the late 1980s is remarkable. In 1886 when the company was founded by C.O.G. Miller and Walter B. Cline, its primary business was renting gas lamps to saloons and other commercial establishments in San Francisco. Over a century later, the firm operated the largest natural gas distribution system in the world; it held major interests in oil and gas exploration and development in the United States and abroad; and it owned one of the largest retail chains in the country. The company's evolution is all the more extraordinary because it occurred under the direction of three members of the same family: C.O.G. Miller, Robert W. Miller, and Paul A. Miller.

A key to Pacific Lighting's success has been its ability to adapt. As the firm grew, it absorbed other operating companies when opportunities presented themselves. Pacific Lighting also embraced technological improvements and new marketing techniques, applied skills in corporate finance through periods of economic growth and stagnation, and otherwise tailored its policies to meet changing historical circumstances.

In its early years as Pacific Lighting evolved into a southern California gas distribution company, the firm seized chances to acquire other organizations in critical markets. This aggressive approach toward expansion was intitially tempered by the conservative policy of concentrating corporate energies on one industry and one geographic region — gas distribution in southern California — thus enabling Pacific Lighting to focus its expertise. Entrepreneurial and financial skills typified the firm's management in this era of competition and consolidation, while all workers brought to their jobs pride, loyalty, and a dedication to serve their communities.

New strategies for success evolved after Pacific Lighting had unified its position in the southern California gas distribution business. As the region became increasingly populated, newcomers placed ever greater demands on the company's system. Pacific Lighting responded in a variety of innovative ways. These included seeking out-of-state gas supplies, creating huge underground storage facilities, and developing an interruptible gas market to absorb periodic surpluses. The changes and the continuing commitment of its employees allowed Pacific Lighting to maintain operations in the face of rapid population increases while offering some of the lowest natural gas rates in the United States.

When southern California's rate of growth peaked and began to taper off, Pacific Lighting again adapted to changing circumstances and looked to new horizons. Recognizing that the future of the energy market was likely to remain uncertain, diversification became corporate policy. This new strategy laid the foundations to meet the challenges of the company's second century of service, and it prompted the firm to change its name to Pacific Enterprises in 1988. The adaptability demonstrated by the diversification program — like the other strategic changes during the first century of operations — and the skills and dedication of the firm's many employees underscored that the company's past truly had been dominated by "The Spirit of Enterprise."

Notes

NOTES TO CHAPTER ONE

1 Pacific Lighting Corporation, *Annual Report of Pacific Lighting Corporation for the Year Ended December 31, 1936* (San Francisco: Taylor and Taylor, [1937]), p. 4.

2 James T. Van Rensselaer, "The Lamplighters," typewritten manuscript, 1967, chap. 7, p. 2, historical files, Southern California Gas Company Research and Information Center, Los Angeles, California.

3 Ibid., foreword, pp. 1-4, chap. 7, p. 2.

4 Ibid., chap. 7, pp. 2-3.

5 "In Memoriam: C.O.G. Miller, Oct. 1, 1865 - April 23, 1952" [bound volume of C.O.G. Miller's obituaries], Miller Family Collection, Pacific Enterprises, Los Angeles, California; Lewis Francis Byington and Oscar Lewis, eds., *The History of San Francisco*, 3 vols. (Chicago: S.J. Clarke Publishing Company, 1931), vol. 2, pp. 395-398; "C.O.G. Miller, Utilities Executive, Dies at 86," *San Francisco Examiner*, April 24, 1952; Allen L. Chickering, "In Memoriam," *California Historical Society Quarterly* 31 (1952): 176-177; "C.O.G. Miller Elected Board Chairman," *American Trust Company Recap* 5 (March 1948): 1.

6 Van Rensselaer, "The Lamplighters," chap. 7, pp. 3-4.

7 Ibid.

8 Ibid., chap. 1, pp. 4-5; W.W. Robinson, *Los Angeles from the Days of the Pueblo* (Los Angeles: California Historical Society, 1977), pp. 54-55.

9 Van Rensselaer, "The Lamplighters," chap. 1, p. 5; W.H. Hutchinson, *Oil, Land and Politics: The Career of Thomas Robert Bard*, 2 vols. (Norman: University of Oklahoma Press, 1965), vol. 1, pp. 61, 140.

10 Van Rensselaer, "The Lamplighters," chap. 1, pp. 2-8.

11 *Los Angeles Semi-Weekly News*, Oct. 1, 1867; ibid., Dec. 3, 1867; Van Rensselaer, "The Lamplighters," chap. 1, p. 1.

12 *Los Angeles Semi-Weekly News*, Dec. 3, 1867.

13 Quoted in Harris Newmark, *Sixty Years in Southern California, 1853-1913* (4th ed., Los Angeles: Leitlen and Ver Brugge, 1970), p. 370.

14 Gas company bill, July 1868, box b2288, Abel Stearns/Common Council Collection, Los Angeles City Archives, Los Angeles, California; Contract for gas lighting, Nov. 1868, ibid.; *Los Angeles Semi-Weekly News*, Dec. 9, 1867; ibid., Dec. 13, 1867; Van Rensselaer, "The Lamplighters," chap. 1, pp. 9-11.

15 *Los Angeles Daily News*, Jan. 4, 1869; ibid., Jan. 20, 1869; Contract between City of Los Angeles and Los Angeles Gas Company to install gas lamps, June 17, 1869, file 1865-0004, historical files, Southern California Gas Company Research and Information Center; Petition to the Los Angeles mayor to have gas street lamps extended along Spring Street, Sept. 25, 1869, file 1865-0002, ibid.

16 Van Rensselaer, "The Lamplighters," chap. 2, pp. 3-4.

17 Ibid., chap. 2, pp. 4-5.

18 City attorney report on gas contract, March 22, 1871, box b2288, Abel Stearns/Common Council Collection; Gas committee report, Jan. 21, 1871, ibid.; *Evening Express*, Jan. 5, 1872; Van Rensselaer, "The Lamplighters," chap. 2, pp. 5-18.

19 *Evening Express*, Dec. 16, 1871; Van Rensselaer, "The Lamplighters," chap. 2, pp. 9-11.

20 "GAS: Light from the Sewers — From the Stables into the Parlor," *Evening Express*, Oct. 18, 1876.

21 [No title], *Evening Express*, Oct. 22, 1873; "Common Council," ibid., Nov. 7, 1873; "Common Council," ibid., Nov. 21, 1873; "Gas and Refining Company," ibid., Jan. 29, 1874; [No title], ibid., Sept. 2, 1875; "Light Wanted," ibid., Oct. 18, 1875.

22 Van Rensselaer, "The Lamplighters," chap. 2, pp. 12-18; Remi Nadeau, *City Makers: The Men Who Transformed Los Angeles from Village to Metropolis, 1850-1930* (Garden City, N.Y.: Doubleday, 1948), pp. 52, 123.

23 Van Rensselaer, "The Lamplighters," chap. 4, pp. 5-10.

24 Ibid.

25 "The Street Light Contract," *Evening Express*, Jan. 14, 1876; J.A. Graves, *My Seventy Years in California, 1852-1923* (Los Angeles: Times-Mirror Press, 1929), p. 96.

26 "Gas Stock in Danger," *Evening Express*, Dec. 24, 1879; Van Rensselaer, "The Lamplighters," chap. 4, pp. 1-27.

27 "Gas Stock in Danger," *Evening Express*, Dec. 24, 1879; Van Rensselaer, "The Lamplighters," chap. 4, pp. 1-27.

28 "The Electric Light," *Evening Express*, Jan. 2, 1883.

29 "The Electric Light," *Evening Express*, Nov. 2, 1885.

30 [Advertisement], *Evening Express*, Jan. 2, 1883.

31 *Evening Express*, Feb. 10, 1883.

32 "City Council," *Evening Express*, Nov. 12, 1884; Newmark, *Sixty Years in Southern California*, p. 535.

33 *Evening Express*, Oct. 1, 1884; ibid., Jan. 8, 1886; Newmark, *Sixty Years in Southern California*, p. 535; Charles Coleman, *The P.G. and E. of California: The Centennial Story of the Pacific Gas and Electric Company, 1852-1952* (New York: McGraw-Hill, 1953), p. 63.

34 Los Angeles Gas Company, "Annual Statement of [the] Los Angeles Gas Company for the Year Ending June 2, 1885," [dated June 8, 1885], file 1880-0001, historical files, Southern California Gas Company Research and Information Center.

35 Glenn S. Dumke, *Boom of the Eighties in Southern California* (San Marino, Ca.: Huntington Library, 1944), passim.

36 *Evening Express*, Nov. 6, 1885; Dumke, *Boom of the Eighties in Southern California*, passim.

37 C.O.G. Miller, "One Hundred Years of Gas Service: A Good Deal of History and a Little of Prophecy," Pacific Coast Gas Association, *Annual Report*, No. 21 [1931], p. 13, historical files, Southern California Gas Company Research and Information Center; *Evening Express*, Dec. 9, 1886; Van Rensselaer, "The Lamplighters," chap. 6, pp. 4-21; Judith Elias, *Los Angeles: Dream to Reality, 1885-1915* (Northridge, Ca.: Santa Suzanna Press, 1983), p. 34-36; Robert Glass Cleland, *March of Industry* (San Francisco: Powell, 1929), pp. 272-273.

38 Van Rensselaer, "The Lamplighters," chap. 6, pp. 4-21.

NOTES TO CHAPTER TWO

1 Assistant Auditor, Los Angeles Gas and Electric Corporation, "Los Angeles Gas and Electric Corporation Meters in Circuit January 1 of Each Year," May 11, 1928, file 1925-0010, historical files, Southern California Gas Company Research and Information Center, Los Angeles, California; Clem A. Copeland, unidentified document, file 1925-0011, ibid.; Los Angeles Lighting Company bills, Jan. 2, 1895, file 1880-0002, ibid.; James T. Van Rensselaer, "The Lamplighters," typewritten manuscript, 1967, chap. 8, pp. 1-2, historical files, ibid.

2 Van Rensselaer, "The Lamplighters," chap. 6, pp. 2-5; Eugene B. Block, *Above the Civil War: The Story of Thaddeus Lowe, Balloonist, Inventor, Railway Builder* (Berkeley: Howell-North Books, 1966); Fred C. Shoop, "Prof. Lowe Hero 70 Years Ago," clipping from *Independent Star News*, Aug. 21, 1963, in "People" album of clippings, Pasadena Historical Society, Pasadena, California; William H. Knight, "The Lowe Passenger Airship," *Out West Magazine*, Jan. 31, 1910; Jane Porter, *Thaddeus of Warsaw* (London: Longman and O. Rees, 1804).

3 C.O.G. Miller, "Foreword," in Pacific Lighting Corporation, *Annual Report of the Pacific Lighting Corporation for 1936* (San Francisco: Taylor and Taylor, [1937]), pp. 3-5.

4 Los Angeles Lighting Company, "All About Gas Stoves and Some Choice Recipes" [booklet], May 14, 1890, file 1890-0005, historical files, Southern California Gas Company Research and Information Center.

5 Ibid.

6 Marion Harland, "The Comfort of Cooking and Heating by Gas" [booklet], 1898, file 1895-0006, historical files, Southern California Gas Company Research and Information Center.

7 C.O.G. Miller, "One Hundred Years of Gas Service: A Good Deal of History And a Little of Prophecy," in Pacific Coast Gas Association, *Annual Report,* No. 21 [1931], historical files, Southern California Gas Company Research and Information Center.

8 Los Angeles Lighting Company bill, Sept. 29, 1898, file 1880-0002, historical files, Southern California Gas Company Research and Information Center.

9 C.W. Koiner to W.J. Dorr, July 16, 1907, letter on display, Public Affairs Department, Southern California Gas Company, Los Angeles, California.

10 Horace Cline, "Old Settler's Story," *L.A. Gas Monthly* [Old Guard Number] 2 (March 1924): 2.

11 Van Rensselaer, "The Lamplighters," chap. 9, pp. 1-4.

12 Pacific Lighting Company, "Trial Balance" [Annual Report], June 30, 1892, Pacific Enterprises files, Los Angeles, California; C.O.G. Miller, "A Short Report on the Pacific Lighting Co." [Annual Report], June 3, 1895, ibid.

13 Pacific Lighting Company, "Trial Balance" [Annual Report], June 30, 1892, Pacific Enterprises files; "Fifty Years of Electric Service: Our Pioneer System Celebrates Its Golden Anniversary," *L.A. Service Review* 7 (Jan. 1, 1933): 2-16.

14 "William G. Kerckhoff," [Southern California Gas Company] *Gas News* 6 (April 30, 1929): 2-4.

15 "Fifty Years of Electric Service: Our Pioneer System Celebrates Its Golden Anniversary," *L.A. Service Review* 7 (Jan. 1, 1933): 2-16.

16 C.O.G. Miller, "A Short Report on the Pacific Lighting Co." [Annual Report], June 3, 1895, Pacific Enterprises files.

17 Ibid.; Van Rensselaer, "The Lamplighters," chap. 9, pp. 1-8.

18 Van Rensselaer, "The Lamplighters," chap. 9, pp. 1-8.

19 Extracted from C.O.G. Miller's "Recollection of the Earthquake and Fire of April 1906," [undated], typewritten manuscript, Pacific Enterprises files.

20 Judith Elias, *Los Angeles: Dream to Reality, 1885-1915* (Northridge, Ca.: Santa Suzanna Press, 1983), pp. 33-35; Carey McWilliams, *Southern California Country: An Island on the Land* (N.Y.: Duell, Sloane, and Pearce, 1946), p. 135; C.O.G. Miller, "One Hundred Years of Gas Service: A Good Deal of History and a Little of Prophecy," p. 13; Oscar Winther, "The Rise of Metropolitan Los Angeles, 1870-1900," *Huntington Library Quarterly* 10 (Aug. 1947): 404-405.

21 Andrew F. Rolle, *California: A History* (3rd ed., Arlington Heights, Ill.: AHM Publishing Corporation, 1978), pp. 414-415.

22 C.A. Bartlett, "Gas Works Reminiscences," *L.A. Service Review* 1 (June 1, 1926): 12-14.

23 Gene Shepherd, "Wade Interview (Bowron)," typewritten manuscript, Nov. 5, 1962, historical files, Southern California Gas Company Research and Information Center.

24 *Los Angeles Daily Times,* Jan. 4, 1907.

25 See reports in the *Los Angeles Express,* Dec. 1906 - Jan. 1907.

26 Norman L. Hoff, "Historical Review of the Development of the Southern California Gas Company," typewritten manuscript, Feb. 2, 1939, historical files, Southern California Gas Company Research and Information Center.

27 Los Angeles Gas and Electric Company, "Important Information for Our Gas and Electric Consumers" [advertising brochure], 1907, file 1905-0002, historical files, Southern California Gas Company Research and Information Center; Robert M. Fogelson, *The Fragmented Metropolis: Los Angeles, 1850-1930* (Cambridge, Mass.: Harvard University Press, 1967), p. 232.

28 Stock ownership records, Pacific Enterprises files.

29 Van Rensselaer, "The Lamplighters," chap. 10, pp. 1-8.

30 Ibid., chap. 11, pp. 1-8.

31 Ibid., chap. 8, pp. 6-7.

32 Ibid., chap. 12, pp. 1-8.

33 Ibid.

34 Ibid.

35 Ibid.

36 C.O.G. Miller to the Stockholders of the Pacific Lighting Corporation, Feb. 10, 1914 [Annual Report], Pacific Enterprises files; Van Rensselaer, "The Lamplighters," chap. 13, pp. 1-15.

37 Van Rensselaer, "The Lamplighters," chap. 13, pp. 1-15.

NOTES TO CHAPTER THREE

1 Spencer C. Olin, Jr., *California's Prodigal Sons: Hiram Johnson and the Progressives, 1911-1917* (Berkeley: University of California Press, 1968), p. 192; Charles Coleman, *The P.G. and E. of California: The Centennial Story of the Pacific Gas and Electric Company, 1852-1952* (New York: McGraw-Hill, 1953), p. 36; *Los Angeles Daily Times,* Feb. 28, 1906; Robert M. Fogelson, *The Fragmented Metropolis: Los Angeles, 1850-1930* (Cambridge: Harvard University Press, 1967), pp. 230-231; "Los Angeles Politics, 1902-1906," box 55, John R. Haynes Collection (1241), Special Collections, University Research Library, University of California, Los Angeles, California; Norman L. Hoff, "History of Gas Rates, Los Angeles Gas and Electric Corporation," [March 28, 1934], historical files, Southern California Gas Company Research and Information Center, Los Angeles, California.

2 *Los Angeles Express,* Nov. 1, 1906.

3 *Los Angeles Express,* Dec. 1, 6, and 14, 1906; *Los Angeles Herald,* Nov. 6, 1908.

4 *Los Angeles Express,* Jan. 17, 1907; *Los Angeles Daily Times,* Jan. 4, 1907.

5 *Los Angeles Daily Times,* Feb. 14, 1907; *Los Angeles Express,* Feb. 13, 1907.

6 Olin, *California's Prodigal Sons,* p. 10; Walton S. Bean, *California: An Interpretive History* (New York: McGraw-Hill, 1968), pp. 312-318.

7 Fogelson, *Fragmented Metropolis,* p. 229.

8 See generally boxes 55 and 57, John R. Haynes Collection. See also Martin Schiesl, "Progressive Reform in Los Angeles under Mayor Alexander, 1909-1913," *California Historical Quarterly* 54 (1975): 40-43.

9 Fogelson, *Fragmented Metropolis,* pp. 232-234; Nelson Van Valen, "A Neglected Aspect of the Owens Valley Aqueduct: The Inception of the Los Angeles Municipal System," *Southern California Quarterly* 59 (1977): 92-93, 101-103.

10 Carey McWilliams, *Southern California Country: An Island on the Land* (New York: Duell, Sloan & Pearce, 1946), pp. 216-220; box 55, John R. Haynes Collection; F. J. Schafer, "Story of the Southern [California Gas Company]," [Southern California Gas Company] *Gas News* 2 (1925): 9; Schiesl, "Progressive Reform in Los Angeles," pp. 45-47.

11 C.O.G. Miller, "President's Address" in "Minutes of the Sixteenth Annual Meeting of the Pacific Coast Gas Association," Santa Cruz, Sept. 15-17, 1908, pp. 155-159.

12 Gerald Nash, "The California Railroad Commission, 1876-1911," *Southern California Quarterly* 44 (1962): 288, 289, 298, 301.

13 Eugene R. Hallett, comp., *Public Utilities Act of 1912* (San Francisco: Louis Sloss & Co., 1912), preface; Max Thelen, *Report . . . on Railroad and Public Service Commissions* (Sacramento: State of California, 1912); Nash, "The California Railroad Commission, 1876-1911," p. 301.

14 Norman L. Hoff, "Historical Review of the Development of the Southern California Gas Company," [Feb. 2, 1939], historical files, Southern California Gas Company Research and Information Center; Vincent Ostrom, *Water and Politics: A Study of Water Policies and Administration in the Development of Los Angeles* (Los Angeles: Haynes Foundation, 1953), p. 55.

15 Quoted in Fogelson, *The Fragmented Metropolis,* p. 232; Beatrice Dinerman and Winston Crouch, *The Southern California Metropolis: A Study in Development for a Metropolitan Area* (Berkeley: University of California Press, 1964), pp. 44-45.

16 Fogelson, *Fragmented Metropolis,* pp. 233, 245.

17 "Breakfast Deal," *Time* 29 (Feb. 15, 1937): 73-74; "Haynes Resume of Cases" in the "Los Angeles Gas and Electric Corporation" folder, box 147, John R. Haynes Collection; *Los Angeles Daily Times,* March 20, 1915.

18 Fogelson, *Fragmented Metropolis,* pp. 235-236.

19 James T. Van Rensselaer, "The Lamplighters," typewritten manuscript, 1967, chap. 16, pp. 1-18, historical files, Southern California Gas Company Research and Information Center.

20 "Haynes Resume of Cases" in "Los Angeles Gas and Electric Corporation" folder, box 147, John R. Haynes Collection; "Los Angeles — Department of Water and Power" folder, ibid.; "Los Angeles Gas and Electric Corporation — Rates" folder, box 118, ibid.; Van Rensselaer, "The Lamplighters," chap. 16, pp. 1-18.

21 "Department of Information: Why It is Needed and What It Tries To Do," [Southern California Gas Company] *Gas News* 2 (Nov. 1925): 17; ibid. 5 (Jan. 1928): 3; ibid. 6 (Feb. 1929): 11.

22 "Relations with Customers," [Southern California Gas Company] *Gas News* 4 (May 1927): 1-2. See also *L.A. Service Review*, vols. 1 (1926) to 7 (1933) and [Southern California Gas Company] *Gas News*, vols. 1 (1924) to 4 (1927).

23 "Bonds Defeated," [Southern California Gas Company] *Gas News* 7 (Oct. 1930): 15.

24 Van Rensselaer, "The Lamplighters," chap. 15, pp. 1-32; Dinerman and Crouch, *Southern California Metropolis*, pp. 44-45.

25 Robert W. Miller, "The Position of the Holding Company," *L.A. Service Review* 5 (July 1, 1931): 2-4.

26 Fogelson, *Fragmented Metropolis*, pp. 239-241.

27 "Haynes Resume of Cases" in "Los Angeles Gas and Electric Corporation" folder, box 147, John R. Haynes Collection; Ostrom, *Water and Politics*, pp. 208-209; "New Electric Rates in Effect," *L.A. Service Review* 3 (Nov. 1, 1928): 11.

28 "Court Gives Decision In Franchise Case," *L.A. Service Review* 6 (April 1, 1931): 6; "Los Angeles Gas and Electric Corporation" folder, box 147, John R. Haynes Collection; "Los Angeles Gas and Electric Corporation, Corporate History" folder, ibid.

29 "Department Heads Hear Bauer and Banks," [Southern California Gas Company] *Gas News* 9 (Dec. 1932): 7; "Public Ownership of Utilities," ibid. 8 (April 1931): 10.

30 "Electric Sale Refused," *Los Angeles Times,* Dec. 28, 1929.

31 "Department of Water and Power — Clippings" envelope, box 117, John R. Haynes Collection.

32 Joseph Gregg Layne, *Water and Power for a Great City* (Los Angeles: Department of Water and Power, 1957), p. 244.

33 F.J. Schafer, "Increasing Public Confidence," [Southern California Gas Company] *Gas News* 9 (March 1932): 18.

34 *Los Angeles Times,* July 21, 1934.

35 *Los Angeles Times,* Aug. 6, 1934. See also ibid., Aug. 2-4, 1934.

36 "Los Angeles Gas and Electric Corporation, Franchises" folder, box 147, John R. Haynes Collection.

37 "Los Angeles — Water and Power — Bonds — Election" folder, box 147, John R. Haynes Collection; "Los Angeles Gas and Electric — Haynes Corporate History" folder, box 138, ibid.

38 *End Poverty News* 1 (Feb. 1935): 4, copy in box 138, John R. Haynes Collection; "Los Angeles Gas and Electric Corporation, Franchises" folder, box 147, ibid.

39 W. Morton Jacobs, interview by Tanis C. Thorne, July 3, 1989, interview transcript, Pacific Enterprises files, Los Angeles, California.

40 *Power* [Published by the Municipal Light and Power Defense League] 5 (Dec. 7, 1936): passim, copy in historical files, Southern California Gas Company Research and Information Center.

41 "Breakfast Deal," pp. 73-74; Layne, *Water and Power for a Great City,* pp. 256-258.

NOTES TO CHAPTER FOUR

1 Pacific Lighting Corporation, *Annual Report of Pacific Lighting Corporation for the Year Ended December 31, 1936* (San Francisco: Taylor and Taylor, [1937]), p. 4.

2 "Local Listed Stocks, Pacific Lighting Corporation," unidentified clipping, [late 1936 or early 1937], copy in file 1955-0050, historical files, Southern California Gas Company Research and Information Center, Los Angeles, California.

3 James T. Van Rensselaer, "The Lamplighters," typewritten manuscript, 1967, chap. 15, pp. 1-32, historical files, Southern California Gas Company Research and Information Center.

4 Ibid.

5 Ibid.

6 "Commercial and Industrial Uses of Gas," [Southern California Gas Company] *Gas News* 1 (July 1924): 4; "Utility Rates," ibid. 4 (Feb. 1927): 1-2; "Recapitalization," ibid. 4 (April 1927), p. 8.

7 "Pages From History," [Southern Counties Gas Company] *Gas News* 2 (Oct. 12, 1943): 2; "Pages from History," ibid. 2 (Nov. 9, 1943): 2.

8 Van Rensselaer, "The Lamplighters," chap. 13, pp. 1-15.

9 Arlon Tussing and Connie Barlow, *The Natural Gas Industry* (Cambridge, Mass.: Ballinger, 1984), p. 13; E.J. Strickland, "Direct Mail Campaign — Heating," Sept. 29, 1937, copy in file 1935-0044, historical files, Southern California Gas Company Research and Information Center.

10 Van Rensselaer, "The Lamplighters," chap. 13, pp. 1-15.

11 "Pages from History," [Southern Counties Gas Company] *Gas News* 2 (Nov. 23, 1943): 2; H.L. Masser, "Natural Gas Production and Utilization in Southern California: Summary of Operations," *California Oil Fields* 8 (1923): 5-37 and passim.

12 Addison B. Day, "Growth of the Natural Gas Industry in Los Angeles," *California Journal of Development* 21 (Sept. 1931): 10-11.

13 "Pages from History," [Southern Counties Gas Company] *Gas News* 3 (Jan. 18, 1944): 2.

14 "Pages from History," ibid. 2 (Dec. 21, 1943): 2; "Pages from History," ibid. 3 (Jan. 1, 1944): 2; Southern Counties Gas Company, "Compliments — Southern Counties Gas Company," [n.d.], file 1925-0009, historical files, Southern California Gas Company Research and Information Center.

15 "Shifting the Load," *L.A. Gas Monthly* 2 (Feb. 1924): 1-2; Van Rensselaer, "Lamplighters," chap. 15, pp. 1-32.

16 Van Rensselaer, "Lamplighters," chap. 15, pp. 1-32.

17 *Los Angeles Gas and Electric Corporation: Its Properties and Operating Statistics,* copy in file 1920, historical files, Southern California Gas Company Research and Information Center.

18 Ibid.

19 "Making Gas Mains," [Southern California Gas Company] *Gas News* 1 (April, 1, 1924): 5.

20 Van Rensselaer, "The Lamplighters," chap. 15, pp. 1-32.

21 Ibid.

22 *Pacific Lighting Corporation: A Description of the History and Development of One of America's Oldest Utility Groups,* [1931], copy in file 1930-0004, historical files, Southern California Gas Company Research and Information Center.

23 "Southern California Gas Corporation," [Southern California Gas Company] *Gas News* 4 (Dec. 1927): 1; "Recapitalization and Analysis of Growth," ibid. 4 (Feb. 1927): 1-13; "Consolidation," ibid. 4 (Aug. 1927): 1-2; "Amalgamation," ibid. 4 (Nov. 1927): 4.

24 "Pacific Lighting in Big Merger," *L.A. Service Review* 4 (April 1, 1929): 10.

25 *Pacific Lighting Corporation*, p. 13.

26 Ibid., pp. 13, 32.

27 "Cheap Gas Boon for Industries," *Los Angeles Times,* Aug. 1, 1927; "New Gas Rates Held Unreasonable," *L.A. Service Review* 6 (Jan. 1, 1931): 12-13; "Gas Rate Cases Appealed to U.S. Supreme Court," ibid. 7 (July 1, 1932): 16; "Los Angeles Gas and Electric Corporation — Rates" folder, box 147, John R. Haynes Collection, Special Collections, University Research Library, University of California, Los Angeles, California.

28 Day, "Growth of the Natural Gas Industry in Los Angeles," pp. 10-11, 51; "How Public Utilities Overcome Depression," [Southern California Gas Company] *Gas News* 8 (Nov. 1931): 4.

29 "How Public Utilities Overcome Depression," [Southern California Gas Company] *Gas News* 8 (Nov. 1931): 4; "Natural Gas and Industry," ibid. 7 (Aug. 1930): 4; Van Rensselaer, "The Lamplighters," chap. 15, pp. 1-32.

30 "Department Heads Hear Bauer and Banks," [Southern California Gas Company] *Gas News* 9 (Dec. 1932): 5.

31 "May in History," [Southern California Gas Company] *Gas News* 8 (May 1931): 6; John William Ashley, "Some Economic Problems of the Natural Gas Industry," Ph.D. dissertation, University of California, Los Angeles, 1958, pp. 21-29.

32 H.P. George, "The Southern's Twenty Inch Pipe-Line from Kettleman Hills to Buena Vista Hills," [Southern California Gas Company] *Gas News* 7 (May 1930): 16-21; "New Pipe Line Project Organized," *L.A. Service Review* 6 (April 1, 1931): 11; Van Rensselaer, "The Lamplighters," chap. 17, p. 13.

33 Alfred M. Leeston, John A. Crichton, and John C. Jacobs, *The Dynamic Natural Gas Industry* (Norman: University of Oklahoma Press, 1988), pp. 8-10.

34 Tussing and Barlow, *The Natural Gas Industry*, pp. 25-28; "Department Head Meeting," [Southern California Gas Company] *Gas News* 8 (Jan. 1931): 14-17; "Southern Fuel Company Formed," ibid. 8 (Feb. 1931): 1.

35 Bound volumes of advertisements, 1930-1938, Marketing Department, Southern California Gas Company, Los Angeles, California.

36 "Los Angeles Gas and Electric Corporation Cost of Earthquakes of March and October 1933," [Sept. 17, 1935], file 1935-0010, historical files, Southern California Gas Company Research and Information Center; "Southern California Gas Company Flood Report — March 1938 — Northern Division," file 1935-0007, ibid.; "Emergency Proves 'Dependable Service,' " [Southern California Gas Company] *Gas News* 10 (April 1933): 8.

37 "Appliance Laboratory for Pacific Coast," *L.A. Service Review* 6 (April 1931): 5; W. Morton Jacobs, interview by Tanis C. Thorne, July 3, 1989, interview transcript, Pacific Enterprises files, Los Angeles, California.

38 C.O.G. Miller, "One Hundred Years of Gas Service: A Good Deal of History And a Little of Prophecy," Pacific Coast Gas Association, *Annual Report*, No.21 [1931], historical files, Southern California Gas Company Research and Information Center; "Southern's Progress Reviewed," [Southern California Gas Company] *Gas News* 8 (April 1931): 9.

39 W. Morton Jacobs, interview by Tanis C. Thorne, July 3, 1989, interview transcript, Pacific Enterprises files.

40 "Local Listed Stocks, Pacific Lighting Corporation," [Southern California Gas Company] *Gas News* 10 (Jan. 1933): 9.

41 Gary Kyle, "Public Utility Holding Company Act: Why, What and Where" [transcript of speech], Feb. 14, 1986, Pacific Enterprises files.

42 Van Rensselaer, "The Lamplighters," chap. 17, pp. 1-23.

NOTES TO CHAPTER FIVE

1 C.A. Bartlett, "Gas Works Reminiscences," *L.A. Service Review* 1 (June 1, 1926): 12; W.F. Spooner, "Our Equipment for Transportation," *L.A. Service Review* 1 (Sept. 1926): 8; F.J. Schafer, "Story of the Southern," [Southern California Gas Company] *Gas News* 1 (Nov. 1924): 3; ibid. 4 (April 1927): 11.

2 Charles Coleman, *The P.G. and E. of California: The Centennial Story of the Pacific Gas and Electric Company, 1852-1952* (New York:McGraw-Hill, 1953), pp. 280, 253.

3 Herbert C. Hoover, "Regulation," [Southern California Gas Company] *Gas News* 2 (Sept. 1925): 1-2.

4 "President's Address," Pacific Coast Gas Association, *Annual Report*, 1920, pp. 332, 335-336.

5 [President's Message], [Southern California Gas Company] *Gas News* 4 (Feb. 1927): 14-15.

6 Robert A. Hornby, "Notes on Southern California and Natural Gas," [Sept. 8, 1948], file 1945-0008, historical files, Southern California Gas Company Research and Information Center, Los Angeles, California.

7 Letter from William Baurhyte to employees, *L.A. Gas Monthly* 2 (Feb.-March 1924): 1.

8 *L.A. Gas Monthly* 1 (Jan. 1923): 7. Early employee publications included: *The Bunch* 1 (1922); *Gasometer* 1 (1923); *L.A. Gas Monthly* 1-3 (1923-1925); and *L.A. Service Review* 1-8 (1926-1933).

9 "Introducing the Southern and Midway *Gas News*," [Southern California Gas Company] *Gas News* 1 (Jan. 1924): 1.

10 H.B. Wells, "What Our Association Plans to Do," *L.A. Service Review* 1 (Sept. 1926): 4, 15.

11 "Employees Install New Officers," *L.A. Service Review* 2 (Sept. 1927): 3-4; William Baurhyte, "A Merry Christmas," ibid. 2 (Dec. 1927): 1.

12 J.C. (Jake) Cowan, interview by Bruce B. Harris, June 29, 1989, interview transcript, Pacific Enterprises files, Los Angeles, California; Robert M. McIntyre, interview by Tanis C. Thorne, July 11, 1989, interview transcript, ibid.

13 Los Angeles Gas and Electric Corporation, *Manual of Standard Practice for Regular Collectors*, [Jan. 20, 1925], pp. E1-E6, F1-F8, copy in file 1925-0021, historical files, Southern California Gas Company Research and Information Center.

14 Ibid.

15 Ibid.

16 "Addison B. Day Passes," [Southern California Gas Company] *Gas News* 16 (Nov. 1939): 2; "Breakfast Deal," *Time* 29 (Feb. 15, 1937): 73-74.

17 "Is Woman a Failure in Business?" [Southern California Gas Company] *Gas News* 5 (April 1928): 14.

18 Addison B. Day, "Why We Have a Women's Committee," *L.A. Service Review* 6 (Jan. 1931): 6-7.

19 "October Department Head Meeting," [Southern California Gas Company] *Gas News* 6 (Nov. 1929): 21.

20 Gladys B. Price, interview by Tanis C. Thorne, July 15, 1989, interview transcript, Pacific Enterprises files; [Southern California Gas Company] *Gas News* 9 (Jan. 1932): 8; ibid. 8 (Nov. 1931): 5.

21 Doncaster G. Humm and Guy W. Wadsworth, Jr., "The Humm-Wadsworth Temperament Scale," *Personnel Journal* 12 (1934): 314-323; Doncaster Humm and Guy Wadsworth, Jr., "The Humm-Wadsworth Temperament Scale," *American Journal of Psychiatry* 92 (July 1935): 163-200; James T. Van Rensselaer, "The Lamplighters," typewritten manuscript, 1967, chap. 17, p. 7, historical files, Southern California Gas Company Research and Information Center.

22 Los Angeles Gas and Electric Corporation, *Manual of Standard Practice*, passim.

23 "November Department Head Meeting," [Southern California Gas Company] *Gas News* 6 (Dec. 1929): 14-18; "Every Employee a Business Builder," ibid. 11 (Jan. 1934): 1-2.

24 [Report of Annual Stockholders' Meeting], *L.A. Service Review* 7 (Dec. 1932): 4.

25 J.S. Spaulding, "Mr. Burke's Radio Presentation," memo, Feb. 7, 1940, file 1940-0003, historical files, Southern California Gas Company Research and Information Center; Joan Bennet, "Evening Concert: Forty-four Years of a Little Night Music," [Southern California Gas Company] *Gas News* 43 (Feb. 1984): 2-3; "Waltz Ends at KFAC as New Crew Gears Up for Rock Format," *Los Angeles Times*, Sept. 20, 1989; "Evening Concert Program on KFAC to End," *Southern California Gas Management Newsletter* 21 (Sept. 5, 1989): 1.

26 Guy W. Wadsworth, Jr., "How to Pick the Men You Want," *Personnel Journal* 14 (March 1936): 330-335.

27 "Labor Board Hearing," [Southern California Gas Company] *Gas News* 15 (June 1938): 2-3.

28 "Equal Employment Opportunity Report No. 1," 1965, Human Resources Department files, Southern California Gas Company, Los Angeles, California; "SoCalGas Underutilization Report," Dec. 31, 1988, ibid.; "Workforce Control Report," Dec. 31, 1988, ibid.; "Affirmative Action: A Statementof Commitment and Accomplishments by the Southern California Gas Company — A Status Report," [1987], ibid.; "History of Pension, Disability and Life Insurance Plans of Pacific Lighting Companies," 1971, ibid.; *Gasco Retiree Times*, May 1989; "SoCalGas Announces New Service-Oriented Campaign," *Southern California Gas Management Newsletter*, 21 (Sept. 11, 1989); "Glad to be of Service!" [Southern California Gas Company] *Gas News* 48 (Sept. 21, 1989): 1.

29 Robert B. Young, "Summary of Union and Company Negotiations, 1938-1955," [Jan. 1, 1955], part 1, Human Resources Department files, Southern California Gas Company.

30 Robert B. Young, "Labor Relations Training Package," [Jan. 1, 1966], Human Resources Department files, Southern California Gas Company; *Light* [Utility Workers Union of America, AFL-CIO, Convention Issue], Southern California Gas Company Research and Information Center.

31 Southern Counties Gas Company, *Supervisor's Rating Manual*, [Dec. 31, 1939], pp. 4, 7, file 1935-0003, historical files, Southern California Gas Company Research and Information Center.

32 Robert A. Hornby, "Notes on Southern California and Natural Gas" [Sept. 8, 1948], file 1945-0008, historical files, Southern California Gas Company Research and Information Center; "P.C.G.A. Honor Awards," [Southern California Gas Company] *Gas News* 18 (Sept. 1941): 16; Marjorie A. Harden, telephone interview by Tanis C. Thorne, Aug. 7, 1989.

33 "Gas Company Rejects Union Strike Threat," *Los Angeles Times*, April 8, 1950; "Gas Workers Due Back Monday as Strike Ends," ibid., April 10, 1953.

34 Sam Weinstein, interview by Tanis C. Thorne, July 18, 1989; Howard Everett, telephone interview by Tanis C. Thorne, Aug. 7, 1989; "Company Offers Savings Plan — Union-SCPEA Negotiations to Continue," [Southern California Gas Company] *Gas News* 23 (Feb. 1964): 1-2.

NOTES TO CHAPTER SIX

1 "If You Are 'In the Draft,'" [Southern California Gas Company] *Gas News* 17 (Oct. 1, 1940): 12; James T. Van Rensselaer, "The Lamplighters," typewritten manuscript, 1967, chap. 18, pp. 1-26, historical files, Southern California Gas Company Research and Information Center, Los Angeles, California.

2 "Women's Activities," unidentified clipping, [1940?], file 1940-0007, historical files, Southern California Gas Company Research and Information Center; Van Rensselaer, "The Lamplighters," chap. 18, pp. 1-26.

3 Gerald Adams, [no title], *San Francisco Examiner*, Sept. 13, 1964; Herb Caen, [no title], *San Francisco Chronicle*, undated clipping, Miller Family Collection, Pacific Enterprises, Los Angeles, California.

4 "Our Boys In Uniform," [Southern California Gas Company] *Gas News* 1 (Aug. 1, 1942): 4-5, 13; "Office and Home," ibid., 4 (Aug. 1, 1945): 14; Pacific Lighting Corporation, *The Big Potato*, June 1944, file 1940-0016, historical files, Southern California Gas Company Research and Information Center.

5 F.M. Banks, "Voluntary Conservation of Natural Gas," [Southern California Gas Company] *Gas News* 2 (July 1, 1943): 3.

6 "Rush Order! Cooked by Gas!" [advertisement, 1942?], file 1940, historical files, Southern California Gas Company Research and Information Center.

7 See for example, "Gas Shut Off from 100 'Non-Essential' Firms," *San Bernardino Telegram*, Dec. 29, 1943; "Natural Gas Supply in County Curtailed," *Santa Ana Register*, Dec. 30, 1943; "Gas Shut-Off Cripples Many Local Plants," *Riverside News*, Dec. 30, 1943; F.M. Banks to Barbara Ann Baking Company, Dec. 16, 1941, file 1940-0015, historical files, Southern California Gas Company Research and Information Center.

8 "Cash for Tire Saving Suggestions," [Southern California Gas Company] *Gas News* 1 (Jan. 1, 1942): 3; "If Bombs Should Fall — Here!" ibid. 2 (March 1, 1943): 4; "We Work for Victory," ibid. 5 (July 1, 1944): 3.

9 J.C. (Jake) Cowan, interview by Bruce B. Harris, June 29, 1989, interview transcript, Pacific Enterprises files; "Holder Marks Sky Highway," *Gas News Pictorial*, Dec. 31, 1947.

10 Harvey A. Proctor, interview by Douglas R. Littlefield, July 13, 1989, interview transcript, Pacific Enterprises files; Van Rensselaer, "The Lamplighters," chap. 18, pp. 1-26.

11 "City Hunting for Source of 'Gas Attack,'" *Los Angeles Times*, July 27, 1943.

12 City Council Minutes, Aug. 11, 1943, Los Angeles City Archives, Los Angeles, California.

13 Ibid.; "Relief from Gas Fumes Promised in December," *Los Angeles Times*, Sept. 15, 1943.

14 Harvey A. Proctor, interview by Douglas R. Littlefield, July 13, 1989, interview transcript, Pacific Enterprises files; "Action Planned to End City's 'Gas Attacks,'" *Los Angeles Times*, Sept. 21, 1943; "City Files Suit to Halt Fumes From Aliso St. Rubber Plant," ibid., Oct. 19, 1943; City Council Minutes, Oct. 22, 1943, Los Angeles City Archives.

15 Harvey A. Proctor, interview by Douglas R. Littlefield, July 13, 1989, interview transcript, Pacific Enterprises files; "Action Planned to End City's 'Gas Attacks,'" *Los Angeles Times*, Sept. 21, 1943; "City Files Suit to Halt Fumes From Aliso St. Rubber Plant," ibid., Oct. 19, 1943; City Council Minutes, Oct. 22, 1943, Los Angeles City Archives.

16 Harvey A. Proctor, interview by Douglas R. Littlefield, July 13, 1989, interview transcript, Pacific Enterprises files; "$73,000,000 Synthetic Rubber Industry of Southland Deflating," *Los Angeles Times*, Aug. 10, 1947.

17 Charles Coleman, *The P.G. and E. of California; The Centennial Story of the Pacific Gas and Electric Company, 1852-1952* (New York: McGraw-Hill, 1953), pp. 306, 333; "A Short History of the Southern California Gas Company (1867-1954)" [report, 1954?], file 1950-0004, historical files, Southern California Gas Company Research and Information Center.

18 Harvey A. Proctor, interview by Douglas R. Littlefield, July 13, 1989, interview transcript, Pacific Enterprises files; "Goleta's Gas: California Uses Nature's Underground 'Tank' to Store Surplus Fuel," *Wall Street Journal*, June 14, 1944; "Huge Pipeline to Solve Gas Problems of Los Angeles Nears End of Long Journey," *Los Angeles Daily News*, Jan. 10, 1945; "Highest Pressure Gas Line," *Western Construction News*, Jan. 1945, pp. 79-166; "Gas Companies Finish Pipe Line," *Los Angeles Times*, April 23, 1945.

19 J.H. Northrop Ellis, interview by Bruce B. Harris, July 12, 1989, interview transcript, Pacific Enterprises files; Harvey A. Proctor, interview by Douglas R. Littlefield, July 13, 1989, interview transcript, ibid.; "A Short History of the Southern California Gas Company (1867-1954)" [report, 1954?], file 1950-0004, historical files, Southern California Gas Company Research and Information Center.

20 Van Rensselaer, "The Lamplighters," chap. 19, pp. 1-18.

21 F.S. Wade, "Background Memo for Division and District Managers from F.S. Wade, President," 1945, file 1945-0028, historical files, Southern California Gas Company Research and Information Center; "Gas Shortage May Curtail Plants," [Monrovia, California] *News-Post*, May 28, 1947; Van Rensselaer, "The Lamplighters," chap. 19, pp. 1-18.

22 W.M. Jacobs, interview by Tanis C. Thorne, July 3, 1989, interview transcript, Pacific Enterprises files; "Gas — The West's Vital Domestic and Industrial Fuel and the Related Appliance Industry," *The Goodall News*, April 30, 1952; Van Rensselaer, "The Lamplighters," chap. 19, pp. 1-18.

23 "Cal.-Tex. Gas Line Planned," *Los Angeles Examiner*, Oct. 14, 1944; "Gas Pipe Line from Texas Oil Fields Planned," *Los Angeles Times*, Oct. 14, 1944; "Gas Pipeline Approval Sought," *Redlands Facts*, Oct. 14, 1944; "1000 Mile Long Gasline May Aid So. Calif." *Los Angeles Daily News*, Oct. 14, 1944; "Texas Gas to be Piped Overland to California," *San Bernardino Sun*, Oct. 15, 1944.

24 "Early Completion of Pipeline Seen," [Tulare, California] *Bee*, Aug. 22, 1947; Van Rensselaer, "The Lamplighters," chap. 19, pp. 1-18.

25 "Opinion and Order," *Opinions and Orders of the Public Utilities Commission* 47 (Aug. 26, 1947): 417-422; Van Rensselaer, "The Lamplighters," chap. 19, pp. 1-18.

26 "Opinion and Order," *Federal Power Commission Reports* 5 (May 31, 1946): 115; *Public Utilities Fortnightly* 38 (Nov. 7, 1946): 602-609; ibid. 38 (Oct. 10, 1946): 499-500; Dahl M. Duff, "FPC Approves Record-Size Texas California Pipe Line," *Oil and Gas Journal* 45 (June 15, 1946): 76; "Section to Be Storage Tank," [Redlands, California] *Facts*, Sept. 11, 1947; "Biggest Inch Finished," [Southern California Gas Company] *Gas News* 6 (Oct. 7, 1947): 1; "Gas Now Being Delivered Thru 1200 Mile Line," [Indio, California] *News*, Nov. 6, 1947; "First Texas Gas is Here," *Los Angeles Times*, Nov. 14, 1947.

27 "Federal Government Approves 1200-Mile Gas Pipeline" [advertisement, 1946], file 1940-0013, historical files, Southern California Gas Company Research and Information Center; "'Biggest Inch' Line is Laid 1000 Miles Across Desert," [Blythe, California] *Palo Verde Times*, May 8, 1947.

28 "Engineers Overcome Many Difficulties in Construction of Huge Gas Pipe Line," [Banning, California] *Record*, July 3, 1947; "$25,000 Payroll a Week Here by Building Gas Line," [Corona, California] *Independent*, July 29, 1947.

29 Russell E. Ward, "*Gas News* Interviews Robert W. Miller," [Southern Counties Gas Company] *Gas News* 17 (Sept. 23, 1958): 1; Robert A. Hornby, "Pacific Lighting Corporation: 73 and Still Growing" [booklet], Nov. 10, 1959, file 1955-0006, historical files, Southern California Gas Company Research and Information Center.

30 W.M. Jacobs, interview by Tanis C. Thorne, July 3, 1989, interview transcript, Pacific Enterprises files; "Completion of Transwestern Pipeline Adds 25% to Southern California Gas Supplies," *Gas Age*, Dec. 22, 1960.

31 Pacific Lighting Corporation, "Pacific Lighting Corporation and Subsidiaries; Selected Statistical Information" [report, 1964], file 1940-0005, historical files, Southern California Gas Company Research and Information Center; J. Fred Ebdon, "The Pacific Lighting System," *Gas: The Nation's Natural Gas Authority*, Aug. 1958; "Gas Company Installs Its Millionth Meter," *Kings County News*, March 4, 1948.

32 Van Rensselaer, "The Lamplighters," chap. 20, pp. 1-23.

33 Charles T. Dierker, interview by Douglas R. Littlefield, July 13, 1989, interview transcript, Pacific Enterprises files; W.M. Jacobs, interview by Tanis C. Thorne, July 3, 1989, interview transcript, Pacific Enterprises files; "Prospect Campaign

Proves Popular," [Southern California Gas Company] *Gas News* 7 (July 6, 1948): 1; Southern Counties Gas Company, "Indoctrination Course" [booklet, 1948], file 1945-0010, historical files, Southern California Gas Company Research and Information Center.

34 John C. Abram, interview by Tanis C. Thorne, Aug. 5, 1989, interview transcript, Pacific Enterprises files; Charles T. Dierker, interview by Douglas R. Littlefield, July 13, 1989, interview transcript, Pacific Enterprises files; W.M. Jacobs, interview by Tanis C. Thorne, July 3, 1989, interview transcript, Pacific Enterprises files; "Prospect Campaign Proves Popular," [Southern California Gas Company] *Gas News* 7 (July 6, 1948): 1.

35 Pacific Lighting Corporation, "Pacific Lighting Corporation and Subsidiaries; Selected Statistical Information" [booklet, 1964], file 1940-0005, historical files, Southern California Gas Company Research and Information Center; J. Fred Ebdon, "The Pacific Lighting System," *Gas: The Nation's Natural Gas Authority,* Aug. 1958.

36 Charles T. Dierker, interview by Douglas R. Littlefield, July 13, 1989, interview transcript, Pacific Enterprises files; Southern California Gas and Southern Counties Gas companies, "The Future of Natural Gas for Industry in Southern California" [booklet, 1946], file 1945-0004, historical files, Southern California Gas Company Research and Information Center.

37 Southern California Gas Company, "Some Facts about . . . Growth, Inflation, & Gas Costs" [booklet, 1953?], file 1950-0006, historical files, Southern California Gas Company Research and Information Center.

38 Pacific Lighting Corporation, *1950 Annual Report,* p. 5.

39 Southern California Gas Company, "Some Facts about . . . Growth, Inflation, & Gas Costs" [booklet, 1953?], file 1950-0006, historical files, Southern California Gas Company Research and Information Center.

40 City Council Minutes, Dec. 30, 1952, Nov. 1, 1954, April 1, 1955, Los Angeles City Archives; "Opinion and Order," *Opinions and Orders of the Public Utilities Commission* 54 (April 19, 1955): 131-141; W.M. Jacobs, "Our Public Relations Program," [Southern California Gas Company] *Gas News* 12 (Sept. 1, 1953): 3; "New 'Aid' Program Opens," ibid. 12 (Oct. 30, 1953): 1.

41 John C. Abram, interview by Tanis C. Thorne, Aug. 5, 1989, interview transcript, Pacific Enterprises; W.M. Jacobs, interview by Tanis C. Thorne, July 3, 1989, interview transcript, Pacific Enterprises files; A.F. Bridge, "What Every Employee Should Know About Our New Rates" [booklet, 1953?], file 1950-0007, historical files, Southern California Gas Company Research and Information Center; Southern California Gas Company, "A Guide to Better Public Relations" [booklet, 1959], file 1955-0018, ibid.; Walter Herrman, "Sell the Gas Rate Increase," [Southern California Gas Company] *Gas News* 10 (Aug. 1, 1951): 2.

42 W.M. Jacobs, interview by Tanis C. Thorne, July 3, 1989, interview transcript, Pacific Enterprises files; " 'Enchilada Inch' Announced, Faces Fight," *Southern Counties Gas Memo to Management,* Sept. 26, 1960; "Gas, Electric Rates Seen Tied to Pipeline," *Los Angeles Times,* Oct. 28, 1964; Richard L. Vanderveld, "Explosive Natural Gas Battle Comes to Head," ibid., March 28, 1965; Richard Austin Smith, "They Play Rough in the Gas Business," *Fortune* 73 (Jan. 1966): 132-135; "Opinion and Order," *Federal Power Commission Reports* 36 (July 26, 1966): 177-307.

43 Robert A. Hornby, "Pacific Lighting Corporation: 73 and Still Growing" [booklet], Nov. 10, 1959, file 1955-0006, historical files, Southern California Gas Company Research and Information Center.

44 Van Rensselaer, "The Lamplighters," chap. 20, pp. 1-23.

45 Ibid.

46 *Phillips Petroleum Company vs. State of Wisconsin, et al.,* 347 U.S. 671 (1953).

47 Pacific Lighting Corporation, *Annual Report for 1965,* pp. 1-7.

NOTES TO CHAPTER SEVEN

1 W.M. Jacobs, interview by Tanis C. Thorne, July 3, 1989, interview transcript, Pacific Enterprises files, Los Angeles, California.

2 Pacific Lighting Corporation, *Annual Report for 1970,* p. 9.

3 "Here's A New Mark For The Record Books," *Southern California Gas Company Management News Letter* 4 (Aug. 26, 1957): 1.

4 Gene Shepherd, "Wade Interview (Bowron)," typewritten manuscript, Nov. 5, 1962, historical files, Southern California Gas Company Research and Information Center, Los Angeles, California.

5 Robert A. Hornby, "Pacific Lighting Corporation: 73 and Still Growing" [booklet], Nov. 10, 1959, file 1955-0006, historical files, Southern California Gas Company Research and Information Center.

6 "GasCo, El Paso Pact Will Bring In Canada Gas," [Southern California Gas Company] *Gas News* 16 (Aug. 6, 1957): 1; Robert A. Hornby, "Pacific Lighting Corporation: 73 and Still Growing" [booklet], Nov. 10, 1959, file 1955-0006, historical files, Southern California Gas Company Research and Information Center.

7 Biographical and obituary file, Southern California Gas Company Research and Information Center.

8 W. Morton Jacobs to Lee C. White, Dec. 16, 1968, as cited in "A Distributor Looks at Gas Requirements and Supply," address delivered by W. Morton Jacobs at the 10th Annual Institute on Exploration and Economics of the Petroleum Industry, held at the International Oil and Gas Education Center, Dallas, Texas, March 5, 1970.

9 Pacific Lighting Corporation, *Annual Report for 1972,* p. 5.

10 Pacific Lighting Corporation, *Annual Report for 1973,* p. 14.

11 "Gulf Gas Contract Called 'Significant,' " [Southern California Gas Company] *Gas News* 31 (Dec. 19, 1972): 1; Harry L. Lepape, interview by Douglas R. Littlefield, July 14, 1989, interview transcript, Pacific Enterprises files.

12 "Polar Gas: Natural Gas from the Arctic Islands" [promotional booklet, 1978?], Pacific Enterprises files; "North Slope Gas Decision Advances in Canada, U.S.," [Southern California Gas Company] *Gas News* 36 (May 17, 1977): 1; Pacific Lighting Corporation, *Annual Report for 1976,* p. 11.

13 Harry L. Lepape, interview by Douglas R. Littlefield, July 14, 1989, interview transcript, Pacific Enterprises files; Harvey A. Proctor, interview by Douglas R. Littlefield, July 13, 1989, ibid.; Northwest Alaskan Pipeline Company, "Alaska Natural Gas Transportation System" [map], 1981, Pacific Enterprises files; Pacific Lighting Corporation, *Annual Report for 1976,* pp. 10-11.

14 Harry L. Lepape, interview by Douglas R. Littlefield, July 14, 1989, interview transcript, Pacific Enterprises files; Harvey A. Proctor, interview by Douglas R. Littlefield, July 13, 1989, ibid.; Northwest Alaskan Pipeline Company, "Alaska Natural Gas Transportation System," [map], 1981, Pacific Enterprises files; Pacific Lighting Corporation, *Annual Report for 1976,* pp. 10-11.

15 "LNG: Today's Link with Tomorrow's Energy" [booklet, 1979?], Pacific Enterprises files; Robert A. Hornby, "Pacific Lighting Corporation: 73 and Still Growing" [booklet], Nov. 10, 1959, file 1955-0006, historical files, Southern California Gas Company Research and Information Center.

16 Robert A. Rosenblatt, "Pacific Lighting Set to Develop Supplies of Fuel in Australia," *Los Angeles Times,* June 30, 1972; "Local Utility Asks for Right to Import Gas," ibid., Dec. 1, 1973; "Pacific Lighting Seeks to Build $140 Million Liquid Gas Plant," ibid., Feb. 16, 1974.

17 Jeffery Raimundo, "LNG: Where, When and Why?" *Sierra Club Bulletin* 63 (June 1978): 35-39.

18 John Hurst, "Indians, LNG Firm Open Negotiations," *Los Angeles Times,* May 14, 1978; Michael Seiler, "Indians 'Ready to Die' to Block LNG Plant," ibid., July 10, 1978; Graham L. Jones, "Indians Occupy Site of Disputed LNG Terminal," ibid., Nov. 1, 1979; "Indian Protest on LNG Terminal Fails," ibid., July 3, 1980.

19 Jeffery Raimundo, "LNG: Where, When and Why?" pp. 35-39.

20 " '60 Minutes' Probes the LNG Issues," [Southern California Gas Company] *Gas News* 36 (May 3, 1977): 3.

21 "Decision," in *Decisions of the Public Utilities Commission,* vol. 9, CPUC 2nd, p. 736.

22 Michael Paprian, "Reprieve for Point Conception," *Sierra Club Bulletin* 68 (March 1, 1983): 46-48.

23 "PUC Issues LNG Decision," [Southern California Gas Company] *Gas News* 43 (Sept. 11, 1984): 1.

24 Harvey A. Proctor, interview by Douglas R. Littlefield, July 13, 1989, interview transcript, Pacific Enterprises files; Robert A. Hornby, "Pacific Lighting Corporation: 73 and Still Growing" [booklet], Nov. 10, 1959, file 1955-0006, historical files, Southern California Gas Company Research and Information Center.

25 "Synthetic Gas Project Using New Mexico Coal Set by Three Concerns," *Wall Street Journal*, Oct. 28, 1971; "Gasification Project May Yield New Supplies," [Southern California Gas Company] *Gas News* 30 (Nov. 9, 1971): 1; "Pacific Lighting's President Urges Cooperation on 'Gasifying' Coal," *Los Angeles Times*, June 20, 1972.

26 "Navajos Figure Prominently in Plant Plans," [Southern California Gas Company] *Gas News* 32 (Feb. 27, 1973): 1.

27 Ibid.

28 Robert M. McIntyre, interview by Tanis C. Thorne, July 11, 1989, interview transcript, Pacific Enterprises files; "Advertising Campaign Stresses Critical Supply Story," [Southern California Gas Company] *Gas News* 34 (Sept. 23, 1975): 1.

29 Paul A. Miller, as quoted by J. Foster Hames to Douglas R. Littlefield, September 27, 1989.

30 Pacific Lighting Corporation, *1978 Annual Report*, p. 7; "Inflated Labor, Operating Costs Spur Rate Increase Request," [Southern California Gas Company] *Gas News* 30 (May 25, 1971): 3; Robert A. Rosenblatt, "Gas Shortage Real or a Rate Gambit?" *Los Angeles Times*, April 16, 1972.

31 "Customer Support Program," [Southern California Gas Company] *Gas News* 43 (Dec. 18, 1984): 1; "Residential Customers Face Higher Bills," Ibid. 45 (Oct. 23, 1986): 1; "Operation Cope," Ibid. 41 (Nov. 1, 1982): 1.

32 Paul A. Miller, interview by Douglas R. Littlefield, Edwin J. Perkins, and Tanis C. Thorne, July 11, 1989, interview transcript, Pacific Enterprises files; Joseph R. Rensch, interview by Tanis C. Thorne, July 13, 1989, interview transcript, ibid.; James R. Ukropina, interview by Douglas R. Littlefield and Edwin J. Perkins, July 12, 1989, interview transcript, ibid.

33 Paul A. Miller, interview by Douglas R. Littlefield, Edwin J. Perkins, and Tanis C. Thorne, July 11, 1989, interview transcript, Pacific Enterprises files; Joseph R. Rensch, interview by Tanis C. Thorne, July 13, 1989, interview transcript, ibid.

34 "Air Conditioning Sales Boom," [Southern California Gas Company] *Gas News* 19 (March 29, 1960): 1.

35 Charles T. Dierker, interview by Douglas R. Littlefield, July 13, 1989, interview transcript, Pacific Enterprises files; "Area Gas Company to Build Air Conditioning Units," *Los Angeles Times*, Feb. 8, 1963; "Two New Pacific Lighting Subsidiaries Announced," *Southern Counties Memo to Management*, April 8, 1963; "Century City, the 180-Acre City Within a City," ibid., Aug. 31, 1964.

36 Charles T. Dierker, interview by Douglas R. Littlefield, July 13, 1989, interview transcript, Pacific Enterprises files.

37 "Four Hawaiian Firms Acquired in PLC Diversification Program," [Southern California Gas Company] *Gas News* 29 (Sept. 15, 1970): 1; "Pacific Lighting Decides to Buy Hawaii Developer," *Wall Street Journal*, July 3, 1969.

38 "Pacific Lighting Votes To Buy Two Concerns," *Wall Street Journal*, Dec. 4, 1969; "Dunn Formula Results in Growth," [Southern California Gas Company] *Gas News* 29 (March 3, 1970): 1; "Fredricks Development Travels the Road to Success," ibid. 29 (May 26, 1970): 1; Pacific Lighting Corporation, *1984 Annual Report*, p. 32.

39 Paul A. Miller, interview by Douglas R. Littlefield, Edwin J. Perkins, and Tanis C. Thorne, July 11, 1989, interview transcript, Pacific Enterprises files; James R. Ukropina, interview by Douglas R. Littlefield and Edwin J. Perkins, July 12, 1989, interview transcript, ibid.; Willis B. Wood, Jr., interview by Edwin J. Perkins and Tanis C. Thorne, July 11, 1989, interview transcript, ibid.

40 Charles T. Dierker, interview by Douglas R. Littlefield, July 13, 1989, interview transcript, Pacific Enterprises files; Paul A. Miller, interview by Douglas R. Littlefield, Edwin J. Perkins, and Tanis C. Thorne, July 11, 1989, interview transcript, ibid.

41 "The Sun Rises on the Future of Solar Energy," [Southern California Gas Company] *Gas News* 37 (May 16, 1978): 2; "Solar Water-Heater Program Is Unveiled By California; Utilities to Aid Financing," *Wall Street Journal*, Sept. 17, 1980.

42 Charles T. Dierker, interview by Douglas R. Littlefield, July 13, 1989, interview transcript, Pacific Enterprises files; "Pacific Lighting, Firm to Build Power Plant," *Wall Street Journal*, March 8, 1983.

43 Harry L. Lepape, interview by Douglas R. Littlefield, July 14, 1989, interview transcript, Pacific Enterprises files; Paul A. Miller, interview by Douglas R. Littlefield, Edwin J. Perkins, and Tanis C. Thorne, July 12, 1989, interview transcript, ibid.

44 Harry L. Lepape, interview by Douglas R. Littlefield, July 14, 1989, interview transcript, Pacific Enterprises files; Paul A. Miller, interview by Douglas R. Littlefield, Edwin J. Perkins, and Tanis C. Thorne, July 12, 1989, interview transcript,

ibid.; James R. Ukropina, interview by Douglas R. Littlefield and Edwin J. Perkins, July 12, 1989, interview transcript, ibid.; "Pacific Lighting To Buy Concern For $300 Million," *Wall Street Journal*, June 30, 1983; Donald Woutat, "Pacific Enterprises Plans to Buy Texas Oil Firm for $339 Million," *Los Angeles Times*, March 26, 1988.

45 Harry L. Lepape, interview by Douglas R. Littlefield, July 14, 1989, interview transcript, Pacific Enterprises files; Paul A. Miller, interview by Douglas R. Littlefield, Edwin J. Perkins, and Tanis C. Thorne, July 12, 1989, interview transcript, ibid.; James R. Ukropina, interview by Douglas R. Littlefield and Edwin J. Perkins, July 12, 1989, interview transcript, ibid.; "Pacific Lighting To Buy Concern For $300 Million," *Wall Street Journal*, June 30, 1983; Donald Woutat, "Pacific Enterprises Plans to Buy Texas Oil Firm for $339 Million," *Los Angeles Times*, March 26, 1988.

46 G. Christian Hile, " 'Exempt' Utility Holding Companies' Right to Diversify is Subject of SEC Inquest," *Wall Street Journal*, Nov. 22, 1971.

47 Ibid.

48 "An Analytical Look at the SEC Case," [Southern California Gas Company] *Gas News* 30 (Nov. 23, 1971): 2.

49 Leonard H. Straus, interview by Douglas R. Littlefield, July 14, 1989, interview transcript, Pacific Enterprises files; James R. Ukropina, interview by Edwin J. Perkins and Douglas R. Littlefield, July 12, 1989, ibid.; Thrifty Corporation, "A History of the Thrifty Corporation," supplement contained in *1979 Annual Report: Thrifty Corporation;* John M. Broder, "Pacific Lighting Planned at Length and Acted Quickly," *Los Angeles Times*, May 30, 1986; "Pacific Lighting Officially Acquired Thrifty," ibid., Aug. 6, 1986.

50 Harvey A. Proctor, interview by Douglas R. Littlefield, July 13, 1989, interview transcript, Pacific Enterprises files; John Heins, "Haywire," *Forbes* 142 (Oct. 3, 1988): 52-54; Rhonda L. Rundle, "Pacific Lighting's Plan to Buy Thrifty Draws Little Enthusiasm from Many Shareholders," *Wall Street Journal*, June 2, 1986.

51 James R. Ukropina, interview by Douglas R. Littlefield and Edwin J. Perkins, July 12, 1989, interview transcript, Pacific Enterprises files.

52 "Killer Quake," [Oakland] *Tribune*, Oct. 18, 1989; "Future Shock," ibid., Dec. 5, 1989; Everett O. Byrd and Robert A. Wise, interview by Douglas R. Littlefield, Oct. 18, 1989, interview transcript, Pacific Enterprises files; "P.E. Employees Play Role in Bay Area Earthquake Relief," *Special Spectrum*, Oct. 31, 1989; "SoCalGas Assists PG & E in Restoring Service after Major Temblor," *Management News Letter* 21 (Oct. 23, 1989): 1; F.A. Bernal memo to J. Foster Hames on the "History of the Mutual Assistance Agreements," Nov. 9, 1989, Pacific Enterprises files; Mutual Assistance Agreement between Southern California Gas Company, Pacific Gas and Electric Company, and San Diego Gas & Electric, Feb. 4, 1988, ibid.

53 Paul A. Miller, interview by Douglas R. Littlefield, Edwin J. Perkins, and Tanis C. Thorne, July 12, 1989, interview transcript, Pacific Enterprises files; James R. Ukropina, interview by Douglas R. Littlefield and Edwin J. Perkins, July 12, 1989, interview transcript, ibid.; John M. Broder, "Pacific Lighting Planned at Length and Acted Quickly," *Los Angeles Times*, May 30, 1986; "Pacific Lighting Officially Acquired Thrifty," ibid., Aug. 6, 1986.

54 Paul A. Miller, interview by Douglas R. Littlefield, Edwin J. Perkins, and Tanis C. Thorne, July 12, 1989, interview transcript, Pacific Enterprises files; Leonard H. Straus, interview by Douglas R. Littlefield, July 14, 1989, interview transcript, ibid.; James R. Ukropina, interview by Douglas R. Littlefield and Edwin J. Perkins, July 12, 1989, interview transcript, ibid.; John M. Broder, "Pacific Lighting Planned at Length and Acted Quickly," *Los Angeles Times*, May 30, 1986; "Pacific Lighting Officially Acquired Thrifty," ibid., Aug. 6, 1986.

55 James R. Ukropina, interview by Douglas R. Littlefield and Edwin J. Perkins, July 12, 1989, interview transcript, Pacific Enterprises files.

56 Nancy Rivera Brooks, "Pacific Lighting Adopts Name to Reflect Diversity," *Los Angeles Times*, Feb. 15, 1988.

Credits for Photos and Illustrations

American Gas Association: 30 (bottom right).
Bancroft Library, University of California, Berkeley: 38-39.
California Historical Quarterly: 55 (bottom).
California Historical Society: 8 (bottom), 10 (right), 67.
California State Library: 15 (top).
El Paso Natural Gas Company: 123 (bottom).
Forbes magazine archives: 21 (top).
Gas Engineer's Pocket Almanac: 19 (bottom).
Industrial Los Angeles County: 89.
L.A. Gas Monthly: 60.
Littlefield, Douglas R.: 124 (bottom).
Los Angeles City Archives: 13 (bottom), 16.
Los Angeles Department of Water and Power: 57, 65.
Los Angeles Record: 43 (top).
Los Angeles Times: 52.
Maguire Thomas Partners: 143, 175 (top).
Norman, Oscar Edward, *Romance of the Gas Industry*: 18.
Out West Magazine: 30 (top right).
Pacific Enterprises: title page, x, 7, 8 (top), 9, 10 (left), 11 (center and bottom), 13 (top), 37 (top), 44 (bottom), 45 (top), 64, 75, 94-95, 124 (top), 131 (bottom), 145 (bottom), 148, 150, 151 (bottom), 156 (top), 159, 163, 168 (top right, middle right, and middle left), 174, 175 (bottom), 176.
Pacific Enterprises Leasing Co.: 162.
Pacific Enterprises Oil Company: 169 (middle).
Pacific Offshore Pipeline Company: 166 (top), 167.
Pasadena Historical Society: 26 (bottom), 30 (middle left), 32 (middle).

Peter R. Antheil Collection: 23, 26 (top), 37 (bottom).
Sabine Corporation: 166 (bottom).
Saturday Evening Post: 100 (bottom).
Seaver Center for Western History Research, Los Angeles County Museum of Natural History: 14.
Security Pacific Historical Photograph Collection, Los Angeles Public Library: 15 (bottom), 30 (top left), 33 (top), 40, 55 (top), 56, 73.
[Southern California Gas Company] *Gas News*: 102, 103, 105 (bottom), 111 (middle and bottom), 115 (top), 122 (top), 125 (middle), 139, 140 (bottom).
Southern California Gas Company: cover, 12, 17, 20 (top), 20-21 (bottom), 24, 25, 27 (top), 31 (top), 32 (top and bottom), 33 (bottom), 34-36, 42, 43 (bottom), 44 (top), 45 (bottom), 46-49, 51, 53, 54, 58, 61-63, 71, 74, 76-84, 86-88, 90-93, 97-99, 100 (top), 101 (top and middle), 104 (top and bottom), 105 (top and middle), 107-110, 111 (top), 112-114, 115 (bottom), 116, 118-121, 122 (bottom), 123 (top), 125 (top and bottom), 126, 128-130, 131 (top), 133-136, 140 (top), 141, 144, 145 (top), 146, 149, 151 (top), 152-155, 156 (bottom), 157, 158, 160, 161, 164, 165, 169 (top), 173.
Special Collections, University Research Library, University of California Los Angeles: 27 (bottom), 69, 70, 117 (bottom), 127.
Thrifty Corporation: 168 (top left, bottom left), 169 (bottom), 170-172.
Urban Archives Collection, California State University, Northridge: 31 (bottom), 41.
Utility Workers Union of America AFL-CIO, Region V: 101 (bottom), 117 (top and middle).
Wells Fargo Bank: 19 (top), 29.
Willard, Charles D., *The Free Harbor Contest at Los Angeles*: 11 (top).

Selected References

In addition to archival sources, this book has drawn upon many histories of Pacific Enterprises and its subsidiaries produced over the years by company historians. Particularly useful was James T. Van Rensselaer's comprehensive and detailed history, "The Lamplighters: The Story of the Building of the Pacific Lighting Natural Gas System in Southern California . . . 1867-1967" (1967). Manuscript copies of Van Rensselaer's work are in the historical files of the Southern California Gas Company Research and Information Center in Los Angeles. Also very helpful were the histories of Pacific Enterprises' subsidiaries (both past and present): "The Story of the Southern [California Gas Company]," by Fred J. Schafer (serialized in *Gas News* from 1924 TO 1929); "The History of Our Company [Los Angeles Gas and Electric]," by Maurice A. Seeley (serialized in *L.A. Service Review* from 1934 to 1936); and Norman L. Hoff's "Historical Review of the Development of Southern California Gas Company," a 1939 manuscript history in the historical files of the Southern California Gas Company Research and Information Center. C.O.G. Miller's "One Hundred Years of Gas Service: A Good Deal of History and a Little of Prophecy," printed in the 1931 Pacific Coast Gas Association's *Annual Report*, was also insightful. Other corporate histories include: *Pacific Lighting Corporation: Development of a Western Utility* (1928); *Pacific Lighting Corporation: A Description of the History and Development of One of America's Oldest Utility Groups* (circa 1931); *Pacific Lighting Corporation: A Giant of Energy*, by Robert A. Hornby (1968); *Landmarks in Service: Then and Now* (1983); and *Pacific Lighting Corporation: A Century of Commitment*, by Thomas C. Sanger (1986).

Of the published works dealing with the historical development of the gas and oil industry in California, Charles Coleman's *The P.G. and E. of California: Centennial Story of the Pacific Gas and Electric Company, 1852-1952* (1953) chronicles the first hundred years of Pacific Enterprises' sister utility in northern California and provides useful background on the utility industry in the state as a whole. W.H. Hutchinson's many works on the California oil industry are particularly rich in detail and provide important information on this energy field so closely related to the natural gas distribution business. Hutchinson's *Oil, Land, and Politics: The Career of Thomas Robert Bard* (1965) is especially useful. For background on gas entrepreneur T.S.C. Lowe, see Eugene B. Block, *Above the Civil War: The Story of Thaddeus Lowe, Balloonist, Inventor, Railway Builder* (1966), and for broader information on California's economic development, see Robert Glass Cleland and Osgood Hardy, *March of Industry* (1929).

Recent works for those interested in the national development of the gas industry include: Chris Castaneda and Joseph Pratt, "New Markets, Outmoded Manufacturing: The Transition from Manufactured Gas to Natural Gas by Northeastern Utilities after World War II," in *Business and Economic History* (1989); Alfred M. Leeston,

John A. Crichton, and John C. Jacobs, *The Dynamic Natural Gas Industry* (1988); and Arlon Tussing and Connie Barlow, *The Natural Gas Industry* (1984). For a general chronology, see James A. Clark, et al., *A Chronological History of the Petroleum and Natural Gas Industries* (1963). A very useful but dated study is John Ashley's unpublished Ph.D. dissertation, "Some Economic Problems of the Natural Gas Industry in California" (University of California, Los Angeles, 1958).

Works on southern California history useful to the writing of this book include: Walton S. Bean, *California: An Interpretive History* (1968); John and LaRee Caughey, eds., *Los Angeles: Biography of a City* (1977); Beatrice Dinerman and Winston Crouch, *The Southern California Metropolis: A Study in Development for a Metropolitan Area* (1964); Glenn S. Dumke, *Boom of the Eighties in Southern California* (1944); Judith Elias, *Los Angeles: Dream to Reality, 1885-1915* (1983); Robert M. Fogelson, *The Fragmented Metropolis: Los Angeles, 1850-1930* (1967); John Anson Ford, *Thirty Explosive Years in Los Angeles County* (1961); J.A. Graves, *My Seventy Years in California, 1852-1923* (1929); Laurence L. Hill, *La Reina: Los Angeles in Three Centuries* (a pictorial history, 1929); Abraham Hoffman, *Vision or Villainy: Origins of the Owens Valley - Los Angeles Water Controversy* (1981); Norris Hundley, *Water and the West: The Colorado River Compact and the Politics of Water in the American West* (1975); William Kahrl, *Water and Power: The Conflict over Los Angeles' Water Supply in the Owens Valley* (1982); Joseph Gregg Layne, *Water and Power for a Great City* (1957); Carey McWilliams, *Southern California Country: An Island on the Land* (1946); Larry Meyer, *Los Angeles, 1781-1981* (a special bicentennial issue of *California History*, 1981); Remi Nadeau *City-Makers: The Men Who Transformed Los Angeles from Village to Metropolis, 1850-1930* (1948); Gerald Nash, "The California Railroad Commission, 1876-1911," *Southern California Quarterly* (1962); Harris Newmark, *Sixty Years in Southern California* (4th ed., 1970); Spencer Olin, Jr., *California's Prodigal Sons: Hiram Johnson and the Progressives, 1911-1917* (1968); Vincent Ostrom, *Water and Politics: A Study of Water Policies and Administration in the Development of Los Angeles* (1953); David H. Redinger, *The Story of Big Creek* (1949); W.W. Robinson, *Los Angeles from the Days of the Pueblo* (1977); Andrew Rolle, *California: A History* (3rd ed., 1978); Rolle, *Los Angeles from Pueblo to the City of the Future* (1981); Martin Schiesl, "Progressive Reform in Los Angeles Under Mayor Alexander, 1909-1913," *California Historical Quarterly* (1975); Nelson Van Valen, "A Neglected Aspect of the Owens River Aqueduct Story: The Inception of the Los Angeles Municipal System," *Southern California Quarterly* (1977); and Oscar O. Winther, "The Rise of Metropolitan Los Angeles, 1870-1900," *Huntington Library Quarterly* (1947).

Index

The Spirit of Enterprise

was designed and composed with Aldus Pagemaker 3.02

on a Macintosh IICX computer.

———

The primary typeface is

Adobe Garamond, designed by Robert Slimbach

and based upon the original version created by

sixteenth-century type designer Auguste Garamond.

———

The book was printed on 80-pound Karma

bright white text by George Rice & Sons,

Los Angeles, California.

DESIGNED BY VICKIE SAWYER KARTEN
JOSH FREEMAN/ASSOCIATES